GETHSEMANE SOLILOQUY

AN EPITOME OF JESUS' RELIABLE SAYINGS

BRAD LANCASTER

Library of Congress Cataloguing in Publication Data:
Lancaster, Brad.
Gethsemane Soliloquy: An Epitome of Jesus' Reliable Sayings
Includes suggested readings

ISBN 978-0-9986435-2-6

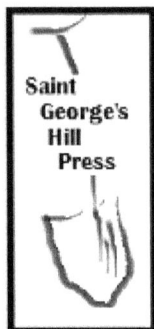

Published by:
Saint George's Hill Press
17503 10th Avenue N.E.
Shoreline, Washington 98155

First Printing: 2017

This book is printed in Times New Roman font.

Printed in the United States of America.

For my sister, Karen,
who loves Jesus,
and broods
over my
soul

TABLE OF CONTENTS

INTRODUCTION

DEPARTING JESUS ECCLESIASTICUS

Many encounter Jesus, or his semblance.[1]

I did. Our meeting came during an initial dive into the New Testament as a high school sophomore in northern Idaho. Jesus won me: his sassiness, blunt wisdom, and that persistent preference for anti-Roman underdogs and unschooled laborers. I savored the Galilean's bemused solitudes, juxtaposed, often uncomfortably, with unbridled chatter and clueless incomprehension from his students. Jesus' metaphors and parables grabbed me, each rooted in his rural conviction that wan urban religiosity had played itself out. Yahweh[2] trembles, in Jesus' rendition, poised to irrupt[3] into human ordinariness. Jesus announced himself as Yahweh's scion,[4] the divine sword of incursion, honed for final judgment. Jesus believed he was the Son of man.[5]

---

[1] In 2016, seventy-eight percent of Americans self-identified as Christians.

[2] "Yahweh" is a transliterated approximation of the Hebrew tetragrammaton (יהוה, rendered in English as "YHVH" or "YHWH"), which is the personal name of the god of Israel (see Genesis 21:33 or Exodus 3:13-15).

[3] To "irrupt" is to suddenly break into something, as in an implosion. See Mark 14:61-62. Note how the gospel writer conflated messianic identity with Son of man language.

[4] A "scion" is a descendant of an aristocratic family, or a shoot grafted onto a mature plant. The concept of branch resides in the eschatological rescue passages of Jeremiah 23:5-6 and Isaiah 11:1-10.

[5] See Daniel 7:9-18, and Mark 2:27-28. In the prophet Daniel's vision, the Son of man stands before the Ancient of Days, who is arrayed in all his divine glory, poised for final judgment upon the four kingdoms of earth. The Ancient of Days gives the Son of man dominion over all peoples of earth, perpetually. He will be served by mankind, as shall all the saints of the Most High. The denomination "son of man" is used in other ways as well in the book of Daniel. At Daniel 8:17, the term is used of Daniel himself, and appears to mean "human." Elsewhere, the term is used to distinguish lowly humankind from the unutterable magnificence of divinity, e.g., Numbers 23:19. The term "son of man" (בן אדם, rendered in English as "ben 'adam") appears 107 times in the Hebrew canon, mostly in the apocalyptic visions of Ezekiel and Daniel. Some interpreters have construed Jesus' use of the term "son of man" as an emphatic form of the personal pronoun. I dispute this construction, since it is inconsistent with the eschatological vision of John the Baptist, to whom Jesus went for baptism and with whose ministry Jesus associated his own (see Mark 1:4-9, Mark 1:14, Mark 9:11-13, Mark 11:30) and with Jesus' own eschatological view of his ministry as the fulfillment of time and the

Parochial eschatology[6] aside, I found Jesus disarmingly heartfelt and alarmingly direct. He captured me. I laid aside my nets. I followed.[7]

A numinous[8] Presbyterian sequel arrived. In the social adhesion of young adults transported by the thrum of guitars and song, I recognized that life exceeds my comprehension of it. I glimpsed *noumena*.[9] We are more—much more—together than alone. I have, in my dotage, clumped together words to describe my youthful song-borne intuition of abyssal existential depth. I presume in that work, probably unsuccessfully, to describe the bramble that is human social interpenetration.[10] At the time, however (it was 1972), the church taught me to call this odd experience a supernal incursion of "the holy spirit." I was, for some months, content enough with my good-hearted pastor's interpretations. I, at that time in my early life, ill-appreciated the mental mutations and mutilations worked by theological jargon. Along with Jesus, who moved me, I imbibed the church, its theology and liturgical habits, and its problematical attitudes. I kept the ecclesiastical bathwater along with its scrubbed and divinized baby Jesus. And I called the burbling batch "faith." I was styled "born again," in the manner evangelicals use those words. At this characterization, I, for reasons I then little understood, chafed. But I shrugged off my misgivings. I chewed at length upon that sinewy muscle that is the church. It proved a tough jerky.

---

leading edge of the oncoming kingdom. See Mark 1:15. As a sophomore in high school, I understood nothing of these eschatological sentiments. I cannot claim greatly improved comprehension now decades later. Perhaps, these logia are intentionally elusive.

6 "Eschatology" refers to ruminations upon the end of the world, and the ultimate destiny of mankind.

7 Mark 1:17-18. Much to the dismay of my parents, I might add. But that is another tale entirely.

8 "Numen" denotes implicit influences that can be perceived, but not by the senses. In the Roman usage, numen trended toward suspicions of divine nudging, though some authors use the term to mean "impressive potency." In sycophantic moments, emperors were applauded for the numen that attended them.

9 "*Noumena*" is a term for things-as-they-are, set over against "*phenomena*," things-as-they-appear to a human. So, the distinction registers recognition that humans see only part of what ultimately exists, bounded as we are by the constraints of our sense organs. Yet, humans imagine (or, possibly, even experience) glimpses of hidden matters. Immanuel Kant denied that humans know anything of *noumena*. See Kant, *Critique of Pure Reason*. I now suspect (but did not always do so) that Kant is right. We unconsciously fabricate much of what we perceive, and (wrongly) call that construction "insight." Reality, as humans experience it, consists in observations pasted together with supposition and superstition. A person spreads that jumble onto a psychic canvas conformed to the survival demands of the African veldt. Gods leak imperceptibly through the canvas, if the divine, in fact, leaks into the cosmos at all.

10 See Lancaster, *Cull: Choosing Well*, Sections I and II, and Lancaster, *Cull: Epitomes* on Berger's *Sacred Canopy*, Buber's *I and Thou*, Cicero, *On Friendship*, and Aristotle, *Nichomachean Ethics*, Books 8 and 9.

Years of study and life among permutations of Christianity ensued.[11] I undertook studies of biblical materials and various theologies at Fuller Theological Seminary in Pasadena, California. I earned a master's degree, and commenced doctoral studies in systematics.[12] Experience and insight grew, as did disillusion. I left seminary, part way through my Ph.D. work under mentor, Paul Jewett. And I forsook the church. My exits were graceless pratfalls, freighted by unresolved anger and trenchant disappointment. Paul Jewett, a quiet and decent man of the church, never plumbed my ecclesiastical dysphoria. The church, for its part, jammed spasmodic fingers in its metaphorical ears, so to remain ignorant of my numerous theological broadsides. Justifiably so. I was obnoxious.

I have, since those dual departures from seminary and churches, nevertheless harbored a grave affection for Yeshua the Galilean.[13] My continuing attachment to Yeshua is grave for two reasons. Interest in Yeshua has been a demanding enterprise. It has taxed me. And many exquisitely painful events in my life emerge from heeding Yeshua. He has asked much. Thoughts often run to the Jewish peasant. Shall I subvert this authority? Shall I comfort that person? What

---

[11] By background, I was Presbyterian. I participated in youth ministry programs with four different congregations of that Scottish ilk. A college friend directed Lutheran youth ministries in the small college town where I spent my sophomore year of college; I worshiped with his congregation occasionally. In my freshman year of college, I helped in youth ministries at a Methodist congregation, one mired in a town awash in immoderate Mormons. I coached an Episcopalian boys' basketball team (which is a measure of just how hard up they were for a coach), and worshiped with the priest's group on campus occasionally. I tasted Pentecostal, Catholic, and non-denominational community churches as opportunities presented themselves. In each community, I found people of good faith attempting to ascertain the will of God for themselves. I also discovered others in their midst devoted to alternative, and to my taste less worthy, purposes.

[12] Systematic theology indulges the presumptuous inquiry of the biblical canon, What is the whole counsel of God? Systematics tends to fold philosophy and alternative religions into the conversation about the meaning of the Jewish and Christian canons. New Testament or Old Testament theology asks of the relevant books, What do these collections, as a whole, teach? Biblical theology focuses on individual books of the canon, asking, What does this book teach? New Testament or Old Testament studies attempt to place a book or collection in its historical circumstance, in an effort to invest obscure language with a then-current human context.

[13] "Yeshua" is the Aramaic name of Jesus, before that name was transliterated into Greek and a Latin masculine suffix added. Matthew 2:23 calls Yeshua a "Nazorean," often dubiously translated in KJV and NRSV as Nazarene. No historical evidence for Nazareth, as a village, exists before the third century A.D. Nazareth probably did not exist in the lifetime of Yeshua. It seems likely that early Christian writers confused the terms Nazirite (Numbers 6:1-23), the third century Galilean village of Nazareth, and a first-century designation for a murky ascetic sect known for fastidious religiosity, the Nazoreans. Toranic Nazirite vows require the worshipper to set himself apart for Yahweh, avoiding alcohol and grapes. The Nazirite did not cut his hair or go near dead bodies (even close family members). If a person died suddenly beside a Nazirite, the Nazirite must shave his head, and make appropriate sacrifices, which are specified. Upon completion of the term of a Nazirite's vow, he made sacrifices and shaved his head at the door of the tent of meeting and burned the hair in the fire of the sacrifices. Then the Nazirite was allowed to drink wine (Numbers 6:1-23). Matthew 2:23 proof-texts to associate Yeshua with the Branch of Yahweh described in Isaiah 11:1. It does appear that Yeshua's early home was Galilee. Matthew 4:23. Thus, I prefer to call this man "Yeshua the Galilean."

matters? Shall I give time or money? How will I make my living? Who may become my friend? What do I owe governments, and my family? How fares my heart? What of enemies? When I make decisions, Yeshua weighs in. He lingers, enigmatically, near the back of every room, close by the exit. He murmurs advice and the occasional snide aside. Yeshua's tongue, and wit, remain whetted edges. They cut. Who, or what, is this Yeshua of Galilee? What did he say? Critically, how is Yeshua the Galilean related to the church's Jesus of Nazareth?

My experience within the Protestant orb falls in two regimes. For five years, I absorbed the church's theology, read the Bible devotionally (but with some intensity), and directed youth programs within the various organizations I attended. The second five years saw formal theological inquiry, critique (sometimes virulent) of churches, and textual criticism of the church's canon. I quested for means to remake the church catholic. Nasty tracts, alternative theologies, and house churches issued. I bluntly castigated ecclesiastical institutions and their unfortunate ciphers, my senior pastors. I offended by arrogant excess and paucity of peacemaking. Maturing, I recognized the church as a matrix of sociologically ossified organizations. After years of painful exchanges, I left my church and the church. We are happier parted.

Passing decades have bequeathed me rubrics[14] more apt, quarried from minds more penetrating than my own, in which to frame theological angst.[15] I found in personalism, both theological and secular, frameworks of utility.[16] Albert Schweitzer's *Quest for the Historical Jesus* exposed the penchant of churches and their opponents to cut-and-paste Jesuses to preference. The final alfalfa leaf that tipped my theological haystack came on a crisp October dawn in 1980. I strolled to seminary beneath a cerulean blue dome, before obscuring smog mashed against Pasadena's hills from the tailpipes of Los Angeles's belching horde of ill-tuned cars, trucks, and buses. A seditious thought dawned, as had the sun. I undoubtedly knew more—no, much more—of Jesus than did Saul of Tarsus, the writer of portions of the New Testament.[17] From that moment, the canon eroded for me. I

---

[14] A "rubric" can mean an explanatory framework or a gloss, or even an organized way of speaking of something.

[15] "Angst" is persistent dread about something that may prove to be essentially trivial.

[16] Consider Martin Buber's *I and Thou*, or Levinas's *Otherwise Than Being*, or the personalist Neo-orthodoxy of Emil Brunner. Brunner's three-volume *Dogmatics* merits a careful reading, if you savor Christianity.

[17] Saul of Tarsus renamed himself the Apostle Paul, after his conversion from Pharisaical Judaism (see Philippians 3:5) to nascent Christianity. Paul never met Jesus, unless one counts the odd event Paul recounts from a trip to Damascus. See Acts 9:1-22. Paul wrote several letters to churches which became part of the canon of the New Testament. Their exact number is indeterminate, because the practice of pseudonymity (attaching a false, and usually more famous or authoritative, author's name to a work) leaves the writer of several New Testament books equivocal.

came to regard the apostles and their successors, as well as subsequent church fathers, not as mentors or icons or heroes. I held them as struggling, relatively narrow, people. The apostles and fathers sought to deflect an existential threat to their affection for Jesus—the revisionist mongrels of the Roman-Hellenic empire. To defeat the syncretist hordes, the church adopted their methods. The church faithful wrote Jesus Ecclesiasticus. Back in Pasadena, church dogma became, for me, equivocal. I recognized in my Christian co-religionists a nasty streak, which rooted also in my heart in a peculiarly putrid manner.[18]

I commenced a search. How might one disentangle Yeshua the Galilean from the church's mash-up, Jesus of Nazareth? This latter is the ecclesiastical god-man, the churches' Messiah, their metaphysical Son of God, and an occasional apocalyptic Son of man. The former, Yeshua, hunkered beneath churchly Jesus. This essay recounts some intellectual components of sorting Yeshua from Jesus.

If you find yourself satisfied with the Jesus whom your church has taught you, do not read this book.[19] Yeshua the Galilean is not Jesus of Nazareth. You will learn next-to-nothing about how to co-exist with Christian people of faith, especially bumptious bible-bangers, by reading this book, except to the extent those brethren are human.

Yeshua belongs to mankind, as do Homer and Plato and Aristotle and Cicero and Augustine and Kant and Wollstonecraft and de Beauvoir. Yeshua shared our struggles and confusions, and ultimately, our death. Jesus, the Jesus invented in those first few centuries of ecclesiastical struggle, belongs to the church, in the way protagonists belong to their novelists. I do no so speak to injure or disparage the church. I use this language because the metaphor is apt.

Jesus Ecclesiasticus hovers, at least a little bit, above our merely mortal fray. What other has been resurrected? Clerical persons claim authorial rights to Jesus. In this, many are more than a bit uppity. Still, their claim has merit. Jesus belongs to the church. For, at least in part, the church made Jesus up. The Fathers painted and prettified their Jesus. They perched their Nazarene, scrubbed and freshly garmented, on a lonely shelf far above pedestrian criticism.

---

[18] A character flaw common to religious ideologues of diverse persuasions, and one from which I, for some years, suffered acutely. I was narrow, and valued narrowness.

[19] Consider yourself warned.

Those clerical dominators have long quashed critics who explore heretical irreverence. They have hoped to silence those who extricate Yeshua from beneath their fractured Jesus—people like me, and possibly, if you are still reading, people like you.[20] Despite the church's fervent obscuring, Yeshua leaked through. I, and many, have whiffed him. We dog Yeshua's trail.

---

[20] Jan Oppermann styles *Gethsemane Soliloquy* a "personal anti-Christology." Oppermann wonders where the author hides amidst the analysis. I certainly have important personal feelings about the topics touched in this little work. But my purpose is not self-revelation (though I do a fair bit of that anyway), but analysis and sorting of the sayings of Yeshua, which I have not found to my satisfaction in other works, followed by a sympathetic summary of Yeshua's residual tuition. Oppermann doubts that I can (or anyone can) follow Yeshua's thoughts from the far side of the two thousand year chasm that separates us. I am sure my friend, Jan, is correct. Yet, Yeshua matters to me. I want to hear him. Ecclesiastical editing excised, I listen. Personal correspondence with the author, spring 2017.

CHAPTER 1
EXCAVATING YESHUA

Yeshua stands, in my view, among the first rank of thinkers. Odd that I can say that at all, for Yeshua wrote nothing.[21] The early church also lacked writings from Yeshua. Early followers, mostly illiterate, relied on the oral accounts told by close friends of Yeshua. Those friends were themselves functionally illiterate. Eventually, those friends of Yeshua began dying. Distressingly, Yeshua had promised it would not be so.[22] The stories of Yeshua, for the first generation of those who loved him, teetered at the precipice of annihilation, death by death. History slights the letterless. Yeshua, their compelling teacher, teetered in peril of being forever inaudible and eventually unfollowed. The Galilean's work was not philosophical, but rather, interpersonal. His thoughts trend to the moral[23] and

---

[21] At least nothing we possess.

[22] See Matthew 10:23, Matthew 16:28, 24:34, Mark 9:1, Mark 13:30, Mark 14:62, and Luke 9:27. (Please note that two different biblical citations formats follow in *Gethsemane Soliloquy*. The citation form I prefer, and have used for decades, is that approved by the Chicago Manual of Style (Thirteenth Edition, §17.63). Biblical citations contain a colon to separate chapter from verse(s). The National Council of the Churches of Christ in the United States of America prefers that biblical citations separate chapter and verse with a period, which is the alternate and less frequent form prescribed by the Chicago Manual of Style (same section). Where required by my license, for the privilege of using portions of the Revised Standard Version of the Bible (for which I have also paid hard cash), I follow that form required by the National Council of Churches. Elsewhere, I follow the more common and familiar citation format.) Note, if you will, the irony. The church still seeks to control access to Jesus, to profit financially from his words, and to define all reference to him, including whether one employs a period or a colon in biblical citation. Testy. Very testy.

[23] A "moral" consideration examines the merits of alternative choices, and the outcomes of those elections.

eschatological,[24] not the analytic.[25] The early church and its dissenters fundamentally muddied Yeshua's ideas by lacing them with their own (not that insightful) theological rhetoric. Perhaps, we can be kind about their plight. It was terribly possible that the Yeshua loved by his first century followers might be swallowed up by the swirling storm of events in Judea, rife as it was with anti-Roman dissent and a herd of messianic claimants. So, the writers of Matthew, Mark, and Luke proof-texted, improved, revised, invented, and distorted some words of Yeshua. The sayings of Yeshua devolve to us trussed in a layered encrustation of pious emendation and ill-considered guesswork.

One is put to a task with her Bible.[26] One may wish to hear Yeshua. Before one can do so, one must tease Yeshua's message from beneath a substantial load of historical detritus obscuring that message, the somewhat-desperate adjustments of his awestruck second-generation followers. Because this task of sorting reliable from suspect sayings is controversial to many people of faith, I show my work at length and plainly state my assumptions in separating wheat from chaff. I identify reliable sayings of Jesus and weed out those that appear less likely or impossible in the mouth of Yeshua. Then I chew over the reliable meat of Yeshua's message. I presume to state Yeshua's teachings.[27]

To illustrate, consider with me Luke 14.27: "[27]Whoever does not bear his own cross and come after me, cannot be my disciple." Jesus admonishes a great multitude that if they decline to be crucified, a fate Jesus will suffer, then Jesus will decline to instruct them. This teaching bears that urgency characteristic of Jesus. Yet it asserts that Jesus foreknew the method of his death. Humans lack such predictive capabilities. And the logion[28] evidences a concern of the later church: Will church members persevere when faced with public execution on account of association with Jesus' followers? After deliberation, I conclude that this much-beloved saying of Jesus is not reliable.[29] Yeshua did not say this. The

---

[24] An "eschatological" concern pertains to the end of times, usually linked to aspects of final judgment by an irritated divinity.

[25] "Analytic" concerns drive one toward counting, investigating historical precedents, offering logical considerations, and dismantling ideas into components. Yeshua's concerns proved persistently more hearty than heady.

[26] All biblical citations in this essay derive from the Revised Standard Version. The Revised Standard Version of the Bible, copyright © 1946, 1952, and 1971, the National Council of the Churches of Christ in the United States of America. Used by permission. All rights reserved.

[27] Authors are arrogant. Writing requires as much. Certainly this topic summons hubris.

[28] "Logion" is a technical term for a saying of Jesus. The term's plural is "logia."

[29] I also deem unreliable Logion 54 (Mark 8:34-37) and Logion 245 (Matthew 16:24-25), which parallel the Lucan version.

church did. The church put these words in Jesus' mouth so their lord might directly address their later-emerging dilemma, the non-return of Jesus and the sporadic persecution of the early church. The gospel author put the screws to the wavering faithful by sleight of hand—invisibly altering Yeshua.

Another sort of problem remains more difficult to assess. What likely events or words in the life of Yeshua can be deduced from the Synoptic texts, even though concerning them the Synoptics are mostly silent?

The early church, having doubled-down on the divinity of Jesus, was most uncomfortable with Jesus' errors and all evidence of psychological development.[30] With some stubborn reading-between-the-lines, one ferrets hints of a human Jesus. A Jesus who learns. A Jesus who falters. Most important, a Jesus who misunderstands himself and his mission. A Jesus who makes adjustments. A man whose religious perceptions mis-describe the reality in which he lives and breathes.

Of Synoptic silences, one asks a core question: What changes did Yeshua make when he sent out the twelve to do their ministries in the local villages, and yet the kingdom of God failed to irrupt upon their numerous successes?

Mark finds Yeshua sending out the twelve,[31] followed by an interpolation of events surrounding the murder of John the Baptist, after which the twelve return to Yeshua, who then, with the disciples, retreats for contemplation and rest.[32] What was Yeshua contemplating in retreat?

Matthew tells the disciples to go out to the villages of Israel (but not to Samaritan or gentile villages), to teach, heal, and do miracles.[33] Teaching segments, the interpolation on John the Baptist's death, and parables intervene. Then, Yeshua withdraws.[34] What did Yeshua consider? Why does the author of Matthew offer no speculation or interpretation of Jesus' respite?

---

[30] So, young Jesus presents a problem. The life events of a child present much that evidences psychological and moral development. How could a god, however, lack knowledge or require growth? Thus, in the church's telling, twelve year old Jesus ditches his parents to remain at the Jerusalem Temple to pepper its teachers with questions. Luke 2:41-49. See Luke 2:40 and 2:52. Jesus grew and became filled with wisdom.

[31] Mark 6:7-13.

[32] Mark 6:30-32.

[33] Matthew 10:5-15.

[34] Matthew 13:14.

In Luke, one finds Yeshua sending out the disciples (first twelve, and then, in likely distorted dittography,[35] seventy)[36] to serve the villages without Yeshua's supervision.[37] Immediately[38] Yeshua learns of the success of their ministries. Then Yeshua retreats. What upset Yeshua? What was Yeshua working out in his mind? Had Yeshua expected Yahweh to irrupt upon successful completion of the disciples' diminutive journeys? After all, "time" has expired. The kingdom of God trembles to irrupt. Yeshua, the Son of man, has arrived, taught, and summoned all to repentance. John, the Elijah precursor, has preached and fallen.[39] Was Yeshua crestfallen and confused when Yahweh failed to elevate Yeshua with onrushing glory in response to the disciples' effective peripatetic outreach?[40]

When Yeshua emerged from his retreat, his teaching took a new tack. He was going up to Jerusalem, there to confront the Temple powers and to be killed. Yeshua was confident that he, once murdered, would be resurrected by Yahweh, to launch the kingdom of God among men.[41] Yeshua creatively wedded the Son of man eschatology to the suffering servant of Yahweh in Isaiah 52-53.[42] Note the resistance or incomprehension of the disciples at Yeshua's revised teaching. The disciples expected an outcome glorious. They anticipated seats of power, as Yeshua had promised them.[43] Now Yeshua unilaterally changed his deal with the disciples. Not only is Yeshua going up to Jerusalem to be killed. But the disciples

---

[35] "Dittography" means the erroneous repetition of a phrase (or word or letter) by a copyist. Here, it is more likely that the author of Luke had two stories of Jesus, one sending out the twelve, and one sending seventy unidentified students. Luke felt incompetent to conflate the stories or delete one of them, and so reports both.

[36] Luke 10:1-12.

[37] Luke 9:1-6.

[38] Luke 9:10; without teaching segment interpolations.

[39] See Mark 1:15, and Mark 9:13.

[40] Mark 6:30-31. Consider also Matthew 10.23b. See Logion 190 for my commentary on this problematically-located logion.

[41] See Luke 18:31-34, Luke 9:43b-45, Matthew 20:17-19, Matthew 16:21-23 (note the language "from that time Jesus began to show . . ."), and, critically, Mark 8:31-33. Note that Jesus "began" to teach, at Mark 8:31.

[42] See Mark 9:12. All of Yeshua's ministry was deeply influenced by the three writers who constructed the book of Isaiah. Note especially Isaiah 11, 24, 25, 26, 28, 29, 30, 35, 40, 42, 45, 49, 50, 52, 53, 55, 56, 58, 59, 61, 64, 65, and 66. It would appear that not Isaiah 52-53 alone, but the general sentiments of proto-Isaiah, deutero-Isaiah, and trito-Isaiah, re-routed Yeshua's ministry toward its more troubled end. All of the eighth century prophets seem to have been influential with Yeshua, especially Daniel 7 and Isaiah 53. Yeshua was taken with prophetic "heartfulness," and put off by the Temple's pride-suffused rigor and narrowness and finance.

[43] Luke 12:28, Matthew 19:28, Mark 10:35-41.

are expected to die ignominiously as well.[44] This is not the outcome for which the disciples enlisted. Peter objects. Messiahs do not die as criminals; they prevail wondrously over Israel's enemies. Yeshua rebukes Peter with urgent harshness.[45] Yeshua promises, in response to the disciples' disappointment, that Yeshua, as the Son of man, will return in Yahweh's glory before they all die.[46]

By this style of analysis, I sort a reliable batch of sayings excavated from the church's pedagogical injections and pious bootstrapping. That is my overarching purpose, at any rate. I wish to hear the Yeshua of history, and to edit away Jesus Ecclesiasticus. Perhaps you might like to hear Yeshua teach as well, being full up with the church's rendition. To that end, after paring the sayings of Jesus to a reliable core, I epitomize Yeshua's teachings as a fictional monologue. I imagine Yeshua issuing a summation of his semi-ascetic discipline to his sleeping students in his favorite garden, Gethsemane.[47] As with most of Yeshua's teaching, his students nodded off, actually or metaphorically, during lessons. The spirit was willing, but their flesh, and perhaps their minds, were weak.[48]

---

[44] Perhaps this grim disappointment sets Judas's sedition in a context.

[45] Mark 8:31-35.

[46] Mark 8:38.

[47] See Chapter 4 of this book for Yeshua's lesson in the garden.

[48] Mark 4:34, Mark 14:38.

CHAPTER 2
WHO OWNS JESUS?

Books have powers. In a manner that, to some extent, defies description, a good book grants entry, perhaps only slightly, to the mental foyer of another human. As an illiterate "author," Yeshua has been trammeled by church interpreters. He has also been trampled by the rush of billions to see Yeshua take up the bat and slug the biblical baseball. We sit in the nose-bleed section of that stadium. Yeshua bats far from our failing vision, inaudible to our noise-blasted ears. Despite being present, one might miss Yeshua altogether. For his distance is great, the crunch of his bat not so loud.

Yet Yeshua whispers toward me from his troubled past. My cheap seat is not insuperable. In this strained perception, I am not alone. Yeshua affects many: Tolstoy, Gandhi, Te Whiti, King, and we pedestrian rabble numbering billions. Apparently, the cheap seats are many and moderately popular. Who or what mumbles at us from the first century?

The question is not easily answered. Freud alleges we ourselves are the mumblers, projecting psychic fractures onto an imaginary companion to achieve neurotic self-deception.[49] Tolstoy found in Yeshua a firebrand pacifist revolutionary.[50] Gandhi clung to a mentor in non-violent resistance.[51] Nietzsche spat Yeshua out, cursing him as a castrating Jewish slavemaker.[52] Yeshua evokes response. Me, Yeshua troubles.

---

[49] Freud, *The Future of an Illusion.*

[50] Tolstoy, *The Kingdom of God is Within You.*

[51] Gandhi, *Satyagraha.*

[52] Nietzsche, *Beyond Good and Evil*, and *Genealogy of Morals.*

I frequently epitomize the works of core thinkers in ethics, among whom I count Yeshua.[53] My purpose in this exercise is to tease out Yeshua's reliable sayings so that one may hear his voice among the wisdom teachers of history, without the cackle and crush of his many subsequent adapters, all fastidiously bending Jesus to their diverse purposes. As we will see in a final section to this essay, one must ask whether, in the course of this task, I have not achieved little more than adding yet one more well-edited Jesus-of-preference to a horde of earlier (per)versions. I suppose one never knows certainly of such matters.

Churches, and their defenders, object. The only Jesus that exists is their Jesus, that man-god delivered to us by New Testament oracles and church Fathers. Authors, such as the writer of *Gethsemane Soliloquy*, who presume to identify another Jesus more pure or authoritative or clarion from the Synoptic morass, self-deceive. There exists only the One, the Word of God, His Son, the Messiah, the Christ, the Son of man, who will come to judge (as promised). All other characterizations of Jesus expose, not the inwardness of Jesus of Nazareth, but instead the imaginative decadence of some faithless writer. The church has long dealt with such enthusiasts as these. It once burned them. It now employs less hideous, but no less effective, exclusions.[54] For, plainly, the church owns Jesus. The church is Jesus' sole authorized interpreter, his keeper, the treasure-chest of Jesus' thoughts. The keys delivered to Peter are just those keys to Jesus' legacy.[55] Peter opens or shuts the gate to seekers after Jesus. No others have access. Jesus' teaching has always been, so the church asserts, proprietary.

I, apparently, disagree. People need faith(s). We humans suffer perpetual insecurity, imagining, as we so frequently do, unpleasant outcomes. We crave more assurances than prove available. Lacking certainty, we fabricate some. Then we strain credulity. We convince ourselves and others of the veracity of our inventions, or attempt such. In religion, we know nothing of divinity. Yet we long for a supernal voice, some deep comfort, and a warm hug from a more-than-human person in the beyond beyond. Much of religion is, as Freud argued, a projection of fractured inwardness. Yet, human religious sensibility exceeds Freud's derogation. Our wish for supra-sensual perception originates primordially, from hominids older than the human line. There has never been a non-religious human. Faith is as natural to humans as bipedalism. Faith rummages our bones, and necessarily so. Religion binds people into communities. Faiths answer

---

[53] You might inspect Lancaster, *Cull: Epitomes*, in this regard.

[54] Excommunications, nasty polemics, benign neglect, and assiduous ear-plugging.

[55] Matthew 16:18-19.

unanswerable questions, some of which are crucial to survival.[56] Faith endures as a human resource, like innate cleverness or running. True, exuberant faiths regularly drive men toward silliness. Yet, only the unwise attempt to tear religious sentiment altogether from mankind's fabric. For faith knits us. Faith guides, yet sometimes misleads, people. The difficult task lies in sorting wisdom from inanity with a modicum of regularity. In that endeavor, humans have often failed.

Yeshua, for his part, never contemplated the existence of a church.[57] He preached an imminently in-breaking kingdom of God, with respect to which Yeshua himself was Yahweh's right hand of apocalyptic judgment. Yeshua utterly failed to anticipate the problems his disciples would face when he died and did not return in power as promised.[58] Yeshua can hardly be blamed for this oversight. To contemplate such problems would have been to admit that he misunderstood his own mission and the sentiments of Yahweh. It would have required Yeshua to admit that his teachings were, in not insignificant ways, erroneous. The firebrand sage could not travel to these psychological vistas and remain himself. Yeshua was, though we tend to forget this, a young man, probably no more than thirty when he commenced his fated public teaching. Yeshua, with the burning enthusiasm and warrantless overconfidence of a young male, was willing to die for his self-concept. He, in fact, did perish in the grip of this Son-of-man-and-suffering-servant vision of his personal role in human eschatology.[59] I often wonder, with regret, what Yeshua might have taught mankind, had he just walked

---

[56] Consider the assurance that our perceptions of the good will of others are not mere fabrications, our need to believe that loved ones exist despite persistent empirical doubts about the continuity and reliability of human perceptions, and the convictions of heartfelt hope surpassing the depredations of grim pessimisms.

[57] The early church suffered terribly when Yeshua, contrary to his promises, failed to return in power (the parousia). Yeshua's non-return drove formation of the early church. Yeshua created no congregation of normal people, living out their lifetimes, for Yeshua anticipated imminent resurrection to power as God's scion. Nascent Christianity adapted. Critically, it blended some unblendable ideas. The "Son of man" is a Danielic heavenly wielder of judgment upon mankind. A "messiah" is an earthly warrior who defeats the opponents of Israel (hence, Cyrus of Persia is a "messiah." See Isaiah 44:28-45:1). A "Son of god" is a Hellenic or Mythraic or Zoroastrian metaphysical being, whose filial origin is divine, who may appear human, but is, in fact, a person more deeply divine than might any mere human pretend. The early church, in its illiteracy and post-Yeshuan confusions, conflated these three concepts. See the usage in Acts7:56, 9:20, and 9:22. The church's theological mash-up persists to the present, obscuring the historical Yeshua. Yeshua himself contradicted the mash-up (Matthew 26:62-64).

[58] Jan Oppermann suggests that "religion is an inevitable consequence of Yeshua's teaching, whether or not he himself experienced this or wanted this or foresaw it." Personal correspondence with the author, spring 2017.

[59] Sue Morgan asks, reasonably, why one should credit any of Yeshua's teaching if he was wrong about eschatology, his role in it, and his very mission. Private correspondence with the author, spring 2017. I respond that many (most?) of our most cherished thinkers suffered distorted self-perception, a rash of ill habits, and misperceptions concerning their role in history. Gandhi was a rabid ascetic with a fixation on the bathroom habits of others. Thomas Jefferson loved one of his slaves, made a family with her, but hid her away from all scrutiny. Socrates neglected his wife and children to jabber

back to Galilee from Gethsemane, discouraged, but alive. What might we have learned if Yeshua had lived only a few years longer, ripening his insights? We might have benefited from Yeshua's thoughts on human communities and their governance. We might have the treasure of Yeshua's prescription for worthy leaders among men. How might Yeshua have jostled the train of political and moral developments, if only he had gone on teaching? What was gained by letting Temple aristocrats and Roman puppets vent themselves upon Yeshua? I find the church's response to my questions implausible.[60]

Yeshua can hardly be held to account for the panicked bootstrapping Jesus suffered at the hands of his beleaguered friends and followers. Some sidled Yeshua up to Mithras of Zoroastrian mythology.[61] Some "resurrected" Yeshua. Jesus' followers invented or borrowed pious fictions which they amalgamated to Yeshua's legacy. Frankly, the early church and its detractors made a mess of Yeshua. Churches set Yeshua in theological concrete. As their pews empty, as they shutter their doors, churches and their orthodoxies leave Yeshua in serious danger of not being heard at all. Were that to happen, we would indeed have lost a pearl of great price. For those of us who have abandoned sanctuaries and even the foyers of churches, this little book aspires to rescue Yeshua from the hoary

---

in the marketplace with sophomores. Alexander the Great, believing himself invulnerable, rode his body to its early grave. All Egyptian pharaohs believed themselves demigods. More than one recent American president thought himself god's gift to women. Martin Luther King Jr. had an insatiable hunger for a potpourri of brief sexual encounters. John Rawls was so shy he could barely teach. Arthur Schopenhauer so hated people that he would buy two seats at dinner just to avoid having a dinner companion. Buddha's exertions in finding nirvana would puzzle any person. Confucius, ever critical of his kings, thought it odd that they did not appoint him regent. Aristotle believed he could tame Alexander of Macedon. Friedrich Nietzsche argued that one of his glories was that no one would read his books. (He may have been right.) One takes help where one finds it, and chalks up eccentricities as foibles of genius.

[60] The church asserts that Jesus died on the Roman cross as a sin offering to placate the Yahweh's righteous anger at human sin. Jesus surrendered his life in expiation for the sins of mankind. See Mark 10:45. (To "expiate" is to make amends, or to offer compensation for wrongdoing.")

[61] Rex Weyler, whose conclusions on the sayings of Yeshua I tend not to follow, argues that Paul, instead of learning of Yeshua, merely wedded Yeshua, of whom he knew little, to Mithras of Zoroastrian mythology. Paul was not alone in that trend. Weyler argues that Tarsus, Paul's home town, was a center of Mithraic cult worship. Weyler asserts that Mithras was a son of god, a member of a sacred trinity, light of the world to his adherents, born of a virgin three days after the winter solstice, and was attended by shepherds with gifts. Mithras ascended into heaven, after a last supper with his twelve disciples, in the midst of which they ate bread and drank wine, which foods were styled the body and blood of Mithras. Weyler, *The Jesus Sayings*, 59-60. My own readings in Mithraic mythology, which are limited, show that two, lightly related, Mithraic traditions exist. The earlier is Mithraism of Iranian Zoroastrianism. Its mythos bears similarities to allegations of the early church about Jesus, but no overwhelming parallelism, such as that Weyler alleges. The later Mithraism is a Roman cult, mostly second century A.D., which may have been influenced by Christianity as much as it influenced Christianity. The larger and important point is this: the church's Jesus was in danger of being aggressively adapted to other traditions in the syncretistic environment of the first century Roman Empire.

glop in which congregations mire him. Yeshua of *Gethsemane Soliloquy* is not orthodox. He is just Yeshua.

Yeshua did not grant his churchly followers possession of his legacy. Yeshua belongs to receptive humankind. Yeshua, by his own words, teaches those who follow. Yeshua, as was his habit, decries presumptuous hierarchies. Perhaps many might hear Yeshua, if only the church would stop strangling Yeshua when he speaks. Please, my church-loving friends, let Yeshua have his voice. Let whoever wishes hear Yeshua. We may misinterpret. As have you. We all may err.

I write knowing I cannot be heard by the church-enamored. The church cannot relent. Harsh imaginative arthritis freezes her joints. Despite the ecclesiastical scowl, some outsiders and apostates will sit on the mount[62] or the plain[63] to hear Yeshua teach. Those who decline Yeshua's tuition impoverish themselves. Those who distort or hide Yeshua's lessons deserve abundant scorn. They have mine.[64]

---

[62] "Sermon on the Mount" (Matthew 5-7).

[63] Jesus comes down to teach at a "level place" (Luke 6:17), hence the attributed name, "Sermon on the Plain." (Luke 6-7).

[64] Not all who disagree do so in bad faith. Some Christian faith proves warm and congenial. Brian Carr writes that my analysis of Yeshua's words is simply wrong-headed. The gospels, indeed the entire New and Old Testament traditions, exist, not for analysis and sorting, but for worship and prayer. Carr writes: ". . . [T]he very project of this sorting is based on a presumption that I have anywhere to stand outside the tradition that has bequeathed me these words. And this just seems to me to be fundamentally untrue. The Church selected these four Gospels, it did the sifting and the sorting, and it decided that just the composite portrait that emerged from the compare-and-contrast exercise of reading them—reading them in church—was what matched the experience of the saints." Private correspondence with the author, spring 2017. Thirty years ago, I shared Carr's confidence in the church's good faith toward and careful attention to Yeshua. Such confidence fled me.

CHAPTER 3
RESURRECTION AND HAGIOGRAPHY

Yeshua the Galilean is dead, as soon shall we all be. I do not, in so asserting, dismiss resurrection. Yeshua died. All historical evidence, including that of his supporters, confirms Yeshua's death. Resurrections lie on the inaccessible side of an epistemological[65] chasm. Death happens before our eyes. We observe, even measure, death. Resurrection recapitulates human hope. None can see resurrection, which belongs to realms absent microscopes and yardsticks. If the dead rise, none observes them.[66] Resurrection, in upending the physical regularities of this universe, could issue only from a supra-cosmic act.

God, too, does not "exist." My atheist friends are correct when they so aver, though they tend to ignore the epistemological chasm, and think things do not exist if humans cannot sense them. Only things of this cosmos exist. God, by

---

[65] "Epistemology" deliberates what can and cannot be known, offering reasons for its conclusions, whatever those might be. For example, an empiricist argues that only sense experience counts as knowledge. Empiricists deem most of our talking pointless jabber, shot through, as it is, with thoughts that exceed what mere sense experience warrants. At the other end of the spectrum, to be credulous is to believe too easily, which is a state of excessive epistemological laxity. Garbage thoughts, for the credulous, mingle with reliable knowledge. Credulity sloshes an undifferentiated slurry of supposition and observation into one's skull.

[66] My assertion, however, contradicts the gist of accounts of Matthew and Luke, which accounts are deeply equivocal. (Mark contains no resurrection narrative, though some fervent reviser attempted to append one later in church history.) Matthew's and Luke's resurrection accounts assert that Jesus physically appeared to disciples, though they had difficulty recognizing him (Luke 24:16 and Luke 24:28-31) and some doubted that they saw Yeshua (Matthew 28:17). In Luke, Jesus suddenly vanishes (Luke 24:31), is thought to be a spirit (Luke 24:37), shows his hands and feet to prove his identity (Luke 24:39, and possibly the textually-omitted verse 40). So, being in the presence of the resurrected Jesus, according to Luke, does not readily identify him as that Yeshua with whom the disciples spent three years. Jesus eats broiled fish, to prove his physicality (Luke 24:42-43). Such accounts leave readers ambivalent about exactly what disciples allege they have seen. This reader suspects improvisation and hagiographical excess.

definition, stands beyond this cosmos. God lives[67] beyond human ken. Much that exists might be examined, even known. God cannot. Whatever we say of God, we say it knowing our talk lacks accuracy.

Theologies cower in metaphor's shadow. Theological talk is non-talk. What can be said of god is that nothing sensical can be said.[68] Some imagine. Their mouths stutter theology, as toddlers babble grammatical gibberish. Nonsense troubles the air around theologians. In the end, one either has an intuition of the supra-empirical or lacks it. God-talk is for blind people who see. Theology is faith's semi-psychotic rant. I do not mean to say that mythic and mystic expression lack content. I do mean to say that such content constitutes the raw material from which people fashion human meaning. Perception of meaning employs sensitivities beyond our five natural capabilities. Meaning is aggregative, not elemental. Meaning is more than intuition, but less than insight. It remains unclear that humans have any perceptions other than those of five senses. Yet, we fashion meaning. Meaning pertains, at least in part, to what cannot be known. Some meaning talk lacks comprehensible content. I am unwilling to say all theology is such. But then, the sense[69] for the supra-empirical has long rooted in me.

Yeshua the Galilean, however, inhabited our side of the epistemological[70] crevasse. Like all humans, Yeshua was born, matured, spoke, worked, suffered, wondered, loved, aged, and died. Yeshua had faith in his god; he embraced the supra-empirical. Yeshua spoke of Yahweh and man. There lies the rub. One wants to mull what Yeshua said, but one finds Yeshua's words mired in cacophonous rubble of first century mumblers. Yeshua's words, as I have said, must be sifted from church hagiography,[71] that is, the church's historical miscomprehen-

---

[67] If such an idea is possible.

[68] Theologians, perhaps with some warrant, ignore Ludwig Wittgenstein's admonition: "Whereof one cannot speak, thereof one must be silent." Wittgenstein, *Tractatus Logico-Philosophicus*, 108 (Section 7). Wittgenstein spoke from his early hyper-empirical (logical positivist) stance. It is not clear that the later Wittgenstein of the perspective-shifting duck-rabbit may not have found some sliver of viable speaking for theologians. Wittgenstein, *Philosophical Investigations*, 165e-166e.

[69] Possibly delusional. Empirically, there is no such sense.

[70] To exist on "our side of the epistemological crevasse" is to dwell in a realm in which human senses might prove of some critical utility. A "supra-empirical" perception wallows in suspicion of divine intrusion into, say, trips to the grocery store or taking out the garbage.

[71] "Hagiography" is writing that praises another greatly, usually by idealizing, or otherwise improving, that person. Hence, hagiography intentionally misrepresents a person for the purpose of promoting him or her in the eyes of others. At law, intentional misrepresentation is "fraud." In theology, hagiography is less deeply stigmatized. The theologian recognizes the human propensity to praise those for whom we have affection, to elevate them for purposes deeply related to our own need for self-praise, and to generate steely heroes from the dross of normal humans.

sions and fictional attributions and pious bootstrapping and enamored story-telling. Sorting that jumble, and restating what emerges of Yeshua from the cleanup, occupies the remainder of this little book.

If one finds this rescue operation to excavate Yeshua a compelling enterprise, a large literature concerning the historical Jesus and his authentic sayings awaits your reading (for some such, see the Reading Suggestions at the end of this book).[72] This essay makes no attempt to survey those other thinkers' conclusions. The Jesus Seminar thinkers seem too ready to welcome Gnostic thoughts into the Yeshua logia. Weyler shares this flaw, most plainly with respect to his view of the reliability of the Thomas logia. Albert Schweitzer's book, *The Quest of the Historical Jesus*, recognizes and adheres to Yeshua's core apocalypticism. Since I have written this book, you can surmise that I find the deliberations of others unsatisfactory. I limit this essay to my own ruminations and conclusions. I seek, and have found, to my own satisfaction,[73] what of Yeshua remains.

---

[72] Thomas Jefferson made a contribution. He sliced elements of the Synoptics and John, piecing together what he thought authentic in stories (not logia only) about Jesus. Sections he rejected Jefferson called a "dunghill." Jefferson, *The Jefferson Bible*.

[73] But probably not yours.

CHAPTER 4
GETHSEMANE SOLILOQUY

For the convenience of readers daunted by the hard work of sorting reliable from suspect sayings of Yeshua within the Synoptic gospels, I offer my epitome of Yeshua's teaching here near the beginning of this little book. The detailed sorting of the Yeshua logia follows, for those who share interest and endurance. Here, I epitomize the body of those sayings I deem reliable. Later, I state why I find each logion reliable or suspect. I exclude anachronisms and translations for Gentiles. I exclude sayings I deem to have been added by the church to bolster its messianic and deeply christological revisions of Yeshua.[74] That ecclesiastical view of Yeshua remains, to this day, equivocal. Yeshua stands wild and unbridled, as are all great thinkers. The Galilean is a human resource, available to any who bother to hear him.

Epitomes, while distorting, also clarify and crystallize. Our age suffers torrential communication. Epitomes redress over-stimulation and render thought, otherwise avoided, accessible, at least in nutshell. I have culled the sayings of Yeshua, to the extent they can be extricated from the detritus in which they are embedded. I have attempted to do so with generosity, but without apology. I have pondered and masticated Yeshua's words. Chewed, they taste of wonder.

So, I now epitomize.

---

[74] "Christology" considers Jesus as a person of two metaphysical natures, imagining his divine and human aspects and their interaction. The church eventually declared Jesus fully god and fully man, disposing of the conundrum haplessly by means of antinomy. Metaphysical inquiries concerning Jesus also speculate upon Jesus' relation to God, which the church eventually defined in the dogma of the trinity: three coequal persons in the Godhead: Father, Son, and Holy Spirit. Considered christologically, the Yeshua of history recedes toward oblivion.

YESHUA'S GETHSEMANE SOLILOQUY

In Gethsemane[75], on the night before his execution, Yeshua implored his disciples to watch with him. They napped instead. What might Yeshua have said to his somnolent peasant companions?

Slumber. So much weakness, my friends. You sleep; events crash over you, heedless. It has been so from the beginning. Even now, you do not grasp the good news. The kingdom of God is upon us, breaking into this world. In our work together, we have ushered the kingdom's leading edge: the sick are well, the lame walk, the dead rise, the possessed are freed, sins are forgiven. Yahweh is about to right the scales of justice and invert our diseased social order. I am to be his strong right hand in so doing. I am the Son of man of the prophet Daniel's vision.

I know you have wished I were a messiah. You would have me mount an insurrection and throw off our odious Roman yoke. You aim too low, my friends. You would shed blood for nominal gains. You would have more of the same, only more to your liking. You would be satisfied with mere political retribution. The onrushing kingdom of God is not an earthly dominion. The Son of man is no mere messiah. Yahweh's kingdom is a realm where the words of peaceful men crush the wiles of the violent. It is a kingdom that rewards those who give all. In the kingdom, the weak find power and the low find exaltation. The arsenal of the kingdom is the heart, not the sword. Let nothing hinder you. Give yourselves utterly to Yahweh's inbreaking kingdom. Hear me! Perhaps you would do so, if only you were awake.

Vindication. Tonight, if Judas's absence is as I suspect, I will suffer torments fashioned by my religious enemies. Take a deep breath. Be

[75] Gethsemane is a garden at the foot of the Mount of Olives across the Kidron Valley from the ancient walled city of Jerusalem. Jesus and his followers often spent time in Gethsemane. See Luke 21:37. Jesus spent his last night in this familiar garden, prayed for deliverance from his fate, and suffered his disciples sleeping through his agony. Matthew 26:36-46.

unafraid. Stoke your patience. Yahweh will act to vindicate me. If I am muzzled, stones will shout. If I am bound, my shackles will crumble. Even if this body dies, my Father will resurrect it promptly. Yahweh's kingdom is inexorable. We shall meet again. Then I shall exercise Yahweh's power. Doubt will flee. Faithless men shall perish. The repentant shall prevail.

Kingdom. The kingdom of God is not a bigger and better version of human empires. The kingdom of God shatters what has been. The kingdom of God is Yahweh's square peg in humanity's round hole. Human rulers marshal armies and erect earthworks. In a day, fields are strewn with the dead and realms are won or lost. The kingdom of God is otherwise. It starts puny, hidden, beneath notice. Yahweh's kingdom is like a tiny mustard seed that becomes, once grown, a gigantic bush. In the end, God's kingdom overwhelms utterly, transforming all things. God's kingdom is yeast in a loaf. Unseen, it changes everything from within. In the kingdom, even fruit trees bear out of season.

The kingdom of God takes for its army the human heart; its razor weapons are compassionate action, forthright speech, and resilience. We, in our wanderings, have taken the good news of the kingdom of God to all the Jews of Galilee and Judea. Yahweh intends, however, to take as his citizens any who demonstrate repentant confidence in Yahweh, and reject any who lack that faith. Yahweh's kingdom is bursting its Jewish container. All faithful persons, Jew and gentile alike, will be gathered in my harvest. All chaff will be consumed in fire. A new world dawns.

Do not worry. I have chosen you. You will not die before you see this kingdom of God in its glory. You will see me exercising divine power as Son of man. You will stand beside me, as will all poor, maimed, downtrodden, blind, lame, broken-hearted, peacemaking, diseased, faithful disciples. Yahweh's kingdom is a peasant movement. Be proud to be part of it. Seize it for yourself now. Do not delay. For Yahweh's kingdom thunders toward us with breathtaking rapidity. Do not be overtaken unaware!

John. John announced Yahweh's judgment at the Jordan River. He baptized for the forgiveness of sins, and ignored Temple sacrifices. Yahweh cherishes repentant sinners. I am wholly aligned with John. Yahweh sent John. Yahweh bypassed the Temple and its religious authorities. It would perhaps be more accurate to say that Yahweh, tasting their vile perversions, spat the Temple and its functionaries from his mouth. Those vipers have hidden their evils; they skulk in shadows.

They make their students worse than themselves. Yahweh will expose them. Their sins will be broadcast to all. Then they will be consumed in divine fire.

Hearts. Yahweh wants your hearts. All men violate God's laws in some way. Only hatred of Yahweh himself will not be forgiven. Many believe that if they comply with religious laws, Yahweh will love them. They are wrong. Yahweh loves pure hearts, repentant hearts. God wants mercy more than obedience, and generosity more than alms. All sins emerge from distorted hearts. That is how men become putrid within. Their visible sins reflect ugliness of heart. People proud of their religiosity are the worst: they pray so others can see, they give to be praised for generosity, and they fast for publicity. Do not imitate them. Pray privately, simply, and quietly. Give in secret; don't even take note of your generosity in your own mind. To do so is dangerous. Fast invisibly. Stay focused on your heart. Introspect. Measure your words; do not blurt. Putrid hearts are easy to come by. Pure hearts require some attention to detail. A man's heart is a tree; taste its fruit to know the man. No price is too great when purchasing a pure heart. In the economy of God, to lose much is to gain all.

To know Yahweh is to drown in your inadequacy. Humble people let their inner putrefaction drain away as they cling to God. Humble people become salt, making life tasty. The kingdom of God belongs to people who embrace their inadequacy. This humility comes more easily to people who cannot equivocate their shortcomings. God's kingdom brims with poor people, mourners, quiet persons, people who show mercy, peacemakers, people who ask questions and seek God, people who seek forgiveness readily, people who give to children, people who are persecuted, repentant tax collectors and whores, people who forgive readily, children, people of childlike simplicity, and people who rely upon God for daily needs. These persons are more likely to have hearts pleasing to Yahweh. A man of pure heart builds his life on a solid rock; putrid-hearted men build on sand. The inwardly-ugly will be washed away in the onrushing cataclysm of the kingdom.

Some matters pose grave risks to your heart. Learn the pressing dangers of anxiety, money, talking, and clamor.

Anxiety. Avoid anxiety about food and houses and clothing. Yahweh knows your needs. He cares for all creatures. How much more God cares for you! Stay focused in the present. Of tomorrow you know little and control less. Ask God, confident of his affection. Wait patiently.

Money. Love of money pollutes a clean heart. Hearts follow desire. Riches tempt one to forsake God in favor of self-assertion. Those who amass wealth already have their reward. Do not aggregate possessions or envy others' things. To love money is to hate God. Wealth is transient; God is immutably forever. If you need excess, hoard joy in God. Yahweh rejects the rich. They have no place in his kingdom. Avoid wealth. If you suffer the misfortune of having wealth, give it away. Stay poor. Keep your heart safe.

Talk. The voice exposes the heart. Never boast. If you find yourself boasting, start over again cleaning out your heart. Your spirituality is plastic; what was once in good shape can again become distorted. Beware! All are inclined to pretend more than is true. Just do what I tell you. Let your life do your talking.

Clamor. Remember! When things get tough or we reach a critical juncture, I go to the wilderness or a mountain and spend time alone. Noise erodes the heart. Quiet restores it.

Suffering. The world gushes suffering like a ruptured pipe. Yahweh relieves suffering as a sign of the inbreaking kingdom. I have healed, exorcized, and repaired sufferers. So too have you, my friends. Still, many more suffer than we have helped. Faith heals. Encourage faith. Pray Yahweh will hasten the kingdom, where suffering of innocents shall cease.

Opponents. Do not emulate evil people. Those who think themselves right with God usually are not. If a person proclaims his righteousness, he stinks to Yahweh. Evil people clamor to lead, but cannot see the way themselves. Religious hypocrites are the worst. To mislead others, they utter words that would please Yahweh, were the words issuing from pure hearts. Religious hypocrites impose convoluted religious rules of their own invention, but ignore those very rules themselves. Evil people do not care about the suffering they propagate. Their doubts about Yahweh lead them to demand signs and omens. They ridicule obvious good when it suits their purposes. Evil people make others sin by discouraging and misguiding them. Evil people will be damned for that! Always, evil people corral money. Jerusalem authorities have remodeled Yahweh's Temple into a livestock trading pit. I went to the Temple and kicked over money changer tables, preached a fiery sermon, and brought Temple functions to a halt for a brief period. Temple spirituality is deficient; if you cannot surpass Temple righteousness, you will never enter the kingdom of God.

Evil people ensnare opponents in word tangles. Evil people are never satisfied in their intellectual wrangling; they flip-flop for convenience and without blushing. Corrupt authorities seek to exercise control as though such belonged to them and not to Yahweh. Evil people are, with respect to God, usurpers. They demand animals to kill, thinking themselves meticulously obedient by so doing. Meanwhile, Yahweh demands mercy and justice and faith, all flowing from repentant hearts. He is ignored. Evil people accuse people who do good acts of stinking motives. Evil people think themselves favored by Yahweh. Whores and Roman soldiers will enter the kingdom of God first, and the Temple establishment last, if at all. Theirs is a perilous position. Jerusalem authorities hate prophets; they murder them. It has always been so. Now they intend to kill me, or so I expect. Yahweh will dismantle the Jerusalem authorities and their Temple. Nothing on Temple mount shall stand when the kingdom breaks over it.

Confront evil people. You do not need to seek them out, but when evil people accost you, speak plainly and truthfully. Do not fear calling them disparaging names, provided the names suit them. Do not let your anger rule you, but use your anger to make your voice unmistakable. You have seen me confront opponents over and over. Speak to them frankly. If they plan evil for you, receive those evils humbly. Ask the evildoer if he would prefer another stab at you. If they steal from you, offer them more from your wallet and do not ask for reimbursement. If you are pressed into forced labor, do twice as much as demanded. In the end, love evil people, as you would yourself wish to be loved. Doing so leaves their hearts to stew. Some may change their paths, which would be a great joy for Yahweh. But if not, you have shielded your own heart from their reeking vomit.

Recognize evil people without judging them. One's vision blurs when examining one's own sins, but grows terribly clear when inspecting the faults of others. To avoid judging evildoers demands balance. One must recognize evil people to avoid following them. One must recognize evil people to confront them. But yours is not to condemn. Yahweh judges. Speak plainly to evildoers of their deeds. Keep your heart from slamming the door on perpetrators. Unanticipated repentance remains possible. Barring that, God will judge soon enough. Their damnation lies beyond those concerns appropriate to humble, open-hearted seekers of Yahweh.

Law. Give political governments what they ask for, if the request is indifferent. Reserve your heartfelt loyalty for the kingdom of God.

Among political persons, much evil resides. Know you may be called to confront that evil.

Religious governments are much more dangerous. In Jerusalem, they preserve Yahweh's laws, but hedge them all around with man-made prescriptions and pointless distinctions. Keep God's law; break human law when necessary. Remember! As the Son of man ushers in the kingdom of God, Yahweh's law will fall to the wayside, utterly fulfilled.

One must find some perspective about divine law. When God says, Keep the Sabbath holy, does he mean that one cannot do good on the Sabbath? No. The Sabbath exists to help, not injure, man. One is free to work hard on the Sabbath doing good, despite Temple rules.

Men cannot bind or release divine law. Even with a Temple-sanctioned divorce, one has not ceased to fornicate when he remarries. God binds marital partners. Man cannot unbind them. The law forbids murder. The kingdom, however, demands more. Anger is heart-murder; so too, impudent insults. Lust is heart-adultery. Swearing is abusive god-mongering; just say "yes" or "no." Do not let conflicts lie. Resolving disputes matters more than Temple compliance. Honor your parents. No priest can relieve you of that obligation. Look within. Who loves God more?—the Jew who keeps divine ordinances, or the gentile who saves a crime victim's life? This is no easy question. Do both.

All the hundreds of rules in the Torah boil down to two: Love Yahweh wholly, and your neighbor as yourself. God sees every person individually. He embraces the sacrifice of a poor person donating a pittance. He scoffs at the ostentatious largesse of the rich.

You will experience this change of perspective regarding the law as a violent upheaval. That it is!

Mission. You have walked with me from Capernaum, around Galilee, and south, up to Jerusalem. We have seen remarkable healings and exorcisms, announced the kingdom, encouraged repentance, confronted opponents, and loved one another. We have had good days and bad days. Capernaum scoffed at us. Five thousand picnickers cheered our message. If you have been paying attention at all (which is not in evidence tonight), you know that Yahweh sent me on this mission. I called you to join me.

You noticed that my understanding of our task changed midstream. When we began at Galilee's lakeside, I believed that I would preach and train you. When I sent you out to the countryside without me, I expected a great groundswell of enthusiasm to erupt. Yahweh would act, so I thought. The kingdom would roll over us, and I would be installed as Son of man in the clouds with power. But you went and returned. Believe me, you did well! Still, Yahweh checked his divine hand. I struggled to understand, and slowly comprehension dawned. I saw that the Son of man must suffer, as did Isaiah's suffering servant, as did the prophets, as did John. Only then is the Son of man qualified to supervise the kingdom of God. I surmised that my tormentors would be Jerusalem authorities. I resigned myself to my restated role, though not without my own measure of objections and trepidation. You, however, did not receive this mission revision politely. Peter, you corrected me, and I rebuffed you. Judas harbored his disappointment, and tonight seeks to compel me toward a messianic insurrection which he imagines preferable. He is wrong, but cannot be deterred, if I read Judas aright.

So, the time is upon us. I will suffer. You will fear and flee in disarray. But then, the kingdom will arrive in power. I will call you to myself.

I remind you now of other matters we have discussed in the course of our travels and work with the poor of the land.

Preaching. Our mission is to tell people about the kingdom of God. Its time is now. That is why I left home. That is why you left your fields and nets and families, and followed me. We just tell people the news. What happens after that is a matter for them to work out. We are lamps in darkness. When we go places, we let people know what we need. If they welcome us, we stay. If not, we leave. We do not coerce. Do not worry about money as you go on your way. Yahweh provides; besides, the time is short. So long as you follow me, you will have no permanent home. You must teach others to announce the news. The harvest needs workers.

Family. This journey is a demanding one. Every fellow traveler must realign priorities. Families and jobs must take second place. The family of God has become our first task. When your father or mother needs burial, you may not be able to help dig. If your family disapproves of your choice to follow, let that be. The kingdom brings conflict aplenty. You must stay focused on the kingdom. That may mean that you never have sex again. That may mean you seldom parent your children. You give up nothing when you follow me that Yahweh will not more than compensate.

Rest. We have rested along the way when necessary. We have also sought solitude.

Competitors. Those who heal in the name of the kingdom, leave them be. But do not be fooled. Only those who are with us are with us.

Honors. Some of you have requested honors. Honors, in the kingdom, belong to those who serve. Have you been paying attention?

Forgiveness. Set no limit to forgiveness. When a brother sins, confront him. When he repents, forgive him. Just keep forgiving and forging onward.

Children. Children matter. They always have access to me. Open your arms to children. In Yahweh's kingdom, all citizens resemble children.

Giving. Give freely. Do not ask for terms or reimbursement. If someone asks, give.

Discipleship. Your path will be mine; prepare to suffer. Yahweh has linked glory and suffering inextricably. You will be disparaged. Find encouragement in one another.

Prayer. I have often prayed. Do so yourselves. Find a quiet place and immerse yourself in Yahweh. Pray also with others. Yahweh hears. Persistence matters. Faith and persistence move mountains.

Sadness. I have been sad, even tonight. I have asked Yahweh to grant me a different path. He has not done so. I accept that outcome. Shortly, Yahweh will vindicate our faith and suffering. I shall overcome whatever our opponents do to me. Have faith.

Now I must be going. Wake, friends!

Judas, is that you, there in the shadows?

CHAPTER 5
THE SYNOPTIC INSIGHT

One requires tools for the task of sifting the literary rubble in which the sayings of Yeshua lie embedded. The canonical texts themselves suggest sieves.

The Synoptic problem[76] is not really a problem, but an insight. The core narratives of Matthew and Luke lean heavily, but not exclusively, upon Mark's earlier tale of Yeshua's life. Mark's story captures the oral tradition associated with Yeshua, recounting Yeshua's adult baptism by John, temptation in times of much-needed solitude, selection of disciples, peripatetic teaching of growing crowds of the poor, occasional dust-ups with religious authorities, sending disciples to preach in Galilean towns, rising to the attention of political authorities, a sea change in Yeshua's teaching, Yeshua's recognition that things were not going to turn out well for him, travel up to Jerusalem from Galilee in the north, confrontations at the Jerusalem Temple, a last meal with the disciples, betrayal by Judas to Jewish authorities, priestly arrest at the Gethsemane garden, trial before Roman Pilate, condemnation, crucifixion, death, burial, and the empty tomb. Matthew approaches the Marcan storyline with a later, Hellenized Jewish writer's concerns. Luke approaches the Marcan narrative from a yet later, Hellenic gentile point of view. Both Matthew and Luke vigorously advance the hagiography of Yeshua,

---

[76] The synoptic gospels share a viewpoint; hence, the designation. The synoptic problem, summarized, explores the fact that Matthew and Luke utilized Mark's narrative as the backbone of their gospels, adding to Mark's storyline other sayings of common source (technically, identified by the German term, *Quelle*, meaning "source"), unique sayings, and new narrative elements. Matthew, Mark, and Luke exhibit a complex chronological and sourcing interrelationship. The "problem" of the synoptics lies in sorting this complexity.

which enthusiastic bootstrapping was already well-entrenched at the time of the earlier composition of Mark.[77]

The Synoptic problem reveals, first, that neither Matthew nor Luke knew the course of historical events in Yeshua's life except from Mark's story. This fact excludes the apostle Matthew as the author of Matthew. Matthew and Luke wrote at a time when eyewitness testimony had entered the oral traditions. Neither Matthew nor Luke was troubled by the possibility of eye-witness disconfirmation, nor aided by living eyewitness recollection. This fact dates these gospels to the late first century, when the first generation of Yeshua's students had passed. One seeks an impetus that would have driven the eschatological church awaiting Yeshua's imminent return to the extremity of memorializing its story and forming a fledgling institution. That impetus was the recognition that Yeshua, contrary to his express promise, was not returning any time soon. The church's oral tradition was too plastic, wholly too fragile to abandon to history's vagaries. The tradition needed to be captured, or, perhaps more accurately, rescued. The Synoptic problem further reveals rising political tides within the early Christian community about its Yeshua story. Mark, in the view of later writers, required augmentation. Matthew (perhaps with misguided ardor) connected Yeshua to Jewish messianic expectations, especially in his Old Testament proof-texting. Luke (perhaps with devotional gullibility) adapts Yeshua for gentile audiences utilizing such sources as were available to him (Luke 1:1-4).

Second, both Matthew and Luke retrieve Yeshua sayings firmly entrenched in the oral tradition but excluded from the Marcan narrative.[78] Each utilizes material from a (hypothetical) logia collection, commonly called Q (for the German term "Quelle," meaning source). The Q materials are a compendium of sayings of Yeshua, not a narrative. Matthew and Luke do not utilize these Q sayings in consistent ways.[79] Matthew and Luke each include logia and stories not contained in Mark.[80] Matthew and Luke each use logia not found in the other or in Mark.[81]

The Synoptic problem reveals that Matthew and Luke are ignorant of the context in which these Yeshua snippets were uttered. These later gospel

---

[77] See Mark 1:11 and Mark 9:2-7 and Mark 14:61-62a.

[78] One wonders why Mark excluded the Q sayings, compelling as they are. Perhaps the sayings document was not available to Mark, or perhaps it had not yet coalesced. The compiler of Quelle is an unrecognized gospeller, whose name should be, but is not, as familiar as Matthew, Mark, Luke, and John.

[79] Compare Matthew 5-7 (Sermon on the Mount) and Luke 6:17-49 (Sermon on the Plain), for example.

[80] Consider the Lord's Prayer (Matthew 6:9-14 and Luke 11:2-4).

[81] Consider Matthew 5:17 (though one might roughly compare Luke 16:16-17) and Luke 15:11-32.

writers are not reporting events, but fictionalizing contexts for logia, organized in a manner that serves their respective rhetorical purposes. One might ask whether Matthew and Luke considered Mark's contextualizing of Yeshua's sayings authoritative. They did not.[82] Matthew and Luke extract Marcan Yeshua logia and reutilize them in different contexts. It is safe to say that for Matthew and Luke, the contexts Mark employs for Yeshua logia are speculative enough to permit fluid readaptation.

So, one learns from the Synoptic tangle that Matthew, Mark, and Luke injected contextless sayings (logia) of Yeshua into a traditional bare bones narrative with largely unconstrained literary license. Theirs was a building block process. Matthew and Luke added narrative elements bolstering Yeshua's credentials: virgin birth, astronomical phenomena, childhood lectures, and resurrection accounts, or fantastical exorcisms and healings, for example. When searching for reliable Yeshua sayings in the Synoptic morass, our interest lies in the logia themselves, not in the uses or contexts supplied by Mark, Matthew, or Luke. Which among the Synoptic Yeshua sayings should be credited, and which set aside, when attempting to hear Yeshua the Galilean?

From the Synoptic structure of the gospels, one arrives at a ***first sieve*** for the sayings of Yeshua. Later sayings inconsistent with the Marcan Yeshua are suspect. Mark came first. The author of Mark may have composed during a period when eyewitnesses might have corrected or contradicted Mark's rendition of Yeshua's sayings or events. Matthew and Luke lean upon Mark's storyline. In sorting the Yeshua sayings, logia inconsistent with the Marcan Yeshua should be suspect.[83] Having surmounted this hurdle, a Yeshua saying has not escaped oblivion. Mark too transmitted material of which he had no direct knowledge. The materials Mark utilized had also suffered decades-long transmission in oral form, which transmission pruned, distorted, deleted, and augmented Yeshua's words. Still, Mark and Q and Matthew's and Luke's independent sources of Yeshua logia remain as close as one may approach the words of Yeshua. This fact leaves us with a sobering prospect. **No sorting of the Synoptic logia leaves one with an indisputable rendering of Yeshua's teachings. The best one can hope, based on the extant materials, is a penultimate, and deeply equivocal, sketch of the public instruction that Yeshua delivered to his various audiences.**

---

[82] Consider, for example, Mark 4:1, Matthew 13:1, Luke 8:4, or Mark 9:35 (in Capernaum), Matthew 23:11 (in the Woe Sermon), Luke 22:26 (after the Last Supper).

[83] The process of sorting for Marcan consistency is, however, dialectical. The gospel of Mark, like the other Synoptics, needs some culling to remove elements introduced by the early church. Hence, there is a necessary circularity in working one's way back to the Marcan essentials. One must edit Mark to unearth a Marcan Yeshua with which to be consistent. In argumentation, this is a less-than-optimal logical structure, suffering substantial circularity.

A ***second sieve*** also springs from the Synoptics. Does the logion evidence Yeshua expressing his self-concept as Son of man (Daniel 7), wedded to the Suffering Servant of Isaiah 52-53? The church, for reasons that are difficult to assess after so many centuries, desperately wanted Yeshua to be received as the Son of God, the messiah of the Jews, and the Son of man of eschatological judgment. Perhaps these urgencies represent the need to present Yeshua winningly to various constituencies of the Greco-Roman world at the eastern end of the Mediterranean. The early churches' mash-up of these distinct concepts, however, leaves Jesus Ecclesiasticus a breath-taking distance from everyday humanity. Yeshua repeatedly denied that he was one of the several messiahs of the Jews. He never claimed to be the Son of God, except when the church inserted such language into his mouth. I call this second sieve Danielic Son of Man. If one finds in a logion the term "Son of man" or finds Yeshua exercising the prerogatives granted to the Son of Man in the Book of Daniel, or finds Yeshua assuming he is in charge of what transpires in his presence, then one sees Yeshua acting as the eschatological Son of man.

A ***third sieve*** is the urgency of repentance. Yeshua taught that the kingdom of God trembles to break into this world with judgment and wonder. One enters that new realm by repenting. Hence, repentance is urgent. Logia that lack such urgency reflect the later church's sentiments, suffering as it was from the interminable delay of the celestial arrival of the Son of man—one has years or decades, not days or weeks, in which to repent.

A ***fourth sieve*** I call a hagiographical hurdle. Some logia transgress the hagiographic impulse and require the church to surmount embarrassment. These logia I take to be the most secure among Yeshua's sayings. Far from elevating Yeshua, these sayings discredit him or present Yeshua in a disfavorable light. These unflattering logia survived the hagiographical surge of the church because they were too deeply-entrenched in the oral tradition to be excised by a gospel writer (except John). For that reason, embarrassing logia (for example the repeated promise of imminent return in glory or the curse of the fig tree) this author deems the most reliable of all Yeshua logia.

A ***fifth sieve*** sorts logia into those that present a possible historical Yeshua, and those that make of Yeshua a magician, or plenipotent demigod, or miracle worker, or frightful exorcist, one born impossibly, in a manner that conforms to various sayings of eighth century prophets, resurrected and eating fish, and transmitting holiness by contagion to those with whom Yeshua associated or even objects he touched. This sieve, which I call hagiographical excess, leaves me doubting that Yeshua uttered the logion. The Marcan Yeshua was too bare for the soaring faith of Matthew's or Luke's audiences. In Matthew and yet more in Luke, detailed resurrection narratives encumber the empty tomb of Mark. Yeshua, like

Mithras, springs from the womb of a virgin, has Persian birth attendants and astronomical marvels, teaches elders while a child, opposes evil persons, and is resurrected. Events mutate into miracles, rendering a Yeshua akin to Greek demigods.

When death steals a beloved human from us, we tend to recall the deceased's virtues and forget her detriments. Hopes and superstitions and wishful mis-recollections augment, and ultimately distort, biography. This is, as I have said, the hagiographic impulse. At some level, hagiography is a remedial grief response. At another, hagiography quenches our thirst for heroes elevated from humankind's mass of muddlers. Gospel sayings or events that exhibit hagiographical excess are suspect, if one seeks the teachings of Yeshua the Galilean. I assume that Yeshua the Galilean was a talented human possessed of thoughts, relationships, and actions, but lacking, as do we all, extraordinary divine resources. So, this fifth sieve asks, Does a logion portray Yeshua as possessing supernatural powers or knowledge of the unknowable, vaulting Yeshua above the common ruck of humankind? If so, the logion is suspect.

This assumption offends some among the Christian orthodox faithful. For that offense, I apologize, without relenting. I intend no blasphemy. I intend to audit Yeshua, suppressing the cacophonous chatter and pious emendations with which the church has burdened and distorted those teachings.

A ***sixth sieve*** comes to light in the gospel writers' tendency to project their post-Yeshua concerns and knowledge into Yeshua's past and sayings. The early church faced many problems, primary among which were: A) how should the church cope with Yeshua's failure to return in power as promised and the consequent despair of the faithful at this failure,[84] and B) how and under what terms should the community welcome gentiles into Christian faith.[85] Logia that place such post-Yeshuan concerns in the mouth of Yeshua are suspect.

A ***seventh and final sieve*** might affect a very small number of logia, which appear to be translations for the benefit of non-Aramaic-speaking readers. I take any such snippet to be mere literary license, and hence no reliable part of Yeshua's sayings.

---

[84] Luke 19:11 expressly acknowledges this problem. Yeshua's non-return put the early church to the task of institutionalizing Christians, to which task Yeshua's students were ill-adapted. Yeshua's first companions were fishermen and commoners, not bureaucrats.

[85] See the debates between Paul and the Jerusalem church over gentile compliance with dietary and circumcision laws, which issue occupies Paul's Epistle to the Romans.

CHAPTER 6
JOHN, PAUL, AND THE REMAINDER

The gospel of John is easily the most striking literary composition of the New Testament, comparable only to Paul's I Corinthians 13 paean to love for soaring eloquence. John's Jesus endears. Yeshua becomes, in John's rendition, the shepherd, the Way, the very Word of God, the friend of humankind, the Greeks logos. The problem with John's gospel resides in its lack of interest in the historical person, Yeshua the Galilean. John's Jesus is the cosmic conduit for seven homiletically-polished sermons hot off the Divine press. John's Jesus is not Yeshua the Galilean. John's gospel was polished long after the Synoptics. Effectively, John repudiates the Synoptic Jesus and the Marcan Synoptic narrative. John's Jesus has suffered a theogonic make-over under the scalpel of a Gnostic surgeon. John's Jesus, while lovely, is suspect.

Saul of Tarsus, who renames himself Paul and self-nominates as an apostle, also evidences little interest in Yeshua. Paul never met Yeshua. Paul's work remains the pinnacle of New Testament intellectual effort, but in Paul's hands, Jesus becomes a messianic cipher for a new Hellenistic religion which Paul frames. Jesus appears shorn of words and deeds, recast as the incarnate god, Christ. To Paul, Jesus' being, not his words and deeds, matter. Gone is the provocative apocalyptist from Galilee, the man who bound himself as friend to poor villagers. Paul invents what we now call Christianity. At the core of Pauline theology lies neglect of Yeshua the Galilean. The church, historically, mimics Pauline and Johannine disinterest in Yeshua. The Yeshua this writer finds compelling has been shoved aside by Paul's indomitable risen Christ.

The New Testament's remaining epistles and apocalypse transmit thoughts milling about the later Hellenized and Paulinized gentile church. All evidence scant interest in the man Yeshua.

To find Yeshua's sayings, then, one must linger in the Synoptics, and consider, at least briefly, texts that failed to make the Synoptic writers' cuts for genuine sayings of Yeshua.

CHAPTER 7
THE GOSPEL OF THOMAS

The most credible among the extra-canonical Yeshua logia is the collection of sayings mistitled The Gospel of Thomas. This collection, discovered in the Nag Hammadi Gnostic library (1945), which was preserved in a cave, and fragments of the same work at Oxyrhynchus, in a desiccated Egyptian garbage pit, draws together sayings attributed to Yeshua. The Thomas collection lacks the narrative elements that might categorize it as a gospel. Thomas logia will be identified TL followed by the Brill numbering, for the sake of brevity.[86]

Some Thomas logia track sayings **familiar** from the Synoptic Yeshua:

- TL2 concerning seeking and finding,
- TL5 and TL6 regarding hidden things being revealed,
- TL10 about judgment,
- TL11 about alteration of the basic rules of living by Yahweh's intervention,
- TL12 concerning disciple debates about greatness,
- TL14 about what goes into and comes out of a man,
- TL16 on creating divisions, not peace, in the world,
- TL20 about the mustard seed,
- the little children saying of TL22,
- the few at TL23,

[86] One can find an acceptable translation of the Gospel of Thomas with the Brill numbering at: http://earlychristianwritings.com/text/thomas-anon.html.

- light of the world at TL24,
- loving others at TL25,
- motes and beams in eyes at TL26,
- TL32 about the city on the hill,
- TL33 about lights and bushels,
- TL34 concerning the blind leading the blind,
- TL35 about robbers in one's house,
- TL36 about anxiety over clothing,
- TL38,[87] TL39 on serpents and doves,
- TL41 about taking and having,
- TL44 regarding blasphemy against the holy spirit,
- TL45 about acts proceeding from hearts,
- TL46 about John the Baptist and little children in the kingdom,
- TL47 about serving two masters, new and old wineskins, and patching garments,
- TL51 about the hidden kingdom,
- TL54 about the poor and the kingdom,
- TL55 about leaving family to follow,
- TL57 about wheat and weeds,
- TL58 about suffering and life,
- TL61A about judgment,
- TL62B about right and left hands,
- TL63 about the rich man and his barns,
- TL64 about the spurned dinner invitation,
- TL65 about the vineyard owner's son,
- TL66 about the cornerstone,
- TL68 about blessing in persecution,
- TL69 about blessing in persecution and hunger,
- TL70 about the fruits of what lies within,
- TL73 about the harvest and laborers,
- TL76 about the pearl and imperishability of the kingdom,
- TL86 about foxes, birds, and having no place to lay his head,
- TL89 about the outside and inside,
- TL90 about Yeshua's easy yoke,
- TL92 about seeking and finding,
- TL93 about pearls before swine,
- TL94 about seeking and knocking,

---

[87]Compare Matthew 26:11.

- TL95 about giving without compensation,
- TL96 about leaven in bread,
- TL99 about Yeshua's mother and brothers and the kingdom,
- TL107 about finding the straying sheep,
- TL110 about the rich giving away their wealth, and
- TL111 about the apocalypse and judgment.

Some Thomas logia broach subjects addressed by the Synoptic Yeshua, but **twist** the import of those sayings in unfamiliar directions:

- TL8 concerning men fishing,
- TL12's emphasis on James's preeminence,
- TL21 recasting the parable of the field,
- TL27 about keeping fasts and Sabbaths,
- TL30 about three gods,
- TL31 about physicians and friends,
- TL37 about the second coming,
- TL40 concerning vines and judgment,
- TL48 about peace moving mountains,
- TL49 about solitude and election,
- TL50 about light and election,
- TL53 about the heart and circumcision (late and Pauline),
- TL71 about destroying so none can rebuild,
- TL75 about the few and many emphasizing solitude,
- TL78 about the kingdom and John the Baptist's strength,
- TL79 regarding imminent judgment,
- TL91 about Yeshua's identity,
- TL95 about giving without compensation,
- TL100 about giving Caesar his due,
- TL101 about hating and loving parents like Yeshua did,
- TL104 about fasting and the bridegroom,
- TL106 about moving mountains,
- TL109 about a treasure hidden in a field, and
- TL113 about the hidden kingdom.

Others evidence **influences outside** the work-a-day world of illiterate Jewish subsistence villagers: Consider Thomas's sayings that:

- smack of Gnostic salvation at TL1,
- contain Hellenistic saws at TL3,
- promise Stoic cosmic unification at TL4,
- Gnostic secrets of TL13 and TL17,

- universal transformation in TL22,
- Hellenic body-spirit dualism at TL29 and TL112,
- TL62A about (Gnostic) mysteries,
- TL67 about self-knowledge and salvation, and
- TL108 about transpersonal merger and Gnostic salvation.

A few Thomas logia evidence **hagiographical excess**:
- TL15 about man not born of woman,
- TL18 and TL19 about the deathlessness of those who know Yeshua's beginning,
- TL19 about Yeshua's pre-existence,
- Yeshua speaking after death in judgment at TL28,
- TL43 about disciples challenging Yeshua,
- TL52 about the twenty-four prophets predicting Yeshua,
- TL61B about Christology and light and darkness,
- TL77 about Yeshua's ubiquity,
- TL82 about being near and far from the kingdom, and
- TL83 about the light of the father revealed in a man.

Some Thomas logia are intelligible, but **novel**:
- TL59 about looking for Yahweh,
- TL60 about the Samaritan lamb corpse,
- TL72 about dividing,
- TL80 about finding the body,
- TL85 about Adam's unworthiness and death,
- TL88 about giving to angels,
- TL97 about the trail to the kingdom,
- TL98 about killing a great man,
- TL102 about dogs not letting cattle eat,
- TL103 about preparing for robbers, and
- TL114 about making women male.

A number of Thomas's logia simply **puzzle**:
- TL7 about lion transformation,
- TL42 about becoming passers-by,
- TL56 about finding corpses,
- TL74 about the well,
- TL81 about power and denial,
- TL84 about pre-existent images,
- TL87 about depending on the body, and

- TL105 about sons of harlots.

The Gospel of Thomas lends credence to the hypothesis of a Quelle upon which Matthew and Luke depended, because it shows that contextless compilations of Yeshua sayings existed.

In reading the Gospel of Thomas, one gets a sense for the permutational impetus of intense religious belief interacting with oral and written religious materials. The writer of Thomas undoubtedly transmits sayings of Yeshua as they were delivered to him, but these Yeshua sayings writhe in his hands, adding elements, sopping up extant mystical ideas, twisting to accommodate the author's mythic preferences. The hagiographical, Hellenistic, and Gnostic influences in the Gospel of Thomas are patent. While the Thomas logia may lend credence to Synoptic logia, divergent Thomas logia can neither supplant nor supplement the Synoptic core. The flow of logia runs, not from Thomas to the Synoptic corpus, but rather from the Synoptic logia out toward the Thomas trove. Yeshua's sayings are less numerous than either Thomas or the Synoptic writers would have us believe.

I have chosen to analyze the Gospel of Thomas because I find it to be the most credible of the non-canonical sources for Yeshua logia. I extend the same generally-dismissive sentiment to the remainder of the apocryphal and non-canonical works. The incipient branching tendencies one finds within the Synoptics have run amok in the non-canonical sources. If one admits their multifarious Yeshuas, one forsakes hope of unearthing a comprehensible Yeshua. Freed of first-century roots, the Yeshua corpus writhes in each reader's hands, becoming in the mind of each a different person and a diverse teaching. Surely, this realization must have driven, first, the Synoptic writers, who themselves sorted among the available Yeshua sayings, and, second, the canon-asserters (for example, Athanasius). The church's Yeshua, facing the onslaught of droves of adapters and revisionists, thrashed in ideological quicksand. Insisting upon the Marcan Yeshua threw their mutating savior a rope. Rescued, the church buttressed Yeshua into Jesus Ecclesiasticus.

CHAPTER 8
SORTING LOGIA

To summarize, sieves for Yeshua logia are:

A. **Marcan Consistency.** Is the logion consistent with logia of Yeshua in the Gospel of Mark (as culled by the following principles)? or

B. **Danielic Son of Man.** Does the logion refer to the Son of man as described in Daniel 7, either expressly or by reference to the sort of judgment contemplated in that vision? or

C. **Urgency of Repentance.** Is Yeshua concerned with rapidity of heartfelt response to the gospel message, given that the irruptive kingdom is about to burst into this world? or

D. **Hagiographical Hurdle.** Does the logion pose an obstacle to the early church's hagiographical urgency? or

E. **Hagiographical Excess.** Does the logion attribute to Yeshua powers that are magical, supra-human, or otherwise incredible? Does the logion paint Yeshua in a favorable light that is inconsistent with ideas that an intelligent first-century functionally-illiterate Galilean Jewish peasant, living among people of similar circumstances and capabilities, might possess? Either of these tendencies subjects a logion to allegations of hagiographical excess, or

F. **Anachronisms and Post-Yeshuan Impositions**. Does the logion place in Yeshua's mouth anachronisms or post-Yeshuan theological or historical interests, knowledge, or language? or

G. **Translations for Gentiles.** Is the logion an explanatory interpolation?

In what follows, I identify and number the Yeshua sayings of Mark, then Matthew, then Luke (their historical order of composition), categorizing each as reliable or suspect. Reliable logia are further identified as consistent with the Marcan Yeshua, therefore exhibiting Marcan Consistency ("MC"), identifying Yeshua as the Danielic Son of man ("DSM"), evidencing Yeshua's characteristic urgency about necessity of immediate repentance ("UR"), or embarrassing the early church's intent to elevate Yeshua, therefore posing a hagiographical hurdle ("HH"). Suspect logia are identified as evidencing hagiographical excess ("HE") or presenting anachronisms and post-Yeshuan concerns ("APY"). Translations for Gentiles are helps for non-Aramaic speakers ("TG").

To chart the abbreviations for evaluative sieves for logia, these are:

Marcan Consistency ....MC
Danielic Son of man ....DSM
Urgency of Repentance ....UR
Hagiographical Hurdle ....HH
Hagiographical Excess ....HE
Anachronisms and Post-Yeshuan concerns ....APY
Translations for Gentiles ....TG

In the Synoptic gospels, I identify 549 logia,[88] 439 of which I deem reliable (80%) and 110 of which I deem suspect (20%). Among suspect logia, 38 are HE (7%) and 72 are APY (13%).

In the gospel of **Mark**, I identify 123 logia, 103 of which I deem reliable (84%) and 20 suspect (16%). Among suspect logia, 6 are HE (5%) and 14 APY(11%).

In the gospel of **Matthew**, I identify 215 logia, 170 of which I deem reliable (79%) and 45 suspect (21%). Among suspect logia, 13 are HE (6%) and 32 APY(15%).

In the gospel of **Luke**, I identify 211 logia, 166 of which I deem reliable (79%) and 45 suspect (21%). Among suspect logia, 19 are HE (9%) and 26 APY(12%).

I have categorized reliable logia by six core subjects: irruptive kingdom logia, salvation logia, healing logia, opponent logia, law logia, and mission logia. Each logion is presented once, though it may well contain material that might be differently categorized.

Concerning both reliable and suspect logia, I offer some rationale for my decisions. I sometimes parenthetically offer the gospel writer's context for sayings that would be confusing or opaque without such contextual information. All such

[88] Please note that the logia end at Logion 538. Some logia, after I had numbered them, I broke apart. Such logia are numbered with affixed A or, in one instance, B. The total is 549 logia.

contexts are equivocal and should be disregarded, once the gist of the logion as presented in the Synoptic gospel is clear.

CHAPTER 9
RELIABLE LOGIA OF YESHUA[89]

IRRUPTIVE KINGDOM LOGIA[90]

Yeshua's core message detailed the imminent irruptive kingdom of Yahweh. This eschatological event teetered above the abyss of hell, into which those who failed to repent and embrace that kingdom's ethos were doomed to fall. Yeshua believed time was short, and that he, as Son of man, was the final and critical element of irruption. Hence, Yeshua's urgency lies everywhere, behind every parable, in every lesson. Yeshua sighs relief when one repents heartfully. He grieves at smart skeptics stuck in that manner of thought promoted by Temple authorities. If repentant, Yeshua welcomes rubes, foreigners, and whores. Though they comply with Temple strictures, Yeshua condemns knowledgeable rabbis and Temple bigwigs and fervent adherents of respectable religion. Their hearts reek. Such will be damned.

Logion 1 (Mark 1.15): "The time is fulfilled, and the kingdom of God is at hand; repent, and believe in the gospel."

---

[89] Superscript numbers within New Testament citations indicate RSV versification, not footnotes.

[90] I am asked why I have not translated from the Greek for the purposes of this little book. I learned Greek and translated much of the New Testament during my theological education. What I learned from that dabbling is that the Revised Standard Version was translated, and amended in the New Revised Standard Version, by persons with skills that far exceed my own. Since those days, I have left translation to those whose lives are devoted to such enterprises, and undertaken efforts better fitted to my own gifts. One can, without abandoning rigor, rely upon the work of highly qualified translators of biblical literatures. In comparing the relative skill among translators, mine and theirs, mine are negligible.

MC, DSM, UR.

This core summary of Yeshua's message is consistent with his self-designation as "Son of man," and with the bulk of Yeshua's preaching, which trends toward the message containing information critical to the hearer concerning Yahweh's intention to intervene imminently to disrupt the course of human affairs. Hence, the logion evidences the urgency with which Yeshua conducted his ministry, as is typical in Mark's version.

Logion 8 (Mark 2.10): "[10]But that you may know that the Son of man has authority on earth to forgive sins."

MC, DSM, UR.

Yeshua's self-designation is "Son of man." The name derives from the intertestamental book of Daniel (probably written around the second century B.C., during the period of the Maccabean revolt against the Romans), which was pseudonymously propagated. The apocalyptic vision of Daniel 7.13-14, reads:

"[13]I saw in the night visions, and behold, with the clouds of heaven there came one like a son of man, and he came to the Ancient of Days and was presented before him. [14]And to him was given dominion and glory and kingdom, that all peoples, nations, and languages should serve him; his dominion is an everlasting dominion, which shall not pass away, and his kingdom one that shall not be destroyed."

Yahweh approves his agent, the son of man, to whom Yahweh gives perpetual rule over mankind. The son of man's rule is an apocalyptic inbreaking divine judgment and power, overwhelming earthly political regimes. The Son of man is no messiah. Messiahs are various earthly rulers who defeat Israel's political opponents, presumably with the assistance of Yahweh[91]. That the early church was aware of this distinction is confirmed by the account of Yeshua rebuking Peter.[92] There existed a tendency in the disciples during Yeshua's ministry and in the post-Yeshuan church to conflate the various concepts. Several rejected logia place messianic affirmations in the mouth of Yeshua.

Son of man sayings have heightened reliability because the later Hellenized church preferred to conceive Yeshua as the Son of God, assimilating Yeshua to Greek cultural demi-gods of the Hellenic pantheon. Son of God sayings have reduced reliability because of their late, non-Jewish interests. Son of man sayings have heightened reliability because of their mild embarrassment to the gospel

[91] See Isaiah 44:28-45:1, which identifies Cyrus of Persia as the anointed of Yahweh, which might be translated "messiah," in a semi-transliteration of the Hebrew term.

[92]See Mark 8:33, and Matthew 16:23, and by Luke 21:27.

writers, in that Yeshua plainly failed to establish himself as the Danielic Son of man. Mid-ministry, Yeshua creatively assimilated his Son of man identity to deutero-Isaiah's suffering servant (Isaiah 53), resulting in Yeshua's conviction that the Son of man would be persecuted and killed. Yeshua's innovation caused a stir among the disciples, who had thought they were participating in a messianic revolution at worst, or the divine moment of judgment at best. Yeshua's change of course may have motivated Judas's betrayal, who might have believed that by forcing Yeshua's hand he could compel Yeshua to fight as every good messiah should. Yeshua's evolving sense of identity certainly motivated Peter's dysphoria.[93]

Logion 11 (Mark 2.19-20): "Can the wedding guests fast while the bridegroom is with them? As long as they have the bridegroom with them, they cannot fast. [20]The days will come, when the bridegroom is taken away from them, and they will fast in that day."

MC, DSM, UR.

Note that Yeshua's later conception of his ministry is here transported into his early public work. Yet, the sense of personal import, the irruptive onslaught of Yahweh's direct rule, guides the passage.

Logion 12 (Mark 2.21): "[21]No one sews a piece of unshrunk cloth on an old garment; if he does, the patch tears away from it, the new from the old, and a worse tear is made."

MC, DSM, UR.

The old and the new juxtaposed. Yeshua's ministry is the cutting-edge of the divine new order. The Danielic Son of man matrix of ideas lies behind the "old-new" dichotomy.

Logion 13 (Mark 2.22): "[22]And no one puts new wine into old wineskins; if he does, the wine will burst the skins, and the wine is lost, and so are the skins; but new wine is for fresh skins."

MC, DSM, UR.

Again, the old and the new are compared, the eschatological contrast. Note the choice of metaphor. Only poor people would be tempted to risk putting new wine in old skins.

---

[93]Mark 8:33.

LOGION SIEVE KEY: Marcan Consistency (MC), Danielic Son of man (DSM), Hagiographical Hurdle (HH), Urgency of Repentance (UR), Hagiographical Excess (HE), Anachronisms and Post-Yeshuan concerns (APY)

Logion 17 (Mark 3.23-27): "How can Satan cast out Satan? [24]If a kingdom is divided against itself, that kingdom cannot stand. [25]And if a house is divided against itself, that house will not be able to stand. [26]And if Satan has risen up against himself and is divided, he cannot stand, but is coming to an end. [27]But no one can enter a strong man's house and plunder his goods, unless he first binds the strong man; then indeed he may plunder his house."

MC, DSM, UR.

The themes of ultimate conflict and urgency echo the Danielic Son of man, without mentioning him.

Logion 24 (Mark 4.26-29): "[26]The kingdom of God is as if a man should scatter seed upon the ground, [27]and should sleep and rise night and day, and the seed should sprout and grow, he knows not how. [28]The earth produces of itself, first the blade, then the ear, then the full grain in the ear. [29]But when the grain is ripe, at once he puts in the sickle, because the harvest has come."

MC, UR, DSM.

Yeshua emphasizes that Yahweh is acting to put the sickle to his grain, so the need to act quickly is apparent. The Son of man lingers beneath the saying, as Yahweh's harvester of judgment.

Logion 25 (Mark 4.30-32): "With what can we compare the kingdom of God, or what parable shall we use for it? [31]It is like a grain of mustard seed, which, when sown upon the ground, is the smallest of all the seeds on earth; [32]yet when it is sown it grows up and becomes the greatest of all shrubs, and puts forth large branches, so that the birds of the air can make nests in its shade."

MC, DSM, UR.

Yeshua teaches that the kingdom's greatness lies hidden, and so not presently apparent to the many. Despite appearances, the need for repentance remains great. Unstated is the onrushing judgment of the Son of man.

Logion 56 (Mark 8.38): "[38]For whoever is ashamed of me and of my words in this adulterous and sinful generation, of him will the Son of man also be ashamed, when he comes in the glory of his Father with the holy angels."

MC, DSM, UR.

Yeshua specifies the result of the irruptive kingdom, its judgment, and his role.

Logion 57 (Mark 9.1): "Truly, I say to you, there are some standing here who will not taste death before they see the kingdom of God come in power."

MC, UR, DSM, HH.

In my view, this logion, and its correlates, are the most reliable sayings of Yeshua in the Synoptics, for they posed a grave embarrassment and created troubles for the early church, which struggled to explain the non-return of Yeshua. The logion exhibits all the other characteristics of reliable logia. The hagiographical hurdle of the early church's embarrassment at Yeshua's errant prediction is expressly acknowledged at Luke 19.11.

Logion 58 (Mark 9.12-13): (The disciples ask about Malachi 4.5) "Elijah does come first to restore all things; and how is it written of the Son of man, that he should suffer many things and be treated with contempt? [13]But I tell you that Elijah has come, and they did to him whatever they pleased, as it is written of him."

MC, DSM, UR.

Yeshua again associates himself, as Son of man, with John the Baptist's ministry, which he takes to be the return of Elijah, prophesied at Malachi 4.5. The kingdom has arrived, its signs fulfilled.

Logion 68 (Mark 9.43-48): "[43]And if your hand causes you to sin, cut it off; it is better for you to enter life maimed than with two hands to go to hell, to the unquenchable fire. [45]And if your foot causes you to sin, cut it off; it is better for you to enter life lame than with two feet to be thrown into hell. [47]And if your eye causes you to sin, pluck it out; it is better for you to enter the kingdom of God with one eye than with two eyes to be thrown into hell, [48]where their worm does not die, and the fire is not quenched."

MC, DSM, UR.

Yeshua uses hyperbole to underline urgency of repentance. Judgment is imminent at the hands of Yahweh's Son of man.

Logion 69 (Mark 9.49): "[49]For every one will be salted with fire."

MC, DSM, UR.

Yeshua warns of burning judgment at the hands of the Son of man. Repentance is the essence of wisdom. None escapes.

Logion 74 (Mark 10.18): "Why do you call me good? No one is good but God alone."

MC.

Yeshua confronts the common practices of his culture, here, its mode of respectful address. There may be in this logion a hint of hagiographic excess, seeking to intimate that Jesus is god. To that extent, the logion is suspect as an interpolation of the early church's later Hellenistic syncretism. All things considered, I credited the logion.

Logion 87 (Mark 11.2-3): "Go into the village opposite you, and immediately as you enter it you will find a colt tied, on which no one has ever sat; untie it and bring it. If any one says to you 'Why are you doing this?' say, 'The Lord has need of it and will send it back here immediately.'"

MC, DSM, UR, HH.

Yeshua seeks a symbolic enactment of the text of Zechariah 9.9: "Rejoice greatly, O daughter of Zion! Shout aloud, O daughter of Jerusalem! Lo, your king comes to you; triumphant and victorious is he, humble and riding on an ass, on a colt the foal of an ass." The church bent sayings related to the return of members of Israel from the Babylonian Captivity toward an eschatological image of final judgment. Note the resonances that this Zechariah passage has with the Danielic Son of man apocalypse. The language about returning the colt, which is missing from Luke's version, evidences the discomfort of the early church about Jesus' command to steal an equine.

Logion 88 (Mark 11.14, 22): (to the fruitless out-of-season fig tree) "May no one ever eat fruit from you again. . . . Have faith in God."

MC, DSM, UR, HH.

This is another of those most-secure Synoptic logia. Yeshua, in a saying that makes him seem a bit unhinged, curses an out-of-season fig tree for failing to bear winter fruit. Yeshua's outburst embarrassed the early church. Here, Mark has rescued the day by conjoining the curse with a saying Jesus may have often uttered, to have faith. Mark has the fig tree withering overnight (Mark 11.20), a fine example of hagiographical excess. No human words cause trees to die. No fig trees waste overnight. Mark turns Yeshua's odd curse into a metaphor for

LOGION SIEVE KEY: Marcan Consistency (MC), Danielic Son of man (DSM), Hagiographical Hurdle (HH), Urgency of Repentance (UR), Hagiographical Excess (HE), Anachronisms and Post-Yeshuan concerns (APY)

fruitless disciples, whose malady lies in absent or dormant faith. One need not adopt the Marcan innovation. Yet, it seems likely that Yeshua cursed the fig tree in a bit of hungry pique, and also that he commonly advised followers to have faith.

Logion 102 (Mark 13.2): "Do you see these great buildings? There will not be left here one stone upon another, that will not be thrown down."

MC, DSM, UR.

The inbreaking kingdom demolishes the most stable artifacts of Yeshua's culture. Note the emphasis that the Temple regime, so disfavored by John the Baptist and Yeshua, will be dismantled. All will be undone in favor of Yahweh's rule through the Son of man.

Logion 103A (Mark 13.26): "[26]And then they will see the Son of man coming in clouds with great power and glory."

MC, DSM, UR.

Interpolated in the midst of a great apocalyptic vision of the early church lies this typical saying of Yeshua, recounting the judgment event promised in Daniel 7. The contextual material for this saying reflects, not Yeshua's view, but that of the early church, suffering as it did from Yeshua's non-return. A great deal of wrangling indeed followed upon that parousia[94] *disappointment.*

Logion 104 (Mark 13.30): "[30]Truly, I say to you, this generation will not pass away before all these things take place."

MC, DSM, UR, HH.

Yeshua's promise of return, the disappointment of which proved the greatest hurdle for the early church and transformed its theology, reiterated. Yeshua promised he would be raised by Yahweh, because the divine scion cannot long be defeated.

Logion 105 (Mark 14.6-8): (when disciples reproached a woman for pouring expensive oil on Yeshua) "Let her alone; why do you trouble her? She has done a beautiful thing to me. [7]For you always have the poor with you, and whenever you will, you can do good to them; but you will not always have me. [8]She has done what she could; she has anointed my body beforehand for burying."

---

[94] "Parousia" means, in biblical Greek, the presence or arrival of a regal dignitary.

MC, DSM, UR.

Yeshua rebukes his disciples for their penurious critique. Yeshua will soon be killed. The woman prepares his body for burial. There is a time to spend, and let the poor be poor. The Son of man, in Yeshua's conflation of his ministry with the suffering servant of Isaiah 53, must be badly handled and killed. Only then can Yahweh glorify the Son of man properly with resurrection and power from on high.

Logion 120 (Mark 14.62b): "You will see the Son of man sitting at the right hand of Power, and coming with the clouds of heaven."

MC, DSM, UR, HH.

Yeshua reiterates the role of the Son of man in judgment and power. This saying proves a hagiographical hurdle, for Yeshua failed to return. Note the church's wriggling here. Considering the whole passage (Mark 14.61-62), the writer places in Jesus' mouth a confession that he is the Christ and the son of God, both later confessional confusions. The three disparate concepts are mashed together in this passage, quite uncomfortably.

Logion 121 (Mark 15.2b): (to Pilate asking if Yeshua is the Christ) "You have said so."

MC, DSM, HH.

Yeshua "renders unto Caesar" a non-response response. The logion sounds like Yeshua. He does the service of a single answer, but declines to be interrogated further. Yeshua's contempt for Roman power, as well as that of the Temple authorities, proved his undoing. Note in this response to Pilate, as we read through Yeshua's logia, the familiar flavor of parlay that he renders to Pharisees and Sadducees and Temple elders and scribes in their attempts to trap Yeshua in verbal stumbling.

Logion 122 (Mark 15.34): "Eloi, Eloi, lama sabachthani?"

MC, HH.

Mark believes this phrase means "My God, my God, why hast thou forsaken me?" If so, it references Psalm 22.1, and invokes the remainder of that psalm. The similarity of the psalm's description to the events the gospel of Mark describes in Yeshua's execution leads one to doubt the historical reliability of the crucifixion account. Nevertheless, the saying may well have come from the mouth of Yeshua. Yeshua was inclined to make biblical references; consider his own Son of man allegations and Mark 12 confrontations.

Logion 125 (Matthew 4.17): "Repent, for the kingdom of heaven is at hand."

MC, DSM, UR.

The logion represents Matthew's abbreviation of the Mark 1.15's summary of Yeshua's mission and teaching.

Logion 146 (Matthew 5.29-30): "[29]If your right eye causes you to sin, pluck it out and throw it away; it is better that you lose one of your members than that your whole body be thrown into hell. [30]And if your right hand causes you to sin, cut it off and throw it away; it is better that you lose one of your members than that your whole body go into hell."

MC, DSM, UR, HH.

Marcan urgency dominates this logion. The Son of man has arrived for judgment. Remove all impediments to repentance. There may also be a slight bit of embarrassment to the early church here, since Yeshua advocates self-mutilation. This sort of entertaining hyperbole must have characterized Yeshua's teaching. How else might crowds have gathered to hear?

Logion 180 (Matthew 9.15): "Can the wedding guests mourn as long as the bridegroom is with them? The days will come when the bridegroom is taken away from them, and then they will fast."

MC, DSM, UR.

Yeshua will die. The party will end. Judgment at the hands of the Son of man will come. Fasting will seem appropriate then. Now, festival predominates. Celebrate. Time is short.

Logion 181 (Matthew 9.16): "[16]And no one puts a piece of unshrunk cloth on an old garment, for the patch tears away from the garment, and a worse tear is made."

MC, DSM, UR.

Yeshua teaches that this world and the kingdom of God are incommensurate.

Logion 182 (Matthew 9.17): "Neither is new wine put into old wineskins; if it is, the skins burst, and the wine is spilled, and the skins are destroyed; but new wine is put into fresh wineskins, and so both are preserved."

MC, DSM, UR.

Yeshua employs a different metaphor to teach that the kingdom and this world are poorly matched.

Logion 190 (Matthew 10.23b): "...for truly, I say to you, you will not have gone through all the towns of Israel, before the Son of man comes."

MC, DSM, UR.

Matthew lodges this logion in a passage about the post-Yeshua church's attempts to spread news of Jesus at a time when they were experiencing some persecution. One must fear tossing the baby with the bathwater here. It seems likely, given Yeshua's revised view of his ministry, that Yeshua said things similar to this logion. Still, its location in a patently post-Yeshuan passage gives pause. It seems possible that this fragment represents Yeshua's expectation concerning his ministry ***before*** *he adapted the Suffering Servant tale to interpret his work. Jesus had anticipated that the disciples would go out without him, teach and serve, which event would bear eschatological import for Yahweh, who would trigger apocalyptic upheaval.*

Logion 202 (Matthew 11.7-11, 13-15): "What did you go out into the wilderness to behold? A reed shaken by the wind? [8]Why then did you go out? To see a man clothed in soft raiment? Behold, those who wear soft raiment are in kings' houses. [9]Why then did you go out? To see a prophet? Yes, I tell you, and more than a prophet. [10]This is he of whom it is written, 'Behold, I send my messenger before thy face, who shall prepare thy way before thee.' [11]Truly, I say to you, among those born of women there has risen no one greater than John the Baptist; yet he who is least in the kingdom of heaven is greater than he." . . . [13]For all the prophets and the law prophesied until John; [14]and if you are willing to accept it, he is Elijah who is to come. [15]He who has ears to hear, let him hear."

MC, DSM, UR.

The reference to preparation of the way derives from Malachi 3.1-18, a passage depicting divine judgment and human repentance. He who comes before the great and terrible day of the Lord is Elijah, per Malachi 4.5. Yeshua affirms John the Baptist as greatest among all of Yahweh's prophets. Yeshua styles John's

LOGION SIEVE KEY: Marcan Consistency (MC), Danielic Son of man (DSM), Hagiographical Hurdle (HH), Urgency of Repentance (UR), Hagiographical Excess (HE), Anachronisms and Post-Yeshuan concerns (APY)

ministry as a precursor to the Son of man, whose judgment exceeds John's work. The "hearing" saying rings true to the Marcan emphasis on repentance and its obstacle, hardness of heart.

Logion 224 (Matthew 13.31-32): "The kingdom of heaven is like a grain of mustard seed which a man took and sowed in his field; [32]it is the smallest of all seeds, but when it has grown it is the greatest of shrubs and becomes a tree, so that the birds of the air come and make nests in its branches."

MC, DSM, UR.

Yeshua teaches that the progress of the immense kingdom of God is hidden.

Logion 225 (Matthew 13.33): "The kingdom of heaven is like leaven which a woman took and hid in three measures of meal, till it was all leavened."

MC, DSM, UR.

Yeshua teaches the present invisibility of the irruptive kingdom. It is hidden but growing rapidly. So repent now, before the time for change has lapsed and the kingdom of God bursts upon you unawares.

Logion 230 (Matthew 13.51-52): "[51]Have you understood all this? . . . Therefore every scribe who has been trained for the kingdom of heaven is like a householder who brings out of his treasure what is new and what is old."

DSM, HH.

Yeshua waxes cryptic in this logion. Its obscurity must have proved a mild embarrassment to the church, who did not want Jesus to be incomprehensible. Yet, the logion has vague Marcan parallels: the old and new, the kingdom of heaven, the incomprehension of the many, a scribe. Here, however, the scribe seems approved, rather than condemned. Perhaps the logion presented another embarrassment to the early church? When a logion fails to assist the church in its rhetorical purpose, and yet is retained, I take that as a good indication that the logion was deeply embedded in the oral tradition at the time that Matthew received his source material, and the logion could not be lightly excised.

Logion 246 (Matthew 16.27): "For the Son of man is to come with his angels in the glory of his Father, and then he will repay every man for what he has done."

MC, DSM, UR.

Yeshua recurs to the Son of man judgment scene from Daniel 7. All must repent or suffer.

Logion 247 (Matthew 16.28): "[28]Truly, I say to you, there are some standing here who will not taste death before they see the Son of man coming in his kingdom."

MC, DSM, UR, HH.

The kingdom of God will irrupt imminently. The failure of that irruption proved the greatest post-Yeshua obstacle for the early church. See the Marcan version at Logion 57.

Logion 267 (Matthew 19.17a): "Why do you ask me about what is good? One there is who is good."

MC.

Yeshua probes the speaker about what constitutes goodness. Yahweh's view does not coincide with the views of unrepentant people.

Logion 280 (Matthew 21.2-3): "Go into the village opposite you, and immediately you will find an ass tied, and a colt with her; untie them and bring them to me. [3]If any one says anything to you, you shall say, 'The Lord has need of them,' and he will send them immediately."

MC, DSM, UR, HH.

Yeshua here enacts the image of Zechariah 9.9, turned from its original meaning toward an eschatological drama of humble arrival of Yahweh's agent of judgment, leading to universal peace. Note themes similar to that of the apocalypse of Daniel 7.

Logion 283 (Matthew 21.19): (to a fig tree) "May no fruit ever come from you again!"

MC, DSM, UR, HH.

Yeshua, in a lapse, damns an out-of-season fruit tree.

LOGION SIEVE KEY: Marcan Consistency (MC), Danielic Son of man (DSM), Hagiographical Hurdle (HH), Urgency of Repentance (UR), Hagiographical Excess (HE), Anachronisms and Post-Yeshuan concerns (APY)

Logion 289 (Matthew 22.1-14): "[2]The kingdom of heaven may be compared to a king who gave a marriage feast for his son, [3]and sent his servants to call those who were invited to the marriage feast; but they would not come. [4]Again he sent other servants, saying, 'Tell those who are invited, Behold, I have made ready my dinner, my oxen and my fat calves are killed, and everything is ready; come to the marriage feast.' [5]But they made light of it and went off, one to his farm, another to his business, [6]while the rest seized his servants, treated them shamefully, and killed them. [7]The king was angry, and he sent his troops and destroyed those murderers and burned their city. [8]Then he said to his servants, 'The wedding is ready, but those invited are not worthy. [9]Go therefore to the thoroughfares, and invite to the marriage feast as many as you find.' [10]And those servants went out into the streets and gathered all whom they found, both bad and good; so the wedding hall was filled with guests. [11]But when the king came in to look at the guests, he saw there a man who had no wedding garment; [12]and he said to him, 'Friend, how did you get in here without a wedding garment?' And he was speechless. [13]Then the king said to the attendants, 'Bind him hand and foot, and cast him into the outer darkness; there men will weep and gnash their teeth.' [14]For many are called but few are chosen."

MC, DSM, UR.

Yeshua recurs to his theme of present celebration and coming demolition. Note his strong view of Yahweh as compassionate and welcoming, but willing to slaughter.

Logion 308 (Matthew 24.34): "Truly, I say to you, this generation will not pass away till all these things take place."

MC, DSM, UR, HH.

This logion is embedded in the apocalyptic predictions of Matthew 24, which are rife with post-Yeshuan concerns.

Logion 313 (Matthew 26.10-12): "Why do you trouble the woman? For she has done a beautiful thing to me. [11]For you always have the poor with you, but you will not always have me. [12]In pouring this ointment on my body, she has done it to prepare me for burial."

MC, DSM, UR, HH.

Yeshua reiterates his burial preparations and anticipated abrupt departure from the disciples' company. He demonstrates his customary affection for the poor. Here, Yeshua wastes resources, which likely proved a mild embarrassment to the early church.

Logion 327 (Matthew 26.64): (to the high priest's inquiry whether Yeshua is the Christ, the Son of God) "You have said so. But I tell you, hereafter you will see the Son of man seated at the right hand of Power, and coming on the clouds of heaven."

MC, DSM, UR, HH.

Yeshua declines to affirm a messianic role or the title Son of God, hence embarrassing the early church's nascent christology. Yeshua reaffirms that he is the Son of man, about to be clothed in power and glory.

Logion 345 (Luke 5.34-35): "Can you make wedding guests fast while the bridegroom is with them? The days will come, when the bridegroom is taken away from them, and then they will fast in those days."

MC, DSM, UR.

Yeshua teaches his recurrent theme of celebration juxtaposed with fasting and austerities.

Logion 346 (Luke 5.36): "No one tears a piece from a new garment and puts it upon an old garment; if he does, he will tear the new, and the piece from the new will not match the old."

MC, DSM, UR.

Yeshua teaches the old and new regimes, and their incompatibility.

Logion 347 (Luke 5.37-38): "[37]And no one puts new wine into old wineskins; if he does, the new wine will burst the skins and it will be spilled, and the new skins will be destroyed. [38]But new wine must be put into fresh wineskins. And no one after drinking old wine desires new; for he says, 'The old is good.'"

MC, DSM, UR.

Yeshua teaches the kingdom will burst the old skin of the present culture.

LOGION SIEVE KEY: Marcan Consistency (MC), Danielic Son of man (DSM), Hagiographical Hurdle (HH), Urgency of Repentance (UR), Hagiographical Excess (HE), Anachronisms and Post-Yeshuan concerns (APY)

Logion 375 (Luke 7.24-28): "What did you go out into the wilderness to behold? A reed shaken by the wind? [25]What then did you go out to see? A man clothed in soft raiment? Behold, those who are gorgeously appareled and live in luxury are in kings' courts. [26]What then did you go out to see? A prophet? Yes, I tell you, and more than a prophet. [27]This is he of whom it is written, 'Behold, I send my messenger before thy face, who shall prepare thy way before thee.' [28]I tell you, among those born of women none is greater than John; yet he who is least in the kingdom of God is greater than he."

MC, DSM, UR.

Yeshua allies himself with John, delivering accolades, and affirming his own role, and those of Yeshua's students.

Logion 396A (Luke 9.27): "[27]But I tell you truly, there are some standing here who will not taste death before they see the kingdom of God."

MC, DSM, UR, HH.

Yeshua's promise of imminent return in power proved a disappointment to the early, waiting church.

Logion 418 (Luke 11.21-22): "[21]When a strong man, fully armed, guards his own palace, his goods are in peace; [22]but when one stronger than he assails him and overcomes him, he takes away his armor in which he trusted, and divides his spoil."

MC, DSM, UR.

Here, war images predominate, and the warning of the coming stronger force of overwhelming potency. Change is both urgent and imminent.

Logion 432A (Luke 12.2-3): "[2]Nothing is covered up that will not be revealed, or hidden that will not be known. [3]Whatever you have said in the dark shall be heard in the light, and what you have whispered in private rooms shall be proclaimed upon the housetops."

MC, DSM, UR.

Yeshua forewarns of imminent judgment. All is transparent to Yahweh.

LOGION SIEVE KEY: Marcan Consistency (MC), Danielic Son of man (DSM), Hagiographical Hurdle (HH), Urgency of Repentance (UR), Hagiographical Excess (HE), Anachronisms and Post-Yeshuan concerns (APY)

Logion 444 (Luke 12.49-50): "[49]I came to cast fire upon the earth; and would that it were already kindled! [50]I have a baptism to be baptized with; and how I am constrained until it is accomplished!"

MC, DSM, UR.

Yeshua reiterates his role in the Day of the Lord. He personally will judge, but not until he suffers himself.

Logion 446 (Luke 12.54-56): "When you see a cloud rising in the west, you say at once, 'A shower is coming'; and so it happens. [55]And when you see the south wind blowing, you say, 'There will be scorching heat'; and it happens. [56]You hypocrites! You know how to interpret the appearance of earth and sky; but why do you not know how to interpret the present time?"

MC, DSM, UR.

Yeshua castigates opponents and promises judgment is upon all.

Logion 452 (Luke 13.18-19): "What is the kingdom of God like? And to what shall I compare it? [19]It is like a grain of mustard seed which a man took and sowed in his garden; and it grew and became a tree, and the birds of the air made nests in its branches."

MC, DSM, UR.

Yeshua teaches that the kingdom of God is obscure, and yet will become great.

Logion 453 (Luke 13.20-21): "To what shall I compare the kingdom of God? [21]It is like leaven which a woman took and hid in three measures of meal, till it was all leavened."

MC, DSM, UR.

The kingdom of God is hidden, but potent and emerging to visibility.

Logion 462 (Luke 14.16-24): "A man once gave a great banquet, and invited many; [17]and at the time for the banquet he sent his servant to say to those who had been invited, 'Come; for all is now ready.' [18]But they all alike began to make excuses. The first said to him, 'I have bought a field, and I must go out and see it; I pray you, have me excused.' [19]And another said, 'I have bought five yoke of oxen, and I go to examine them; I pray you, have me excused.' [20]And another said, 'I have married a wife, and therefore I cannot come.' [21]So the servant came and reported this to his master. Then the householder in anger said to his servant, 'Go out quickly to the streets and lanes of the city, and bring in the poor and maimed and blind and lame.' [22]And the servant said, 'Sir, what you commanded has been done, and still there is room.' [23]And the master said to the servant, 'Go compel people to come in, that my house may be filled. [24]For I tell you, none of those men who were invited shall taste my banquet.'"

MC, DSM, UR.

Note the different thrust given the parable by Luke as compared to Matthew's rendition (See Logion 289 (Matthew 22.1-14). *Perhaps, in Luke's version, the parable is turned to address the Jew-Gentile problem of the early church.*

Logion 491 (Luke 18.18-19a): "Why do you call me good? No one is good but God alone."

MC.

Yeshua confronts the cultural norm of habitually calling people "good," referring them to the divine.

Logion 502 (Luke 19.30-31): "Go into the village opposite, where on entering you will find a colt tied, on which no one has ever yet sat; untie it and bring it here. [31]If any one asks you, 'Why are you untying it?' you shall say this, 'The Lord has need of it.'"

MC, DSM, UR, HH.

Yeshua seeks to conform his entry into Jerusalem to Zechariah 9.9.

Logion 503 (Luke 19.40): (on Pharisaical criticism of crowd praise) "I tell you, if these were silent, the very stones would cry out."

MC, DSM, UR.

Yeshua counters the criticism of clerics who urge Yeshua to silence crowds proclaiming Yeshua a king arriving in Yahweh's name. He responds with an eschatological blunderbuss.

Logion 509 (Luke 20.34-38): "The sons of this age marry and are given in marriage; [35]but those who are accounted worthy to attain to that age and to the resurrection from the dead neither marry nor are given in marriage, 36for they cannot die any more, because they are equal to angels and are sons of God, being sons of the resurrection. 37But that the dead are raised, even Moses showed, in the passage about the bush, where he calls the Lord the God of Abraham and the God of Isaac and the God of Jacob. 38Now he is not God of the dead, but of the living; for all live to him."

MC, DSM, UR.

Yeshua answers critics with descriptions of the kingdom and resurrection.

Logion 515 (Luke 21.32): "Truly, I say to you, this generation will not pass away till all has taken place."

MC, DSM, UR, HH.

Yeshua promises the kingdom's arrival is imminent.

SALVATION LOGIA

Yeshua's logia concerning salvation bear deep symmetries to his assertions concerning the irruptive kingdom of God. One finds rescue by aligning oneself with the pulse of that kingdom. One cannot think one's way to admission to the kingdom. The admission ticket is heartful self-criticism, the perception of one's own inadequacy. One's heart conforms to that standard, or it does not. Yeshua credits heartfelt repentance. Such are saved. Yeshua excoriates fine sentiments and careful legalisms and religion that lacks compassion for poor people. Yeshua repeats lessons he learned hearing, probably in synagogue, fiery lessons from Isaiah and Daniel[95] *and other eighth century prophets. He heard those resonances again at the Jordan River from the mouth of iconoclast John who baptized people there.*

Logion 10 (Mark 2.17): "Those who are well have no need of a physician, but those who are sick; I came not to call the righteous, but sinners."

MC, DSM, UR.

Yeshua explains his preference for poor disciples and those who are humbly repentant. He conceives his ministry as "coming for them."

Logion 18 (Mark 3.28-29): "[28]Truly, I say to you, all sins will be forgiven the sons of men, and whatever blasphemies they utter; [29]but whoever blasphemes against the Holy Spirit never has forgiveness, but is guilty of an eternal sin."

MC, DSM, UR, HH.

Yeshua again claims to forgive sins, with one exception. Judgment is upon mankind; repentance must govern every person. This logion may have presented an embarrassment to the early church, because it lacks clarity about what is being eternally forbidden.

---

[95] Daniel is an intertestamental work, probably written in the second century B.C. during the period of the Maccabees. The work purports to be an eighth century B.C. prophetic writing. It seems unlikely that Yeshua or his contemporaries would have known of this misrepresentation.

LOGION SIEVE KEY: Marcan Consistency (MC), Danielic Son of man (DSM), Hagiographical Hurdle (HH), Urgency of Repentance (UR), Hagiographical Excess (HE), Anachronisms and Post-Yeshuan concerns (APY)

Logion 23 (Mark 4.24-25): "Take heed what you hear; the measure you give will be the measure you get, and still more will be given you. [25]For to him who has will more be given; and from him who has not, even what he has will be taken away."

MC, DSM, UR.

Recompense waits, just around the corner. Divine justice respects no human status.

Logion 28 (Mark 4.40): (Yeshua speaks to disciples in a storm-tossed boat) "Why are you afraid? Have you no faith?"

MC, DSM, UR.

Yeshua recurs to his characteristic emphases on salvific faith and fear.

Logion 34 (Mark 5.36): (Yeshua speaks to the synagogue leader, whose daughter has died.) "Do not fear, only believe."

MC, UR.

Yeshua again returns to his characteristic emphases on salvific faith and fear.

Logion 45 (Mark 7.20-23): "What comes out of a man is what defiles a man. [21]For from within, out of the heart of man come evil thoughts, fornication, theft, murder, adultery, [22]coveting, wickedness, deceit, licentiousness, envy, slander, pride, foolishness. [23]All these evil things come from within, and they defile a man."

MC, DSM, UR.

Yeshua teaches the nature of sin and repentance. Sin lies in ill-action, not in dietary observances or ritual punctuality.

Logion 50 (Mark 8.15-21): "Take heed, beware of the leaven of the Pharisees and the leaven of Herod. . . . Why do you discuss the fact that you have no bread? Do you not yet perceive or understand? Are your hearts hardened? [18]Having eyes do you not see, and having ears do you not hear? And do you not remember? [19]When I broke the five loaves for the five thousand, how many baskets full of broken pieces did you take up? . . . [20]And the seven for the four thousand, how many baskets full of broken pieces did you take up? . . . Do you not yet understand?"

MC, DSM, UR.

Yeshua returns to his leaven teaching. A tiny hidden kernel makes or destroys a man. Yeshua is typically critical of his none-too-insightful students. All seem to be missing Yeshua's thrust. A weakness of this logion is its reliance on the two feeding stories, which may well represent the dittography which traditions passed orally suffer.

Logion 70 (Mark 9.50): "[50]Salt is good; but if the salt has lost its saltness, how will you season it? Have salt in yourselves, and be at peace with one another."

MC, UR.

Yeshua uses images familiar to his audience, but asks them to consider odd possibilities, leading to moral conclusions. All trends, in Yeshua's teaching, toward the human heart.

Logion 76 (Mark 10.23): "How hard it will be for those who have riches to enter the kingdom of God!"

MC, DSM, UR.

Yeshua shocks his hearers, as he preferred to do, rejecting external wealth in favor of better riches.

Logion 77 (Mark 10.24): "Children, how hard it is to enter the kingdom of God!"

MC, DSM, UR.

Yeshua stresses the difficulties entailed in entering the kingdom of God.

Logion 78 (Mark 10.25): "[25]It is easier for a camel to go through the eye of a needle than for a rich man to enter the kingdom of God."

MC, DSM, UR.

Yeshua shocks his hearers by derogating riches. His affections lie with the heartfelt poor.

LOGION SIEVE KEY: Marcan Consistency (MC), Danielic Son of man (DSM), Hagiographical Hurdle (HH), Urgency of Repentance (UR), Hagiographical Excess (HE), Anachronisms and Post-Yeshuan concerns (APY)

Logion 79 (Mark 10.27): (of salvation) "With men it is impossible, but not with God; for all things are possible with God."

MC, DSM, UR.

No man can be saved but by God. All merely human efforts are void in meeting the onrushing kingdom.

Logion 81 (Mark 10.31): "[31]But many that are first will be last, and the last first."

MC, DSM, UR.

Yeshua inverts things. The worldly order is passing. The kingdom has arrived.

Logion 90 (Mark 11.23): "[23]Truly, I say to you, whoever says to this mountain, 'Be taken up and cast into the sea,' and does not doubt in his heart, but believes that what he says will come to pass, it will be done for him."

MC, DSM.

Yeshua believes great power lies at hand for the faithful.

Logion 91 (Mark 11.24): "Therefore I tell you, whatever you ask in prayer, believe that you receive it, and you will."

MC, DSM.

Yeshua teaches that Yahweh responds to the devotion of the faithful. Yeshua's confidence in the potency of the inbreaking kingdom knows few bounds.

Logion 92 (Mark 11.25): "[25]And whenever you stand praying, forgive, if you have anything against any one; so that your Father also who is in heaven may forgive you your trespasses."

MC, DSM, UR.

Yeshua teaches reciprocity in the oncoming judgment. Those who forgive are forgiven.

LOGIOS SIEVE KEY: Marcan Consistency (MC), Danielic Son of man (DSM), Hagiographical Hurdle (HH), Urgency of Repentance (UR), Hagiographical Excess (HE), Anachronisms and Post-Yeshuan concerns (APY)

Logion 127 (Matthew 5.3): "[3]Blessed are the poor in spirit, for theirs is the kingdom of heaven."

MC, DSM, UR.

Yeshua prefers poor people, as, he believes, does Yahweh. He emphasizes the heart.

Logion 128 (Matthew 5.4): "[4]Blessed are those who mourn, for they shall be comforted."

MC, DSM, UR.

Yeshua comforts the sufferers. The comfort is eschatological.

Logion 129 (Matthew 5.5): "[5]Blessed are the meek, for they shall inherit the earth."

MC, DSM, UR.

Yeshua again prefers humble people. They are eschatologically favored.

Logion 130 (Matthew 5.6): "[6]Blessed are those who hunger and thirst for righteousness, for they shall be satisfied."

MC, DSM, UR.

Yeshua turns attention to the heart of a person. The kingdom is peopled by such.

Logion 131 (Matthew 5.7): "[7]Blessed are the merciful, for they shall obtain mercy."

MC, DSM, UR.

Yeshua calls people to show mercy. Only such as those receive Yahweh's mercy in the kingdom of God.

Logion 132 (Matthew 5.8): "[8]Blessed are the pure in heart, for they shall see God."

MC, DSM, UR.

Yeshua drives a core point. The human heart determines one's relationship to the kingdom of God.

Logion 133 (Matthew 5.9): "[9]Blessed are the peacemakers, for they shall be called sons of God."

MC, DSM, UR.

Yeshua connects human relations and belonging to the kingdom.

Logion 144 (Matthew 5.25-26): "[25]Make friends quickly with your accuser, while you are going with him to court, lest your accuser hand you over to the judge, and the judge to the guard, and you be put in prison; [26]truly, I say to you, you will never get out till you have paid the last penny."

MC, UR.

Yeshua emphasizes that community harmony precludes suing people. Harsh judicial regimes leave no room for stinting. It is best to avoid them (both the human and divine versions).

Logion 153 (Matthew 6.1): "Beware of practicing your piety before men in order to be seen by them; for then you will have no reward from your Father who is in heaven."

MC, DSM, UR.

Yeshua calls students to their hearts, not to appearances. Judgment in the kingdom of God concerns the heart.

Logion 154 (Matthew 6.2-4): "[2]Thus, when you give alms, sound no trumpet before you, as the hypocrites do in the synagogues and in the streets, that they may be praised by men. Truly, I say to you, they have their reward. [3]But when you give alms, do not let your left hand know what your right hand is doing, [4]so that your alms may be in secret; and your Father who sees in secret will reward you."

MC, DSM, UR.

Yeshua draws a line between charitable giving and human praise. One gets one or the other, not both.

Logion 155 (Matthew 6.5-6): "[5]And when you pray, you must not be like the hypocrites; for they love to stand and pray in the synagogues and at the street corners, that they may be seen by men. Truly, I say to you, they have their reward.

[6]But when you pray, go into your room and shut the door and pray to your Father who is in secret; and your Father who sees in secret will reward you."

MC, DSM, UR.

As with giving, prayer too requires heartfulness, which is compromised by seeking praise. The kingdom belongs to the secret prayer.

Logion 156 (Matthew 6.7-13): "[7]And in praying do not heap up empty phrases as the Gentiles do; for they think that they will be heard for their many words. [8]Do not be like them, for your Father knows what you need before you ask him. [9]Pray then like this: Our Father who art in heaven, Hallowed be thy name. [10]Thy Kingdom come, Thy will be done on earth as it is in heaven. [11]Give us this day our daily bread; [12]And forgive us our debts, as we also have forgiven our debtors; [13]And lead us not into temptation, But deliver us from evil."

MC, DSM, UR.

Yeshua teaches heartfelt prayer.

Logion 157 (Matthew 6.14-15): "[14]For if you forgive men their trespasses, your heavenly Father also will forgive you; [15]but if you do not forgive men their trespasses, neither will your Father forgive your trespasses."

MC, DSM, UR.

Yeshua correlates human forgiveness with divine clemency. There exists divine parallelism.

Logion 158 (Matthew 6.16-18): "[16]And when you fast, do not look dismal, like the hypocrites, for they disfigure their faces that their fasting may be seen by men. Truly, I say to you, they have their reward. [17]But when you fast, anoint your head and wash your face, that your fasting may not be seen by men but by your Father who is in secret; and your Father who sees in secret will reward you."

MC, DSM, UR.

Yeshua extends his heart parallel to fasting. Note that Yeshua twists all the temple practices, as well as those of religious orders of his day. What happens within, not who approves without, governs Yahweh's view of matters. The kingdom of God waits for heartfelt people.

LOGION SIEVE KEY: Marcan Consistency (MC), Danielic Son of man (DSM), Hagiographical Hurdle (HH), Urgency of Repentance (UR), Hagiographical Excess (HE), Anachronisms and Post-Yeshuan concerns (APY)

Logion 159 (Matthew 6.19-21): "[19]Do not lay up for yourselves treasures on earth, where moth and rust consume and where thieves break in and steal, [20]but lay up for yourselves treasures in heaven, where neither moth nor rust consumes and where thieves do not break in and steal. [21]For where your treasure is, there will your heart be also."

MC, DSM, UR.

Yeshua draws his conclusion. The heart determines all in the kingdom of God.

Logion 160 (Matthew 6.22-23): "[22]The eye is the lamp of the body. So, if your eye is sound, your whole body will be full of light; [23]but if your eye is not sound, your whole body will be full of darkness. If then the light in you is darkness, how great is the darkness!"

MC, DSM, UR.

Dubious physiology aside, Yeshua calls all to heartfulness. Other states preclude entry upon the kingdom of God.

Logion 161 (Matthew 6.24): "[24]No one can serve two masters; for either he will hate the one and love the other, or he will be devoted to the one and despise the other. You cannot serve God and mammon."

MC, DSM, UR.

The capacities of the human heart are limited. One master alone is possible. Money is a danger for heartful people.

Logion 162 (Matthew 6.25-34): "[25]Therefore I tell you, do not be anxious about your life, what you shall eat or what you shall drink nor about your body, what you shall put on. Is not life more than food and the body more than clothing? [26]Look at the birds of the air: they neither sow nor reap nor gather into barns, and yet your heavenly Father feeds them. Are you not of more value than they? [27]And which of you by being anxious can add one cubit to his span of life? [28]And why are you anxious about clothing? Consider the lilies of the field, how they grow; they neither toil nor spin; [29]yet I tell you, even Solomon in all his glory was not arrayed like one of these. [30]But if God who clothes the grass of the field, which today is alive and tomorrow is thrown into the oven, will he not much more clothe you, O men of little faith? [31]Therefore do not be anxious, saying, 'What shall we eat?' or "What shall we drink?' or 'What shall we wear?' [32]For the Gentiles seek all these things; and your heavenly Father knows that you need them all. [33]But seek first his kingdom and his righteousness, and all these things shall be yours as well. [34]Therefore, do not be anxious about tomorrow, for tomorrow will be anxious for itself. Let the day's own trouble be sufficient for the day."

MC, DSM, UR.

Yeshua teaches faith, which he conceives as relying upon Yahweh for life's necessities. One's priority must be the kingdom of God today. Abandon anxiety. Unspoken is Yeshua's conviction that the time is very short, so the anxiety is misplaced. One wonders what Yeshua might have taught had he lived longer, and seen living in this world as an ongoing challenge. I would have listened raptly to that discourse.

Logion 163 (Matthew 7.1-5): "Judge not, that you be not judged. [2]For with the judgment you pronounce you will be judged, and the measure you give will be the measure you get. [3]Why do you see the speck that is in your brother's eye, but do not notice the log that is in your own eye? [4]Or how can you say to your brother, 'Let me take the speck out of your eye,' when there is the log in your own eye? [5]You hypocrite, first take the log out of your own eye, and then you will see clearly to take the speck out of your brother's eye."

MC, DSM, UR.

Yeshua warns against judging other people. Yahweh will hold us to our own standards. We are much more likely to be bothered by the flaws of others than by our own flaws. None can be both full of pride and helpful to others.

Logion 164 (Matthew 7.6): "[6]Do not give dogs what is holy; and do not throw your pearls before swine, lest they trample them under foot and turn to attack you."

MC, DSM, UR, HH.

Yeshua warns of the danger of those who do not share confidence in his message. Faithful goodhearted people live at risk. Here, the early church's need to resolve the Gentile admission problem might have found this saying of Yeshua a hurdle and embarrassment.

Logion 165 (Matthew 7.7-11): "[7]Ask, and it will be given you; seek, and you will find; knock, and it will be opened to you. [8]For every one who asks receives, and he who seeks finds, and to him who knocks it will be opened. [9]Or what man of you, if his son asks him for bread, will give him a stone? [10]Or if he asks for a fish, will give him a serpent? [11]If you then, who are evil, know how to give good gifts to your children, how much more will your Father who is in heaven give good things to those who ask him!"

MC, DSM.

Yeshua encourages open heartedness toward Yahweh. We know how to provide for our children. How much more is Yahweh able and willing?

Logion 166 (Matthew 7.13-14): "[13]Enter by the narrow gate; for the gate is wide and the way is easy that leads to destruction, and those who enter by it are many. [14]For the gate is narrow and the way is hard, that leads to life, and those who find it are few."

MC, DSM, UR.

Yeshua warns that many will not be saved.

Logion 168 (Matthew 7.15-20): "[15]Beware of false prophets, who come to you in sheep's clothing but inwardly are ravenous wolves. [16]You will know them by their fruits. Are grapes gathered from thorns, or figs from thistles? [17]So, every sound tree bears good fruit, but the bad tree bears evil fruit. [18]A sound tree cannot bear evil fruit, nor can a bad tree bear good fruit. [19]Every tree that does not bear good fruit is cut down and thrown into the fire. [20]Thus you will know them by their fruits."

MC, DSM, UR.

The kingdom waits impatiently. Misleading teachers must be scrutinized. Good trees bear edible fruit. Every misleader will be condemned. Look to outcomes, not words. This logion might be doubted, because the early church suffered diverse teachings. Yet, the problem existed for Yeshua as well. In the end, I judge the logion reliable, though not without reservation.

Logion 170 (Matthew 7.24-27): "[24]Every one then who hears these words of mine and does them will be like a wise man who built his house upon the rock; [25]and the rain fell, and the floods came, and the winds blew and beat upon that house, but it did not fall, because it had been founded on the rock. [26]And every one who hears these words of mine and does not do them will be like a foolish man who built his house upon the sand; [27]and the rain fell, and the floods came, and the winds blew and beat against that house, and it fell; and great was the fall of it."

MC, DSM, UR.

Yeshua urges his students to heed his words. Judgment is certain.

Logion 200 (Matthew 10.42): "[42]And whoever gives to one of these little ones even a cup of cold water because he is a disciple, truly, I say to you, he shall not lose his reward."

MC, DSM, UR.

Yeshua teaches a direct correlation between human compassion and divine favor.

Logion 213 (Matthew 12.31-32): "[31]Therefore I tell you, every sin and blasphemy will be forgiven men, but blasphemy against the Spirit will not be forgiven. [32]And whoever says a word against the Son of man will be forgiven; but whoever speaks against the Holy Spirit will not be forgiven, either in this age or in the age to come."

MC, DSM, UR, HH.

Yeshua teaches which sins can be forgiven, and which cannot. This logion may have presented a hurdle to the early church because its meaning is so deeply indeterminate, yet its topic so pressing.

Logion 216 (Matthew 12.36-37): "[36]I tell you, on the day of judgment men will render account for every careless word they utter; [37]by your words you will be justified, and by your words you will be condemned."

MC(?), DSM, UR.

Yeshua lays down a hard line, and one that deviates from his emphasis on the heart. To this extent, the logion is suspect. Yet, the logion carries the urgency and concern with salvific judgment so characteristic of Yeshua. I call this logion reliable, without any great conviction in that regard.

Logion 217 (Matthew 12.39, 41-42): "An evil and adulterous generation seeks for a sign; but no sign shall be given to it except the sign of the prophet Jonah. . . . [41]The men of Nineveh will arise at the judgment with this generation and condemn it; for they repented at the preaching of Jonah, and behold, something greater than Jonah is here. [42]The queen of the South will arise at the judgment with this generation and condemn it; for she came from the ends of the earth to hear the wisdom of Solomon, and behold, something greater than Solomon is here."

MC, DSM, UR.

Yeshua warns about sign-seekers. He refers to his ministry as a magnificence, as he had earlier compared himself to the ministry of John the Baptist.

Logion 222 (Matthew 13.11-12): "To you it has been given to know the secrets of the kingdom of heaven, but to them it has not been given. [12]For to him who has will more be given, and he will have abundance; but from him who has not, even what he has will be taken away."

MC, DSM, UR.

Yeshua explains the logic of the kingdom. Divine judgment gives and takes differently than men prefer.

Logion 227 (Matthew 13.44): "[44]The kingdom of heaven is like treasure hidden in a field, which a man found and covered up; then in his joy he goes and sells all that he has and buys that field."

MC, DSM, UR.

Yeshua likens the kingdom to serendipitous treasure. Entry merits giving all.

Logion 228 (Matthew 13.45-46): "[45]Again, the kingdom of heaven is like a merchant in search of fine pearls, [46]who, on finding one pearl of great value, went and sold all that he had and bought it."

MC, DSM, UR.

The kingdom is a surprising find, worth any price.

Logion 229 (Matthew 13.47-50): "[47]Again, the kingdom of heaven is like a net which was thrown into the sea and gathered fish of every kind; [48]when it was full, men drew it ashore and sat down and sorted the good into vessels but threw away the bad. [49]So it will be at the close of the age. The angels will come out and separate the evil from the righteous, [50]and throw them into the furnace of fire; there men will weep and gnash their teeth."

MC, DSM, UR.

Yeshua teaches of judgment and divine sorting among men.

LOGION SIEVE KEY: Marcan Consistency (MC), Danielic Son of man (DSM), Hagiographical Hurdle (HH), Urgency of Repentance (UR), Hagiographical Excess (HE), Anachronisms and Post-Yeshuan concerns (APY)

Logion 241 (Matthew 16.6-11): "Take heed and beware of the leaven of the Pharisees and Sadducees. . . . O men of little faith, why do you discuss among yourselves the fact that you have no bread? [9]Do you not yet perceive? Do you not remember the five loaves of the five thousand, and how many baskets you gathered? [10]Or the seven loaves of the four thousand, and how many baskets you gathered? [11]How is it that you fail to perceive that I did not speak about bread? Beware the leaven of the Pharisees and Sadducees."

MC, UR.

Yeshua teaches leavening. One must be concerned about what the misguided teachers do to one, rather than about lunch. Yeshua expresses frustration at his dense disciples. The duplicate feedings may be oral tradition dittography.

Logion 255 (Matthew 18.3-4): "Truly, I say to you, unless you turn and become like children, you will never enter the kingdom of heaven. [4]Whoever humbles himself like this child, he is the greatest in the kingdom of heaven."

MC, DSM, UR.

Yeshua commends child-like humility. Again, the state of one's heart determines fitness for the kingdom of God.

Logion 257 (Matthew 18.7-9): "[7]Woe to the world for temptations to sin! For it is necessary that temptations come, but woe to the man by whom the temptation comes! [8]And if your hand or your foot causes you to sin, cut it off and throw it from you; it is better for you to enter life maimed or lame than with two hands or two feet to be thrown into the eternal fire. [9]And if your eye causes you to sin, pluck it out and throw it from you; it is better for you to enter life with one eye than with two eyes to be thrown into the hell of fire."

MC, DSM, UR, HH.

Yeshua hyperbolizes to draw attention to the urgency of repentance. Perhaps the early church found such verbal extravagance embarrassing.

Logion 258 (Matthew 18.10-14): "[10]See that you do not despise one of these little ones; for I tell you that in heaven their angels always behold the face of my Father who is in heaven. [12]What do you think? If a man has a hundred sheep, and one of them has gone astray, does he not leave the ninety-nine on the hills and go in search of the one that went astray? [13]And if he finds it, truly, I say to you, he rejoices over it more than over the ninety-nine that never went astray. [14]So it is not the will of my Father who is in heaven that one of these little ones should perish."

MC, DSM, UR.

Yeshua again rhapsodizes children, emphasizing simplicity of heart. Repentance is urgent, in Yahweh's view, and cause for great rejoicing.

Logion 263 (Matthew 18.23-35): "[23]Therefore the kingdom of heaven may be compared to a king who wished to settle accounts with his servants. [24]When he began the reckoning, one was brought to him who owed him ten thousand talents; [25]and as he could not pay, his lord ordered him to be sold, with his wife and children and all that he had, and payment to be made. [26]So the servant fell on his knees, imploring him, 'Lord, have patience with me, and I will pay you everything.' [27]And out of pity for him the lord of the servant released him and forgave him the debt. [28]But that same servant, as he went out, came upon one of his fellow servants who owed him a hundred denarii; and seizing him by the throat he said, 'Pay what you owe.' [29]So his fellow servant fell down and besought him, 'Have patience with me, and I will pay you.' [30]He refused and went and put him in prison till he should pay the debt. [31]When his fellow servants saw what had taken place, they were greatly distressed, and they went and reported to their lord all that had taken place. [32]Then his lord summoned him and said to him, 'You wicked servant! I forgave you all that debt because you besought me; [33]and should not you have had mercy on your fellow servant, as I had mercy on you?' [34]And in anger his lord delivered him to the jailers, till he should pay all his debt. [35]So also my heavenly Father will do to every one of you, if you do not forgive your brother from your heart."

MC, DSM, UR.

Yeshua conjoins forgiveness of others with receipt of divine latitude. Heartfelt reformation presses all urgently.

Logion 268 (Matthew 19.17b, 18b-19, 21b): "If you would enter life, keep the commandments. . . . You shall not kill, You shall not commit adultery, You shall not steal, You shall not bear false witness, [19]Honor your father and mother, and, You shall love your neighbor as yourself. . . . If you would be perfect, go, sell what you possess and give to the poor, and you will have treasure in heaven; and come, follow me."

MC, DSM, UR.

LOGION SIEVE KEY: Marcan Consistency (MC), Danielic Son of man (DSM), Hagiographical Hurdle (HH), Urgency of Repentance (UR), Hagiographical Excess (HE), Anachronisms and Post-Yeshuan concerns (APY)

Yeshua affirms the law's commandments, but elevates heartfelt care for the poor over such observances. To follow Yeshua is preeminently important for entry upon the kingdom of God.

Logion 269 (Matthew 19.23): "Truly, I say to you, it will be hard for a rich man to enter the kingdom of heaven."

MC, DSM, UR.

Yeshua warns of the obstacle that wealth presents to heartfelt repentance.

Logion 270 (Matthew 19.24, 26): "[24]Again I tell you, it is easier for a camel to go through the eye of a needle than for a rich man to enter the kingdom of God."

MC, DSM, UR.

Wealth proves an obstacle to a person's salvation.

Logion 271 (Matthew 19.26b): (of salvation) "With men this is impossible, but with God all things are possible."

MC, DSM, UR.

Entry upon the kingdom of God opens through a divine act.

Logion 273 (Matthew 19.30): "[30]But many that are first will be last, and the last first."

MC, DSM, UR.

The kingdom inverts human perceptions, admitting the downtrodden, and refusing the mighty and powerful.

Logion 274 (Matthew 20.1-16): "For the kingdom of heaven is like a householder who went out early in the morning to hire laborers for his vineyard. [2]After agreeing with the laborers for a denarius a day, he sent them into his vineyard. [3]And going out about the third hour he saw others standing idle in the market place; [4]and to them he said, 'You go into the vineyard too, and whatever is right I will give you.' So they went. [5]Going out again about the sixth hour and the ninth hour, he did the same. [6]And about the eleventh hour he went out and found others standing; and he said to them, 'Why do you stand here idle all day?' [7]They said to him, 'Because no one has hired us.' He said to them, 'You go into the vineyard too.' [8]And when evening came, the owner of the vineyard said to his steward,

'Call the laborers and pay them their wages, beginning with the last, up to the first.' [9]And when those hired about the eleventh hour came, each of them received a denarius. [10]Now when the first came, they thought they would receive more; but each of them also received a denarius. [11]And on receiving it they grumbled at the householder, [12]saying, 'These last worked only one hour, and you have made them equal to us who have borne the burden of the day and the scorching heat.' [13]But he replied to one of them, 'Friend, I am doing you no wrong; did you not agree with me for a denarius? [14]Take what belongs to you, and go; I choose to give to this last as I give to you. [15]Am I not allowed to do what I choose with what belongs to me? Or do you begrudge my generosity? [16]So the last will be first and the first last."

MC, DSM, UR.

Yeshua teaches his recalcitrant students of divine reward. Matthew attaches the first-last, last-first logion to this parable.

Logion 283A (Matthew 21.21b): (Matthew seeks to give Yeshua's curse of the fig tree a context that reduces its petulance.) "Even if you say to this mountain, 'Be taken up and cast into the sea,' it will be done."

MC, DSM.

Yeshua argues that great powers benefit those belonging to the kingdom of God.

Logion 285 (Matthew 21.22): "[22]And whatever you ask in prayer, you will receive it, if you have faith."

MC, DSM.

Yeshua teaches that Yahweh responds to heartfelt faith.

Logion 309A (Matthew 25.29): "[29]For to every one who has will more be given, and he will have abundance; but from him who has not, even what he has will be taken away."

MC, DSM, UR.

Yeshua teaches the core efficacy of heartfelt repentance. He who practices such repentance receives; he who does not, loses.

LOGION SIEVE KEY: Marcan Consistency (MC), Danielic Son of man (DSM), Hagiographical Hurdle (HH), Urgency of Repentance (UR), Hagiographical Excess (HE), Anachronisms and Post-Yeshuan concerns (APY)

Logion 350 (Luke 6.20b): "Blessed are you poor, for yours is the kingdom of God."

MC, DSM, UR.

The kingdom of God belongs to poor people.

Logion 351 (Luke 6.21a): "[21]Blessed are you that hunger now, for you shall be satisfied."

MC, DSM, UR.

Those who know their need will find divine satisfaction.

Logion 352 (Luke 6.21b): "Blessed are you that weep now, for you shall laugh."

MC, DSM, UR.

In the kingdom of God, sadness melts into laughter.

Logion 353 (Luke 6.22-23): "[22]Blessed are you when men hate you, and when they exclude you and revile you, and cast out your name as evil, on account of the Son of man! [23]Rejoice in that day, and leap for joy, for behold, your reward is great in heaven; for so their fathers did to the prophets."

MC, DSM, UR.

Yeshua teaches that suffering due to association with the Son of man will prove fruitful. This logion suffers diversion toward addressing the circumstance after Yeshua's death in which the church was sporadically persecuted, but may be original to Yeshua. During his work, he and his disciples suffered denigration.

Logion 354 (Luke 6.24): "[24]But woe to you that are rich, for you have received your consolation."

MC, DSM, UR.

For the prosperous, there lies little hope of life in the kingdom of God.

Logion 355 (Luke 6.25a): "Woe to you that are full now, for you shall hunger."

MC, DSM, UR.

LOGION SIEVE KEY: Marcan Consistency (MC), Danielic Son of man (DSM), Hagiographical Hurdle (HH), Urgency of Repentance (UR), Hagiographical Excess (HE), Anachronisms and Post-Yeshuan concerns (APY)

Yeshua teaches that reward in this life will be punished under the kingdom's regime.

Logion 356 (Luke 6.25b): "Woe to you that laugh now, for you shall mourn and weep."

MC, DSM, UR.

Present prosperity leads to ultimate despair.

Logion 357 (Luke 6.26): "[26]Woe to you, when all men speak well of you, for so their fathers did to the false prophets."

MC, DSM, UR.

Good reputation is worrisome, when considering salvation.

Logion 365 (Luke 6.37-38): "[37]Judge not, and you will not be judged; condemn not, and you will not be condemned; forgive, and you will be forgiven; [38]give, and it will be given to you; good measure, pressed down, shaken together, running over, will be put into your lap. For the measure you give will be the measure you get back."

MC, DSM, UR.

Divine compensation falls to those who humbly give and forgive.

Logion 366 (Luke 6.39): "Can a blind man lead a blind man? Will they not both fall into a pit?"

MC, DSM, UR.

Teachers other than the Son of man mislead people.

Logion 367 (Luke 6.40): "[40]A disciple is not above his teacher, but every one when he is fully taught will be like his teacher."

MC, DSM, UR.

Yeshua encourages his students to diligence and understanding.

Logion 368 (Luke 6.41-42): "[41]Why do you see the speck that is in your brother's eye, but do not notice the log that is in your own eye? [42]Or how can you say to your brother, 'Brother, let me take out the speck that is in your eye,' when you yourself do not see the log that is in your own eye? You hypocrite, first take the log out of your own eye, and then you will see clearly to take out the speck that is in your brother's eye."

MC, DSM, UR.

Yeshua teaches that we are insensitive to our own flaws, but vigilant toward those of others. He instructs his students to tend themselves first.

Logion 369 (Luke 6.43-45): "[43]For no good tree bears bad fruit, nor again does a bad tree bear good fruit; [44]for each tree is known by its own fruit. For figs are not gathered from thorns, nor are grapes picked from a bramble bush. [45]The good man out of the good treasure of his heart produces good, and the evil man out of his evil treasure produces evil; for out of the abundance of the heart his mouth speaks."

MC, DSM, UR.

Good people do well by others. One's mouth exposes his heart.

Logion 370 (Luke 6.46): "[46]Why do you call me 'Lord, Lord,' and not do what I tell you?"

MC, DSM, UR.

Yeshua expresses frustration with his students' obstinance and incomprehension.

Logion 371 (Luke 6.47-49): "[47]Every one who comes to me and hears my words and does them, I will show you what he is like: [48]he is like a man building a house, who dug deep, and laid the foundation upon rock; and when a flood arose, the stream broke against that house and could not shake it, because it had been well built. [49]But he who hears and does not do them is like a man who built a house on the ground without a foundation; against which the stream broke, and immediately it fell, and the ruin of that house was great."

MC, DSM, UR.

Much is at stake in Yeshua's words. To ignore is to court disaster.

Logion 377 (Luke 7.40-48, 50): (to a hospitable, but judgmental, opponent, concerning a disreputable woman who washed Yeshua's feet with her tears and hair) "Simon, I have something to say to you. . . . [41]A certain creditor had two debtors; one owed five hundred denarii, and the other fifty. [42]When they could not pay, he forgave them both. Now which of them will love him more? . . . You have judged rightly. . . . Do you see this woman? I entered your house, you gave me no water for my feet, but she has wet my feet with her tears and wiped them with her hair. [45]You gave me no kiss, but from the time I came in she has not ceased to kiss my feet. [46]You did not anoint my head with oil, but she has anointed my feet with ointment. [47]Therefore I tell you, her sins, which are many, are forgiven, for she loved much; but he who is forgiven little, loves little. . . . Your sins are forgiven. . . . Your faith has saved you; go in peace."

MC, DSM, UR.

Yeshua teaches a Pharisee of heartfelt repentance in the actions of a poor woman.

Logion 395 (Luke 9.25): "[25]For what does it profit a man if he gains the whole world and loses or forfeits himself?"

MC, DSM, UR.

Yeshua teaches the hearty economics of the imminent kingdom.

Logion 414 (Luke 11.2-4): "When you pray, say: 'Father, hallowed be thy name. Thy kingdom come. [3]Give us each day our daily bread; [4]and forgive us our sins, for we ourselves forgive every one who is indebted to us; and lead us not into temptation."

MC, DSM, UR.

Yeshua teaches students to pray. Compare Logion 156 (at Matthew 6.9-13).

Logion 415 (Luke 11.9-10): "[9]Ask, and it will be given you; seek, and you will find; knock, and it will be opened to you. [10]For every one who asks receives, and he who seeks finds, and to him who knocks it will be opened."

MC, DSM, UR.

Yahweh waits to help those who express need.

Logion 416 (Luke 11.11-13): "[11]What father among you, if his son asks for a fish, will instead of a fish give him a serpent; [12]or if he asks for an egg, will give him a scorpion? [13]If you then, who are evil, know how to give good gifts to your children, how much more will the heavenly Father give the Holy Spirit to those who ask him!"

MC, DSM, UR.

LOGION SIEVE KEY: Marcan Consistency (MC), Danielic Son of man (DSM), Hagiographical Hurdle (HH), Urgency of Repentance (UR), Hagiographical Excess (HE), Anachronisms and Post-Yeshuan concerns (APY)

Yahweh heeds repentant men, and knows their needs. The reference to the Holy Spirit may be an interpolation of the post-Pentecost fledgling church, and casts a shadow over the logion. Note the deviation from the Matthean version of the saying at Logion 165 (Matthew 7.9-11). Still, Yeshua used the formulation "Holy Spirit" when discussing the unforgiveable sin (Logion 435 (Luke12.8-10) and Logion 213 (Matthew 12.31-32)).

Logion 420 (Luke 11.24-26): "[24]When the unclean spirit has gone out of a man, he passes through waterless places seeking rest; and finding none he says, 'I will return to my house from which I came.' [25]And when he comes he finds it swept and put in order. [26]Then he goes and brings seven other spirits more evil than himself, and they enter and dwell there; and the last state of that man becomes worse than the first."

MC, DSM, UR.

Yeshua teaches that demons are persistent and invasive. The subtext remains that it is better that one repent.

Logion 422 (Luke 11.29-32): "This generation is an evil generation; it seeks a sign, but no sign shall be given to it except the sign of Jonah. [30]For as Jonah became a sign to the men of Nineveh, so will the Son of man be to this generation. [31]The queen of the South will arise at the judgment with the men of this generation and condemn them; for she came from the ends of the earth to hear the wisdom of Solomon, and, behold, something greater than Solomon is here. [32]The men of Nineveh will arise at the judgment with this generation and condemn it; for they repented at the preaching of Jonah, and behold, something greater than Jonah is here."

MC, DSM, UR.

Yeshua's work notifies Israel of coming judgment.

Logion 433 (Luke 12.4-5): "[4]I tell you, my friends, do not fear those who kill the body, and after that have no more that they can do. [5]But I will warn you whom to fear: fear him who, after he has killed, has power to cast into hell; yes, I tell you, fear him!"

MC, DSM, UR.

Yeshua warns of mistaken apprehension and imminent judgment.

Logion 435 (Luke 12.8-10): "And I tell you, every one who acknowledges me before men, the Son of man also will acknowledge before the angels of God; but he who denies me before men will be denied before the angels of God. And every one who speaks a word against the Son of man will be forgiven; but he who blasphemes against the Holy Spirit will not be forgiven."

MC, DSM, UR.

Note the increasing complexity of this logion as it mutates from Mark to Matthew to Luke. See the Marcan version at Logion 18, and the Matthean version at Logion 213.

Logion 438 (Luke 12.15): "Take heed, and beware of all covetousness; for a man's life does not consist in the abundance of his possessions."

MC, DSM, UR.

Yeshua calls his students to avoid the lure of things. The kingdom of God presses near, where lies real life.

Logion 439 (Luke 12.16-21): "The land of a rich man brought forth plentifully; [17]and he thought to himself, 'What shall I do, for I have nowhere to store my crops?' [18]And he said, 'I will do this; I will pull down my barns, and build larger ones; and there I will store all my grain and my goods. [19]And I will say to my soul, Soul, you have ample goods laid up for many years; take your ease, eat, drink, be merry.' [20]But God said to him, 'Fool! This night your soul is required of you; and the things you have prepared, whose will they be?' [21]So is he who lays up treasure for himself, and is not rich toward God."

MC, DSM, UR.

Yeshua teaches of misplaced values and imminent irruption of the kingdom of God. The phrase "rich toward God" captures Yeshua's sentiment, whether or not the aphorism issued from his mouth.

Logion 440 (Luke 12.22-31): "Therefore I tell you, do not be anxious about your life, what you shall eat, nor about your body, what you shall put on. [23]For life is more than food, and the body more than clothing. [24]Consider the ravens: They neither sow nor reap, they have neither storehouse nor barn, and yet God feeds them. Of how much more value are you than the birds! [25]And which of you by being anxious can add a cubit to the span of life? [26]If then you are not able to

LOGION SIEVE KEY: Marcan Consistency (MC), Danielic Son of man (DSM), Hagiographical Hurdle (HH), Urgency of Repentance (UR), Hagiographical Excess (HE), Anachronisms and Post-Yeshuan concerns (APY)

do as small a thing as that, why are you anxious about the rest? 27Consider the lilies, how they grow; they neither toil nor spin; yet I tell you, even Solomon in all his glory was not arrayed like one of these. 28But if God so clothes the grass which is alive in the field today and tomorrow is thrown into the oven, how much more will he clothe you, O men of little faith! 29And do not seek what you are to eat and what you are to drink, nor be of anxious mind. 30For all the nations of the world seek these things; and your Father knows that you need them. 31Instead, seek his kingdom, and these things shall be yours as well."

MC, DSM, UR.

Yeshua teaches reliance upon Yahweh's imminent kingdom for sustenance. Not planting or planning, but mere confidence in divine provision, demonstrates Yeshua's perspective on the shortness of time remaining before the kingdom irrupts.

Logion 441 (Luke 12.32-34): "32Fear not, little flock, for it is your Father's good pleasure to give you the kingdom. 33Sell your possessions, and give alms; provide yourselves with purses that do not grow old, with a treasure in the heavens that does not fail, where no thief approaches and no moth destroys. 34For where your treasure is, there will your heart be also."

MC, DSM, UR.

Yeshua warns of the co-opting influence of wealth. Note again Yeshua's emphasis on heartfelt allegiance to the kingdom of God.

Logion 447 (Luke 12.57-59): "57And why do you not judge for yourselves what is right? 58As you go with your accuser before the magistrate, make an effort to settle with him on the way, lest he drag you to the judge, and the judge hand you over to the officer, and the officer put you in prison. 59I tell you, you will never get out till you have paid the very last copper."

MC, DSM, UR.

Yeshua teaches the correlation between social justice and divine approbation.

Logion 448 (Luke 13.2-5): (of murdered political prisoners) "Do you think that these Galileans were worse sinners than all the other Galileans, because they suffered thus? 3I tell you, No; but unless you repent you will all likewise perish. 4Or those eighteen upon whom the tower of Siloam fell and killed them, do you think that they were worse offenders than all the others who dwelt in Jerusalem? [5]I tell you, No; but unless you repent you will all likewise perish."

MC, DSM, UR.

Judgment appears fickle, as are historical outcomes. But judgment is certain.

Logion 449 (Luke 13.6-9): "A man had a fig tree planted in his vineyard; and he came seeking fruit on it and found none. [7]And he said to the vinedresser, 'Lo, these three years I have come seeking fruit on this fig tree, and I find none. Cut it down; why should it use up the ground? [8]And he answered him, 'Let it alone, sir, this year also, till I dig about it and put on manure. [9]And if it bears fruit next year, well and good; but if not, you can cut it down."

MC, DSM, UR, HH.

Luke attempts to explain Yeshua's embarrassing "curse of the fig tree" story of Logion 88 (Mark 11.12-14,20-21). The logion, however, expresses Yeshua's patience with sinners and emphasis on immediate repentance. I find the logion reliable to that extent.

Logion 453A (Luke 13.24): "[24]Strive to enter by the narrow door; for many, I tell you, will seek to enter and will not be able."

MC, DSM, UR.

Yeshua teaches that all shall not enter the kingdom of God, despite their desire to do so.

Logion 454 (Luke 13.25-29): "[25]When once the householder has risen up and shut the door, you will begin to stand outside and to knock at the door, saying, 'Lord, open to us.' He will answer you, 'I do not know where you come from.' [26]Then you will begin to say, 'We ate and drank in your presence, and you taught in our streets.' [27]But he will say, 'I tell you, I do not know where you come from; depart from me, all you workers of iniquity!' [28]There you will weep and gnash your teeth, when you see Abraham and Isaac and Jacob and all the prophets in the kingdom of God and you yourselves thrust out. [29]And men will come from east and west, and from north and south, and sit at table in the kingdom of God."

MC, DSM, UR.

Yeshua breaks the redemptive vessel of Judaism, admitting many whose hearts are rightly oriented toward Yahweh. All others are excluded.

LOGION SIEVE KEY: Marcan Consistency (MC), Danielic Son of man (DSM), Hagiographical Hurdle (HH), Urgency of Repentance (UR), Hagiographical Excess (HE), Anachronisms and Post-Yeshuan concerns (APY)

Logion 455 (Luke 13.30): "[30]And behold, some are last who will be first, and some are first who will be last."

MC, DSM, UR.

Yeshua warns of a divine inversion of social hierarchy.

Logion 461 (Luke 14.12-14): "When you give a dinner or a banquet, do not invite your friends or your brothers or your kinsmen or rich neighbors, lest they also invite you in return, and you be repaid. [13]But when you give a feast, invite the poor, the maimed, the lame, the blind, [14]and you will be blessed, because they cannot repay you. You will be repaid at the resurrection of the just."

MC, DSM, UR.

Yeshua plainly states Yahweh's preference for poor and challenged people, and expresses disdain of money. Resurrection awaits only those possessing good hearts.

Logion 467 (Luke 14.34-35a): "[34]Salt is good; but if salt has lost its taste, how shall its saltness be restored? [35]It is fit neither for the land nor for the dunghill; men throw it away."

MC, DSM, UR.

Yeshua teaches the heartfelt sort of person Yahweh seeks. Those lacking such hearts are discarded.

Logion 468 (Luke 14.35b): "He who has ears to hear, let him hear."

MC, DSM, UR.

Yeshua indicates that the ability to hear his message is not universal. Only those with "hearing ears" enter the kingdom of God.

Logion 469 (Luke 15.4-7): "[4]What man of you, having a hundred sheep, if he has lost one of them, does not leave the ninety-nine in the wilderness, and go after the one which is lost, until he finds it? [5]And when he has found it, he lays it on his shoulders, rejoicing. [6]And when he comes home, he calls together his friends and his neighbors, saying to them, 'Rejoice with me, for I have found my sheep which was lost.' [7]Just so, I tell you, there will be more joy in heaven over one sinner who repents than over ninety-nine righteous persons who need no repentance."

MC, DSM, UR.

Yeshua teaches Yahweh's joy in repentance, and subtly expresses doubt about those whose acts lead them to believe they are righteous.

Logion 470 (Luke 15.8-10): "[8]Or what woman, having ten silver coins, if she loses one coin, does not light a lamp and sweep the house and seek diligently until she finds it? [9]And when she has found it, she calls together her friends and neighbors, saying, 'Rejoice with me, for I have found the coin which I had lost.' [10]Just so, I tell you, there is joy before the angels of God over one sinner who repents."

MC, DSM, UR.

Yeshua teaches Yahweh's view of sinners by a different parable.

Logion 471 (Luke 15.11-32): "There was a man who had two sons; [12]and the younger of them said to his father, 'Father, give me the share of property that falls to me.' And he divided his living between them. [13]Not many days later, the younger son gathered all he had and took his journey into a far country, and there he squandered his property in loose living. [14]And when he had spent everything, a great famine arose in that country, and he began to be in want. [15]So he went and joined himself to one of the citizens of that country, who sent him into his fields to feed swine. [16]And he would gladly have fed on the pods that the swine ate; and no one gave him anything. [17]But when he came to himself he said, 'How many of my father's hired servants have bread enough and to spare, but I perish here with hunger! [18]I will arise and go to my father, and I will say to him, 'Father, I have sinned against heaven and before you; [19]I am no longer worthy to be called your son; treat me as one of your hired servants.' [20]And he arose and came to his father. But while he was yet at a distance, his father saw him and had compassion, and ran and embraced him and kissed him. [21]And the son said to him, 'Father, I have sinned against heaven and before you; I am no longer worthy to be called your son.' [22]But the father said to his servants, 'Bring quickly the best robe, and put it on him; and put a ring on his hand, and shoes on his feet; [23]and bring the fatted calf and kill it, and let us eat and make merry; [24]for this my son was dead, and is alive again; he was lost, and is found.' And they began to make merry. [25]Now his elder son was in the field; and as he came and drew near to the house, he heard music and dancing. [26]And he called one of the servants and asked what this meant. [27]And he said to him, 'Your brother has come, and your father has killed the fatted calf, because he has received him safe and sound.' [28]But he was angry and refused to go in. His father came out and entreated him, [29]but he answered his father, 'Lo, these many years I have served you, and I never disobeyed your command; yet you never gave me a kid, that I might make merry with my friends. [30]But when this son of yours came, who has devoured your living with harlots, you killed the fatted calf!' [31]And he said to him, 'Son, you are always with me, and all that is mine is yours. [32]It was fitting to make merry and be glad, for this your brother was dead, and is alive; he was lost and is found."

MC, DSM, UR.

This is perhaps Yeshua's most famous parable. Yeshua teaches that Yahweh rejoices in repentant sinners. Yahweh (at best) lavishes divine neglect upon the obedient Jewish nation.

Logion 473 (Luke 16.13): "[13]No servant can serve two masters; for either he will hate the one and love the other, or he will be devoted to the one and despise the other. You cannot serve God and mammon."

MC, DSM, UR.

Yeshua discounts prosperity as an indicator of divine approval, and warns of the corruption of the heart caused by wealth.

Logion 479 (Luke 17.1-2): "Temptations to sin are sure to come; but woe to him by whom they come! [2]It would be better for him if a millstone were hung round his neck and he were cast into the sea, than that he should cause one of these little ones to sin."

MC, DSM, UR.

Yeshua teaches Yahweh's overweening love of children, and his wrath toward those who corrupt the young (perhaps youth is here a cipher for the pure of heart).

Logion 487 (Luke 17.33): "[33]Whoever seeks to gain his life will lose it, but whoever loses his life will preserve it."

MC, DSM, UR.

The irruptive kingdom is imminent. Salvation lies in immediate repentance, which may feel like losing one's life.

LOGION SIEVE KEY: Marcan Consistency (MC), Danielic Son of man (DSM), Hagiographical Hurdle (HH), Urgency of Repentance (UR), Hagiographical Excess (HE), Anachronisms and Post-Yeshuan concerns (APY)

Logion 490 (Luke 18.16-17): "Let the children come to me, and do not hinder them; for to such belongs the Kingdom of God. [17]Truly, I say to you, whoever does not receive the kingdom of God like a child shall not enter it."

MC, DSM, UR.

Yeshua teaches that heartfelt adherence, child-like in its innocence, opens the kingdom's door. No other approach gains admittance.

Logion 492 (Luke 18.20, 22): "[20]You know the commandments: 'Do not commit adultery, Do not kill, Do not steal, Do not bear false witness, Honor your father and mother.' . . . One thing you still lack. Sell all that you have and distribute to the poor, and you will have treasure in heaven; and come, follow me."

MC, DSM, UR.

Yeshua teaches that the rich ruler, good in all his acts, cannot enter the kingdom of God, for he adheres to money, not Yeshua.

Logion 493 (Luke 18.24-25): "[24]How hard it is for those who have riches to enter the kingdom of God! [25]For it is easier for a camel to go through the eye of a needle than for a rich man to enter the kingdom of God."

MC, DSM, UR.

Yeshua warns of the dangers of wealth.

Logion 494 (Luke 18.27): (of salvation of the rich) "What is impossible with men is possible with God."

MC, DSM, UR.

Yeshua teaches that Yahweh saves whom he pleases.

Logion 498 (Luke 19.5, 9): (to a repentant, short-of-stature, rich tax collector) "Zacchaeus, make haste and come down; for I must stay at your house today. . . . Today salvation has come to this house, since he also is a son of Abraham."

MC, DSM, UR.

Yeshua commends the sinner (tax-collector) Zacchaeus for his tender heart in giving to the poor and making good his financial wrongs.

Logion 499 (Luke 19.10): "[10]For the Son of man came to seek and to save the lost."

MC, DSM, UR.

Yeshua recurs to his Son of man identity and mission to save the heartfelt repentant sinner.

Logion 501 (Luke 19.26): "[26]I tell you, that to every one who has will more be given; but from him who has not, even what he has will be taken away."

MC, DSM, UR.

Yeshua teaches, with substantial ambiguity, that social priorities differ between this world and the kingdom of God.

HEALING LOGIA

Yeshua, throughout his brief travels in Israel, sought and proclaimed miraculous events that would attend the arrival of the kingdom of God. One need not credit the events themselves to appreciate Yeshua's conviction that such events were to occur. In today's hospitals, some still claim miraculous healings. We may declare that which we little understand miraculous. Of diseases, we remain deeply ignorant. Of the power of bodies to heal themselves, we frequently underestimate. Of what may have happened during Yeshua's ministry, we know only what the early church reports. Of those reports, I remain skeptical. But I am deeply convinced that Yeshua himself believed in remarkable healings, exorcisms, and even resuscitations from the dead. Yeshua was an uneducated commoner of his day, regardless what compelling insights drove his actions and prompted his words. Healing stories, in the mouths of believers, lend themselves to hagiographical extravagance. One proceeds with caution.

Logion 5 (Mark 1.41): (to a leper who requested healing) "I will; be clean."
MC, DSM.

In this story, Yeshua heals a leper. The buried logion might be cast aside as hagiographically excessive. And yet, from Yeshua's other sayings, one might retain the saying as an indicator of Yeshua's preference for people who acknowledge their problems. Humans cannot heal leprosy by speaking to its victims. Yet, the diagnostic capability of Yeshua's peasant companions leaves much to be desired. This healing could be psychosomatic. I remain ambivalent, but find no compelling reason to excise the brief saying. All the healing logia contain a preference for signs, which Yeshua explicitly declines to provide (see, for example, Matthew 16.4).

Logion 6 (Mark 1.44): "See that you say nothing to any one; but go, show yourself to the priest, and offer for your cleansing what Moses commanded, for a proof to the people."
MC, DSM, UR.

LOGION SIEVE KEY: Marcan Consistency (MC), Danielic Son of man (DSM), Hagiographical Hurdle (HH), Urgency of Repentance (UR), Hagiographical Excess (HE), Anachronisms and Post-Yeshuan concerns (APY)

This logion is marred by its messianic secret emphasis, but is otherwise consistent with Yeshua's views. Proving the healing to the people stretches the logion's Marcan Consistency, since Yeshua declined proofs and asserted Yahweh's independence to welcome those whom he will to the kingdom of God. With reservations, I retain the logion.

Logion 7 (Mark 2.5): "My son, your sins are forgiven."

MC, DSM, UR.

Yeshua forgives sin, a divine prerogative delegated to the Son of man, much to the chagrin of his detractors.

Logion 9 (Mark 2.8-11): "Why do you question thus in your hearts? [9]Which is easier, to say to the paralytic, 'Your sins are forgiven,' or to say, 'Rise, take up your pallet and walk'? [10]But that you may know that the Son of man has authority on earth to forgive sins . . . [11]I say to you, rise, take up your pallet and go home."

MC, DSM, UR.

This logion is tainted by its showiness, aimed to bolster Yeshua's authority, but its essence, which is given different settings in Matthew 9.2-8 and Luke 5.18-26, lend the core logion credence.

Logion 29 (Mark 5.8): "Come out of the man, you unclean spirit! . . . What is your name?"

MC, DSM.

Yeshua commands a demon, a prerogative of the scion of Yahweh. Humans cannot command demons, since none exists. Yet, Yeshua believed demons existed, and believed the kingdom of God commanded such creatures. I count the logion reliable.

Logion 30 (Mark 5.19): (to the dispossessed demoniac) "Go home to your friends, and tell them how much the Lord has done for you, and how he has had mercy on you."

MC, DSM, UR.

Contradicting the messianic secret theme of Mark, Yeshua tells the healed demoniac to tell others of Yeshua's mission. I take the messianic secret theme to be a device by which Mark explained why more people did not flock to Yeshua, given his extravagant healings, exorcisms, and other miracles.

LOGION SIEVE KEY: Marcan Consistency (MC), Danielic Son of man (DSM), Hagiographical Hurdle (HH), Urgency of Repentance (UR), Hagiographical Excess (HE), Anachronisms and Post-Yeshuan concerns (APY)

Logion 32 (Mark 5.34): (to the menorrhagic woman) "Daughter, your faith has made you well; go in peace, and be healed of your disease."

MC, DSM, UR, HH.

Yeshua commends a woman healed of her unusual menstrual bleeding. Note that Yeshua commends her faith, a state of the heart, contrary to the gist of the rest of the passage in which Mark has situated the logion. The contextual story makes Yeshua's powers magical and contagious to clothing. Hemorrhage yields to neither magic nor the touch of cloth. The early church may have found this saying an embarrassment, given the context into which Mark inserted the logion. If faith heals, what role remains for Yeshua? The early church missed Yeshua's answer. Yeshua ushers in the kingdom of God, and judges men by their hearts. Yeshua is Yahweh's scion. In the kingdom of God, many unusual things happen.

Logion 33 (Mark 5.36): (addressing a ruler seeking Yeshua's assistance on behalf of a man whose daughter has died) "Do not fear, only believe."

MC, DSM, UR.

Yeshua teaches faith and confidence in Yahweh. The context given to the logion well-exemplifies the hagiographic excess of the early church, but the logion might well have been uttered by Yeshua.

Logion 34A (Mark 5.39, 41): (to the sleeping/dead daughter of Jairus, the ruler of the synagogue) "Why do you make a tumult and weep? The child is not dead but sleeping. . . . Talitha cumi."

MC, DSM, UR.

This odd logion seems an attenuated attempt at hagiographical excess. If the girl slept, as Yeshua asserts, then no hagiographical excess mars the logion. If the girl had died, the matter is a resuscitation. Death is not defeated by human speech. I retain the logion with reservations.

Logion 46 (Mark 7.27-29): (To the Syrophoenician Greek woman, who claims dogs get table crumbs) "Let the children first be fed, for it is not right to take the children's bread and throw it to the dogs. . . . For this saying you may go your way; the demon has left your daughter."

MC, DSM, UR.

LOGION SIEVE KEY: Marcan Consistency (MC), Danielic Son of man (DSM), Hagiographical Hurdle (HH), Urgency of Repentance (UR), Hagiographical Excess (HE), Anachronisms and Post-Yeshuan concerns (APY)

Yeshua teaches that the Jewish community comes first, before the Greek communities. As Son of man, Yeshua claims powers over demons. This troubled logion may be the creation of the early Jewish church to contradict the Hellenizing influence of Paul and the growing numerical dominance of the churches of Asia Minor and Greece. Still, Yeshua conducted his work primarily among Jews. The insult in the saying seems inconsistent with the Marcan Yeshua, who prioritizes faith over ethnicity. I have credited this logion, but am deeply equivocal about it.

Logion 47 (Mark 7.34b): (Upon restoring sight and speech to the Decapoline deaf and dumb man) "Ephphatha."

MC, DSM.

Yeshua, with some semi-magical spittle and ear-poking, heals a deaf and dumb man. Yet, the saying is simple enough, and lacks ostentation. Given Yeshua believed he had been granted divine powers, the logion may be original, with some hagiographic flourishes added.

Logion 51 (Mark 8.23, 26) (to the blind man whose eyes Yeshua spit on and laid on hands, then sent home) "Do you see anything? . . . "Do not even enter the village."

MC, DSM.

Yeshua, again with magical spittle and secret techniques, heals a blind man (on the second try). The first part of this logion might be mere literary license, yet it seems the sort of simple question one attempting to help might ask. The second half of the logion (about not going home) may be a messianic secret invention, but might also reflect Yeshua's concern about being mobbed in the healed man's village. The logion might be accurate, and so is retained, with reservations.

Logion 60 (Mark 9.19-25): (Of a boy possessed by a persistent demon that occasionally afflicts the boy with seizures) "Oh faithless generation, how long am I to be with you? How long am I to bear with you? Bring him to me. . . . How long has he had this? . . . If you can! All things are possible to him who believes. . . . You dumb and deaf spirit, I command you, come out of him and never enter him again. . . . This kind cannot be driven out by anything but prayer."

MC, DSM, UR.

Yeshua strikes his usual themes of faith, possibility, healing, and prayer. The scion of the inbreaking kingdom of God commands such difficulties. Here, the

LOGION SIEVE KEY: Marcan Consistency (MC), Danielic Son of man (DSM), Hagiographical Hurdle (HH), Urgency of Repentance (UR), Hagiographical Excess (HE), Anachronisms and Post-Yeshuan concerns (APY)

miraculous elements trouble one, but most clearly in this story, the commoners' understanding of their physical ailments as spiritual possessions is plain. The story also lacks that showiness that often accompanies hagiographical excess. With reservations, I retain the logion.

Logion 86 (Mark 10.49-52): (to blind Bartimaeus) "Call him. . . . What do you want me to do for you? . . . Go your way; your faith has made you well."

MC, DSM, UR.

Yeshua again heals, but without fanfare. Lacking ostentation, I retain the logion.

Logion 171 (Matthew 8.3-4): (to a leper) "I will; be clean. . . . See that you say nothing to any one; but go, show yourself to the priest, and offer the gift that Moses commanded, for a proof to the people."

MC, DSM, UR.

Yeshua heals, then instructs the beneficiary to both keep his secret and reveal his secret. This stretches Marcan Consistency, since it requires ritual proofs, which Yeshua consistently declined, and indulges the messianic secret theory in Mark, which is inconsistent with Yeshua's purpose of declaring the kingdom of God. The healing is simple enough. Yeshua's subsequent instructions seem both complicated and unlikely. Despite its flaws, I retain the logion, with many reservations.

Logion 172 (Matthew 8.7, 10, 13): (to a centurion) "I will come and heal him. . . . Truly I say to you, not even in Israel have I found such faith. . . . Go; be it done for you as you have believed."

MC, DSM, UR.

Yeshua teaches that the kingdom of God rewards people of faith, even those outside Judaism. The logion might be criticized because it welcomes gentiles, which was a post-Yeshua problem for the early church. Yet, Yeshua's dependence upon the eighth-century prophets, with their emphasis that Yahweh will welcome those who have right hearts, regardless of their origins, leaves this logion's sentiment within the scope of Yeshua's teachings. The logion also avoids Yeshua healing in a manner that might have been spectacularly crowd-pleasing, and so counters the general trend of those writers inclined to hagiographical excess.

LOGION SIEVE KEY: Marcan Consistency (MC), Danielic Son of man (DSM), Hagiographical Hurdle (HH), Urgency of Repentance (UR), Hagiographical Excess (HE), Anachronisms and Post-Yeshuan concerns (APY)

Logion 176 (Matthew 8.32): (to the Gadarene demoniacs) "Go."

MC, DSM, HH.

Yeshua commands the Gadarene (in Luke and Mark, "Gerasene") demoniacs to depart into pigs, which then fled to suicide themselves. The logion portrays Yeshua as a commander of demons, which suffers the flaw of excess praise of Yeshua. No human commands demons because no demons exist. In that Yeshua destroyed someone's herd of swine, the logion may have proved a hurdle to the early church. Also, the story portrays the townspeople as deeply fearful of Yeshua, imploring him to leave. Again, this fact may have proved a hagiographical hurdle for the early church. The logion has the merit of the simple command typical of Yeshua, and is as short as a logion might become. With reservations, I retain the logion.

Logion 177 (Matthew 9.2): (to a paralytic) "Take heart, my son; your sins are forgiven."

MC, DSM, UR.

Yeshua forgives a paralytic's sins, based on the faith of his friends. He exercises the prerogatives of the Son of man.

Logion 178 (Matthew 9.4-6): "Why do you think evil in your hearts? [5]For which is easier, to say 'Your sins are forgiven,' or to say 'Rise and walk'? [6]But that you may know that the Son of man has authority on earth to forgive sins . . . Rise, take up your bed and go home."

MC, DSM, UR.

Yeshua confronts scribal opponents bluntly as the Son of man. A paralytic walks, and the crowd is pleased. The logion suffers for its showiness. Yeshua consistently declined to perform for skeptics. Yet, the logion evidences Yeshua's common themes.

Logion 183 (Matthew 9.22): (to a menorrhagic woman who touched his garment) "Take heart, daughter; your faith has made you well."

MC, DSM, UR.

Yeshua heals a woman with chronic hemorrhage. The logion contains Yeshua's typical emphasis on the salvific effect of faith. The logion's context, however, suffers hagiographical excess, which should be discarded. Yeshua's garments healed no one, as Yeshua himself attempts to make plain to the victim.

Logion 184 (Matthew 9.24): "Depart, for the girl is not dead but sleeping."

MC, DSM, HH.

Yeshua wakes a sleeping (or dead) girl. The crowd believe the girl dead. I retain the logion, despite its emphasis on Yeshua's magical powers, because the logion leaves open the possibility that the girl was merely unconscious, not dead. And that possibility might well have caused the Synoptic writers to omit the logion, were it not deeply embedded in their oral tradition.

Logion 185 (Matthew 9.28-30): (to two blind men) "Do you believe that I am able to do this? . . . According to your faith be it done to you. . . . See that no one knows it."

MC, DSM, UR.

Yeshua heals two blind men, again crediting their faith. The logion suffers from a messianic secret emphasis. Yet, its core message of faith is consistent with the Marcan Yeshua.

Logion 238 (Matthew 15.24-28): (to a Canaanite woman) "I was sent only to the lost sheep of the house of Israel. . . . It is not fair to take the children's bread and throw it to the dogs." . . . O woman, great is your faith! Be it done for you as you desire."

MC, DSM, HH.

Yeshua heals the daughter of a non-Jew, after objecting in that regard. This logion reflects Yeshua's vacillation between a broad, prophetic view of the saving effect of faith, and the narrow view that the Son of man comes to rescue repentant Jews. Vacillation itself might prove a hagiographic hurdle to the church, to the extent it was bent upon proffering Yeshua as possessing supra-human knowledge. Some portion of the early church would have objected to this logion, no matter how it was cast. The role of non-Jews in the early church was a difficult subject. So, the logion may have presented a hagiographic hurdle to some portion of the church, and so may have been deeply embedded in the oral tradition.

LOGION SIEVE KEY: Marcan Consistency (MC), Danielic Son of man (DSM), Hagiographical Hurdle (HH), Urgency of Repentance (UR), Hagiographical Excess (HE), Anachronisms and Post-Yeshuan concerns (APY)

Logion 251 (Matthew 17.17): (to the father of (a possibly) epileptic child) "O faithless and perverse generation, how long am I to be with you? How long am I to bear with you? Bring him here to me."

MC, DSM.

Yeshua complains of his disciples' shortcomings, with warnings about his role as Son of man. There is the distinct possibility that this logion is a post-Yeshuan imposition, addressing the church's angst at the non-return of Yeshua in power. Yet, Yeshua's frustration with the disciples, his emphasis on faith, and his confidence in his role as Son of man predominate. With reservations, I retain the logion.

Logion 252 (Matthew 17.20): (to the disciples who failed to heal the epileptic son) "Because of your little faith. For truly, I say to you, if you have faith as a grain of mustard seed, you will say to this mountain, 'Move hence to yonder place,' and it will move; and nothing will be impossible to you."

MC, DSM, UR.

Yeshua evaluates the faith of his disciples. A little faith goes a long way. In the kingdom of God, no force proves greater.

Logion 279 (Matthew 20.32): (to two blind men) "What do you want me to do for you?"

MC, DSM, UR.

Yeshua heals two blind men. The story may be a re-versioning of Matthew 9.27-31. If so, if offers a good illustration of the freedom that the author of Matthew felt in purposing logia and re-contextualizing them. The duality may also be an artifact of oral transmission, all apart from Matthew's literary license.

Logion 338 (Luke 4.35): "Be silent, and come out of him!"

MC, DSM.

Yeshua publicly, at synagogue, commands a demon to depart. This command is consistent with the simple exercise of authority in the Marcan Yeshua, yet suffers hagiographic excess in its setting. Humans command no demons. No demons exist.

Logion 341 (Luke 5.13-14): (to a leper) "I will; be clean. . . . Go and show yourself to the priest, and make an offering for your cleansing, as Moses commanded, for a proof to the people."

MC, DSM.

Yeshua heals a leper by command. One notes the lack of a reference to the leper's faith in all three of these versions (Mark 1.40-45 and Matthew 8.1-4). Nevertheless, the story appears deeply embedded in the oral tradition. Note the consistency through all three versions. The hagiographic excess of this story diminishes its reliability. On balance, I retain the logion, with reservations.

Logion 342 (Luke 5.20, 22-24): (to a paralytic, and Pharisees) "Man, your sins are forgiven you. . . . Why do you question in your hearts? [23]Which is easier, to say, 'Your sins are forgiven you,' or to say, 'Rise and walk'? [24]But that you may know that the Son of man has authority on earth to forgive sins . . . I say to you, rise, take up your bed and go home."

MC, DSM, UR.

Yeshua heals a paralytic before Pharisees, who question him. The logion suffers showiness, and yet it appears deeply grounded in the Synoptic tradition that Yeshua confronted opponents in a manner intended to embarrass them. With reservations, I retain the logion.

Logion 372 (Luke 7.9): (responding to the centurion's faith in Yeshua' capabilities) "I tell you, not even in Israel have I found such faith."

MC, DSM, UR.

Yeshua praises the Roman's faith, comparing it favorably to what he finds in his fellow Jews. The possibility exists that this logion intends to serve a later purpose, that of letting Yeshua weigh in on the conflict between Jewish Christians and gentile Christians in the church's first century. Still, Yeshua himself seems to have ambivalence on the question of the role of non-Jews in the kingdom of God. I retain the logion, with reservations.

Logion 387 (Luke 8.30, 39): (to the demon Legion) "What is your name? . . . [39]Return to your home, and declare how much God has done for you."

MC, DSM.

LOGION SIEVE KEY: Marcan Consistency (MC), Danielic Son of man (DSM), Hagiographical Hurdle (HH), Urgency of Repentance (UR), Hagiographical Excess (HE), Anachronisms and Post-Yeshuan concerns (APY)

Yeshua exorcises the Gerasene (in Matthew, the Gadarene) demoniac, demonstrating power as Son of man. He encourages the freed sufferer to promote Yeshua in his home town. This differs from Mark's Yeshua, and yet the story appears deeply embedded in the oral tradition.

Logion 389 (Luke 8.48): (to the menorrhagic woman) "Daughter, your faith has made you well; go in peace."

MC, DSM, UR.

Yeshua heals the bleeding woman. Luke's story elevates Yeshua's hagiography, with Yeshua "perceiving that power had gone out from him." This battery theory of divine potency sets Yeshua apart in a manner inconsistent with the Marcan Yeshua. You will find rejected portions of Luke's version at Logion 388 in suspect logia.

Logion 390 (Luke 8.50, 52, 54): (to the father of a dead daughter) "Do not fear; only believe, and she shall be well. . . . Do not weep; for she is not dead but sleeping. . . . Child, arise."

MC, DSM, UR, HH.

Yeshua wakes a sleeping (or dead) child. The logion emphasizes faith, and may have proved a hurdle to the early church, given the ambiguity of what Yeshua accomplished in that home.

Logion 397 (Luke 9.41): (to a man whose son the disciples could not heal) "O faithless and perverse generation, how long am I to be with you and bear with you. Bring your son here."

MC, DSM, UR.

Yeshua criticizes the disciples for missing the point of his teaching. He heals where they failed. As with all the healing logia, they are suspect for their tendency to hagiographical excess. Yet, strong evidence exists that psychological states can create physical disease. So, all such logia may not be mere hagiographical inventions. I retain logia where the "healings" they report might be psychosomatic "cures."

Logion 450 (Luke 13.12) (to a bent woman) "Woman, you are freed from your infirmity."

MC, DSM.

LOGION SIEVE KEY: Marcan Consistency (MC), Danielic Son of man (DSM), Hagiographical Hurdle (HH), Urgency of Repentance (UR), Hagiographical Excess (HE), Anachronisms and Post-Yeshuan concerns (APY)

Yeshua heals in synagogue, before the rulers. The logion has the problem that spinal deformity cannot be repaired by mental states, neither Yeshua's nor that of the bent woman. So, the logion suffers hagiographical excess. Still, the logion confronts Jewish rulers and addresses the needs of a commoner, consistent with the Marcan Yeshua. With many reservations, I retain the logion.

Logion 483 (Luke 17.14, 19): (to ten lepers) "Go and show yourselves to the priests. . . . Rise and go your way; your faith has made you well."

MC, DSM, UR.

This logion may be a re-versioning of the leper healing of Luke 5.13-14 (Logion 341). It suffers the hagiographical excess of larger numbers and impossible healings, and yet retains the emphasis on faith that is the hallmark of the Marcan Yeshua. With reservations, I retain the logion.

Logion 497 (Luke 18.41-42): (to a blind importunate man) "[41]What do you want me to do for you? . . . Receive your sight; your faith has made you well."

MC, DSM, UR.

Yeshua heals the blind man, despite his rudeness. Note the increasing emphasis on command in the Lucan narrative. Here, faith retains the fore, and so I retain the logion.

OPPONENT LOGIA

Much has been made of Yeshua's compassion. Yeshua was indeed kind to humble commoners. Commentators often downplay Yeshua's harshness. The Son of man speaks on behalf of Yahweh, who is about to consign most of a generation of his people to eternal torment. Some words from Yeshua's mouth are brutally blunt. Some actions must be called impolite, and might be styled crass. With opponents, Yeshua minced no words. I construe Yeshua's interactions with opponents as lessons in caring—caring for sorely misguided aristocrats who wantonly confuse or mislead those less intellectually supple than themselves.

Logion 40 (Mark 7.6-8): "Well did Isaiah prophesy of you hypocrites, as it is written 'This people honors me with their lips, but their heart is far from me; [7]in vain do they worship me, teaching as doctrines the precepts of men.' [8]You leave the commandment of God and hold fast the tradition of men."

MC, DSM, UR.

Yeshua confronts opponents harshly with facts about themselves. He does not shy from calling them uncharitable names.

Logion 41 (Mark 7.9-13): "You have a fine way of rejecting the commandment of God, in order to keep your tradition! [10]For Moses said, 'Honor your father and your mother'; and, 'He who speaks evil of father or mother, let him surely die'; [11]but you say, 'If a man tell his father or his mother, What you would have gained from me is Corban . . . [23]then you no longer permit him to do anything for his father or mother, [13]thus making void the word of God through your tradition which you hand on. And many such things you do."

MC, DSM, UR.

Yeshua takes opponents to task on biblical interpretation and the hedge legalists erected around compliance, making more stringent rules to reduce the likelihood of breaching actual Toranic strictures. To know and obey from the heart matters. Priestly add-ons do not matter. This is a core theme in Yeshua's critique of opponents.

LOGION SIEVE KEY: Marcan Consistency (MC), Danielic Son of man (DSM), Hagiographical Hurdle (HH), Urgency of Repentance (UR), Hagiographical Excess (HE), Anachronisms and Post-Yeshuan concerns (APY)

Logion 49 (Mark 8.12): "Why does this generation seek a sign? Truly, I say to you, no sign shall be given to this generation."

MC, DSM, UR.

Yeshua declines to provide signs to the heartless. Note that this sentiment is at odds with the many healing logia of the last section. There, the church makes of Yeshua a source of divine signs, issuing miracles on demand.

Logion 59 (Mark 9.16): "What are you discussing with them?"

MC.

Yeshua interacts with a crowd by asking them a question.

Logion 67 (Mark 9.42): "[42]Whoever causes one of these little ones who believe in me to sin, it would be better for him if a great millstone were hung round his neck and he were thrown into the sea."

MC, DSM, UR.

Yeshua teaches the stakes of repentance. The risks for adults wax when they teach children.

Logion 89 (Mark 11.17): "Is it not written 'My house shall be called a house of prayer for all the nations'? But you have made it a den of robbers."

MC, DSM, UR.

Yeshua refers to Isaiah 56.1-7. This passage serves as his justification for making a commotion in the Temple yard where money was exchanged and sacrificial livestock transacted. Yeshua cuts to the heart of cultic abuses. The Temple honors form, not substance.

Logion 93 (Mark 11.29-30, 33): (to persons questioning his authority) "I will ask you a question; answer me, and I will tell you by what authority I do these things. [30]Was the baptism of John from heaven or from men? Answer me. . . . Neither will I tell you by what authority I do these things."

MC, DSM, UR.

Yeshua traps opponents in their own view of matters. Note Yeshua's insolence toward misguided authority.

LOGION SIEVE KEY: Marcan Consistency (MC), Danielic Son of man (DSM), Hagiographical Hurdle (HH), Urgency of Repentance (UR), Hagiographical Excess (HE), Anachronisms and Post-Yeshuan concerns (APY)

Logion 95 (Mark 12.15-17): (on being asked by Pharisees and Herodians whether one should pay taxes to Caesar or not) "Why put me to the test? Bring me a coin, and let me look at it. . . . Whose likeness and inscription is this? . . . Render to Caesar the things that are Caesar's and to God the things that are God's."

MC, DSM.

Yeshua evades the trap of opponents. He calls people to find what matters in Yahweh's view of things, and do that. Note again the measured insolence Yeshua reserves for opponents.

Logion 96 (Mark 12.24-27): (answering a marriage conundrum created by the doctrine of the resurrection) "Is not this why you are wrong, that you know neither the scriptures nor the power of God? [25]For when they rise from the dead, they neither marry nor are given in marriage, but are like angels in heaven. [26]And as for the dead being raised, have you not read in the book of Moses, in the passage about the bush, how God said to him, 'I am the God of Abraham, and the God of Isaac, and the God of Jacob'? [27]He is not God of the dead, but of the living; you are quite wrong."

MC, DSM, UR.

Yeshua fails to answer the Sadducees, but instead criticizes their paucity of heartfelt knowledge of Yahweh.

Logion 98 (Mark 12.34): (to an agreeable scribe) "You are not far from the kingdom of God."

MC, DSM, UR.

The agreeable scribe recognizes the heartfelt devotion required by the eighth century prophets in their reading of the Torah. Yeshua commends him.

Logion 100 (Mark 12.38-40): "Beware of the scribes, who like to go about in long robes, and to have salutations in the market places [39]and the best seats in the synagogues and the places of honor at feasts, [40]who devour widows' houses and for a pretense make long prayers. They will receive the greater condemnation."

MC, DSM, UR.

Yeshua criticizes misplaced devotion. Damnation awaits such religiosity.

Logion 141 (Matthew 5.20): "[20]For I tell you, unless your righteousness exceeds that of the scribes and Pharisees, you will never enter the kingdom of heaven."

MC, DSM, UR.

Yeshua teaches of deficient practices. If you want to know what not to do, watch scribes and Pharisees.

Logion 179 (Matthew 9.12-13): "Those who are well have no need of a physician, but those who are sick. Go and learn what this means, 'I desire mercy, and not sacrifice.' For I came not to call the righteous, but sinners."

MC, DSM, UR.

Yeshua critiques his critic, who asked why he eats with tax collectors and sinners. Yeshua defines his mission, an inversion of the priorities of Pharisees.

Logion 204 (Matthew 11.16-19): "[16]But to what shall I compare this generation? It is like children sitting in the market places and calling to their playmates, [17]'We piped to you, and you did not dance; we wailed, and you did not mourn.' [18]For John came neither eating nor drinking, and they say, 'He has a demon'; [19]the Son of man came eating and drinking, and they say, 'Behold, a glutton and a drunkard, a friend of tax collectors and sinners!' Yet wisdom is justified by her deeds."

MC, DSM, UR.

Yeshua laments his contemporaries generally. They prove critical, no matter what practices they confront. The citation is not identifiable, though it resembles eighth century prophet sentiment. For the confusing final sentence of this passage, compare Luke 7.35.

Logion 205 (Matthew 11.21-24): "[21]Woe to you, Chorazin! Woe to you Bethsaida! For if the mighty works done in you had been done in Tyre and Sidon, they would have repented long ago in sackcloth and ashes. [22]But I tell you, it shall be more tolerable on the day of judgment for Tyre and Sidon than for you. [23]And you Capernaum, will you be exalted to heaven? You shall be brought down to Hades. For if the mighty works done in you had been done in Sodom, it would have remained until this day. [24]But I tell you that it shall be more tolerable on the day of judgment for the land of Sodom than for you."

MC, DSM, UR, HH.

Yeshua berates his home village (Capernaum) and surrounding villages on the north shore of the Sea of Galilee. They have been present for portions of Yeshua's ministry, but failed to repent. Perhaps Yeshua's pique here presented a hagiographic hurdle for the early church. His criticism is immoderate.

Logion 211 (Matthew 12.25-29): "Every kingdom divided against itself is laid waste, and no city or house divided against itself will stand; 26and if Satan casts out Satan, he is divided against himself; how then will his kingdom stand? 27And if I cast out demons by Be-el'zebul, by whom do your sons cast them out? Therefore they shall be your judges. 28But if it is by the Spirit of God that I cast out demons, then the kingdom of God has come upon you. 29Or how can one enter a strong man's house and plunder his goods, unless he first binds the strong man? Then indeed he may plunder his house."

MC, DSM, UR.

Yeshua takes opponents to task for illogic. He asserts that the Son of Man binds Satan eschatologically, for the kingdom of God soon irrupts.

Logion 214 (Matthew 12.33): "33Either make the tree good, and its fruit good; or make the tree bad, and its fruit bad; for the tree is known by its fruit."

MC, DSM, UR.

Yeshua teaches again that what comes out of man defines that man. Good fruit from the good tree, bad from bad.

Logion 215 (Matthew 12.34-35): "34You brood of vipers! How can you speak good, when you are evil? For out of the abundance of the heart the mouth speaks. 35The good man out of his good treasure brings forth good, and the evil man out of his evil treasure brings forth evil."

MC, DSM, UR.

The state of one's heart determines the merit of every action. This is one of Yeshua's great themes.

Logion 219 (Matthew 12.43-45): "43When the unclean spirit has gone out of a man, he passes through waterless places seeking rest, but he finds none. 44Then he says, 'I will return to my house from which I came.' And when he comes he finds it empty, swept, and put in order. 45Then he goes and brings with him seven other spirits more evil than himself, and they enter and dwell there; and the last state of that man becomes worse than the first. So shall it be also with this evil generation."

MC, DSM, UR.

Yeshua teaches that evil convenes evil. Where goodness fails to occupy the space in one's heart once occupied by evil, one suffers yet greater evil.

Logion 223 (Matthew 13.24-30): "The kingdom of heaven may be compared to a man who sowed good seed in his field; [25]but while men were sleeping, his enemy came and sowed weeds among the wheat, and went away. [26]So when the plants came up and bore grain, then the weeds appeared also. [27]And the servants of the householder came and said to him, 'Sir, did you not sow good seed in your field? How then has it weeds?' [28]He said to them, 'An enemy has done this.' The servants said to him, 'Then do you want us to go and gather them?' [29]But he said, 'No; lest in gathering the weeds you root up the wheat along with them. [30]Let both grow together until the harvest; and at harvest time I will tell the reapers, Gather the weeds first and bind them in bundles to be burned, but gather the wheat into my barn."

MC, DSM, UR.

Yeshua teaches of judgment in the kingdom of God, which belongs to the Son of man. Yahweh discerns among humans, culling those who are "grainy," burning the remainder.

Logion 226 (Matthew 13.37-43): "He who sows the good seed is the Son of man; [38]the field is the world, and the good seed means the sons of the kingdom; the weeds are the sons of the evil one, [39]and the enemy who sowed them is the devil; the harvest is the close of the age, and the reapers are angels. [40]Just as the weeds are gathered and burned with fire, so will it be at the close of the age. [41]The Son of man will send his angels, and they will gather out of his kingdom all causes of sin and all evildoers, [42]and throw them into the furnace of fire; there men will weep and gnash their teeth. [43]Then the righteous will shine like the sun in the kingdom of their Father. He who has ears, let him hear."

MC, DSM, UR.

Yeshua teaches the twelve the elements of his allegory of the good and bad seed. One suspects that the lesson is a Matthean invention. Yet, Yeshua must surely have taught his disciples the meaning of parables and stories directly, as in this passage. With reservations, I retain the logion.

LOGION SIEVE KEY: Marcan Consistency (MC), Danielic Son of man (DSM), Hagiographical Hurdle (HH), Urgency of Repentance (UR), Hagiographical Excess (HE), Anachronisms and Post-Yeshuan concerns (APY)

Logion 236 (Matthew 15.13-14): "Every plant which my heavenly Father has not planted will be rooted up. [14]Let them alone: They are blind guides. And if a blind man leads a blind man, both will fall into a pit."

MC, DSM, UR.

Yeshua evaluates his opponents, and advises non-confrontation. They will perish soon enough in judgment.

Logion 240 (Matthew 16.2-4): "When it is evening, you say, 'It will be fair weather; for the sky is red.' [3]And in the morning, 'It will be stormy today, for the sky is red and threatening.' You know how to interpret the appearance of the sky, but you cannot interpret the signs of the times. [4]An evil and adulterous generation seeks for a sign, but no sign shall be given to it except the sign of Jonah."

MC, DSM, UR.

Yeshua declines to produce heavenly signs for opponents. The "sign of Jonah" exception is a later interpolation. Humans do not know what will happen after their deaths. Yet, Yeshua firmly believed that if he were to die, Yahweh would resurrect him and install him as the Son of man. I retain this logion, with the stated reservation.

Logion 256 (Matthew 18.5-6): "[5]Whoever receives one such child in my name receives me; [6]but whoever causes one of these little ones who believe in me to sin, it would be better for him to have a great millstone fastened round is neck and to be drowned in the depth of the sea."

MC, DSM, UR.

Yeshua teaches the state of heart required in the kingdom of God. Terrible judgment falls upon those who corrupt people well-disposed toward the kingdom of God.

Logion 281 (Matthew 21.13): (after Yeshua drove the merchants and financial exchange people from the Temple) "It is written, 'My house shall be called a house of prayer'; but you make it a den of robbers."

MC, DSM.

Yeshua creates a confrontation to make his point. Here, Yeshua's actions may clarify more than his words. The two seem integrally linked, unlike so many logia which appear pasted into their narrative frames.

LOGION SIEVE KEY: Marcan Consistency (MC), Danielic Son of man (DSM), Hagiographical Hurdle (HH), Urgency of Repentance (UR), Hagiographical Excess (HE), Anachronisms and Post-Yeshuan concerns (APY)

Logion 282 (Matthew 21.16): (of children praising Yeshua) "Yes; have you never read, 'Out of the mouth of babes and sucklings thou hast brought perfect praise'?"

MC, DSM, UR.

Yeshua references a distortion of Psalm 8.2. He does so in criticism of opponents (the chief priest and Temple scribes), who complain of his many healings in the temple. One wonders that the Yeshua who declined to provide heavenly signs (Logion 240 – Matthew 16.4) now does so openly in the most public of places before those very enemies. Still, Yeshua might have spoken in this manner, the language is bluntly critical of opponents, as was Yeshua's style, and no human is steadfastly consistent in all things. I retain the logion.

Logion 286 (Matthew 21.24, 27): (to challengers) "I also will ask you a question; and if you tell me the answer, then I also will tell you by what authority I do these things. [25]The baptism of John, whence was it? From heaven or from men? . . . Neither will I tell you by what authority I do these things."

MC, DSM, UR.

Mysteriously, Yeshua declines to state that he acts as the Son of man, by direct authority of Yahweh. Such a declaration might have resulted in immediate execution.

Logion 287 (Matthew 21.28-32): "[28]What do you think? A man had two sons; and he went to the first and said, 'Son, go and work in the vineyard today.' [29]And he answered, 'I will not'; but afterward he repented and went. [30]And he went to the second and said the same; and he answered, "I go, sir,' but did not go. [31]Which of the two did the will of his father? . . . Truly, I say to you, the tax collectors and the harlots go into the kingdom of God before you. [32]For John came to you in the way of righteousness, and you did not believe him, but the tax collectors and the harlots believed him; and even when you saw it, you did not afterward repent and believe him."

MC, DSM, UR.

Yeshua teaches opponents of their lack of repentance. Such can take a lesson from the attitudes of sinners and Roman agents in response to John the Baptist.

LOGION SIEVE KEY: Marcan Consistency (MC), Danielic Son of man (DSM), Hagiographical Hurdle (HH), Urgency of Repentance (UR), Hagiographical Excess (HE), Anachronisms and Post-Yeshuan concerns (APY)

Logion 290 (Matthew 22.18-22): "Why put me to the test, you hypocrites? [19]Show me the money for the tax. . . . Whose likeness and inscription is this? . . . Render therefore to Caesar the things that are Caesar's, and to God the things that are God's."

MC, DSM.

Yeshua evades detractors with a clever answer. He disparages his opponents' actions.

Logion 291 (Matthew 22.29-32): "You are wrong, because you know neither the scriptures nor the power of God. [30]For in the resurrection they neither marry nor are given in marriage, but are like angels in heaven. [31]And as for the resurrection of the dead, have you not read what was said to you by God, [32]'I am the God of Abraham, and the God of Isaac, and the God of Jacob'? He is not the God of the dead, but of the living."

MC, DSM, UR.

Yeshua criticizes opponents for their biblical exegesis, and for their frigid relation to Yahweh. Yeshua believes in resurrection, as a component of effective judgment.

Logion 294 (Matthew 23.2-7): "[2]The scribes and Pharisees sit on Moses' seat; [3]so practice and observe whatever they tell you, but do not what they do; for they preach, but do not practice. [4]They bind heavy burdens, hard to bear, and lay them on men's shoulders; but they themselves will not move them with their finger. [5]They do all their deeds to be seen by men; for they make their phylacteries broad and their fringes long, [6]and they love the places of honor at feasts and the best seats in the synagogues, [7]and salutations in the market places, and being called rabbi by men."

MC, DSM, UR.

Yeshua teaches heartfelt action. Scribes and Pharisees teach well, but fail to practice what they teach. They make life more difficult for normal people, and seek praise from men. Ultimately, scribes and Pharisees teach how one ought not *to behave.*

LOGION SIEVE KEY: Marcan Consistency (MC), Danielic Son of man (DSM), Hagiographical Hurdle (HH), Urgency of Repentance (UR), Hagiographical Excess (HE), Anachronisms and Post-Yeshuan concerns (APY)

Logion 298 (Matthew 23.13): "[13]But woe to you, scribes and Pharisees, hypocrites! because you shut the kingdom of heaven against men; for you neither enter yourselves, nor allow those who would enter to go in."

MC, DSM, UR.

Yeshua castigates scribes and Pharisees for practicing their religion in a way that bars others. They cannot live in a heartful manner, nor do they allow others to do so.

Logion 299 (Matthew 23.15): "[15]Woe to you, scribes and Pharisees, hypocrites! for you traverse sea and land to make a single proselyte, and when he becomes a proselyte, you make him twice as much a child of hell as yourselves."

MC, DSM, UR.

Yeshua criticizes scribes and Pharisees for converting people to their views, thus rendering them fodder for damnation.

Logion 300 (Matthew 23.16-22): "[16]Woe to you, blind guides, who say, 'If any one swears by the temple, it is nothing; but if any one swears by the gold of the temple, he is bound by his oath.' [17]You blind fools! For which is greater, the gold or the temple that has made the gold sacred? [18]And you say, 'If any one swears by the altar, it is nothing; but if any one swears by the gift that is on the altar, he is bound by his oath.' [19]You blind men! For which is greater, the gift or the altar that makes the gift sacred? [20]So he who swears by the altar, swears by it and by everything on it; [21]and he who swears by the temple, swears by it and by him who dwells in it; [22]and he who swears by heaven, swears by the throne of God and by him who sits upon it."

MC, DSM, UR.

Yeshua confronts the nit-picking of Temple ritual oaths. Note the deeply confrontational language, even disparaging name-calling. Yeshua got worked up about these issues.

Logion 301 (Matthew 23.23-24): "[23]Woe to you, scribes and Pharisees, hypocrites! for you tithe mint and dill and cummin, and have neglected the weightier matters of the law, justice and mercy and faith; these you ought to have done, without neglecting the others. [24]You blind guides, straining out a gnat and swallowing a camel!"

LOGION SIEVE KEY: Marcan Consistency (MC), Danielic Son of man (DSM), Hagiographical Hurdle (HH), Urgency of Repentance (UR), Hagiographical Excess (HE), Anachronisms and Post-Yeshuan concerns (APY)

MC, DSM, UR.

Yeshua delivers a lesson straight from the eighth century prophets. Do not pretend to make yourself pleasant smelling to Yahweh when you have neglected justice and mercy and faith. People become terribly disoriented in such matters, fastidious in minute compliance, but grossly neglectful of weightier matters.

Logion 302 (Matthew 23.25-26): "[25]Woe to you, scribes and Pharisees, hypocrites! for you cleanse the outside of the cup and of the plate, but inside they are full of extortion and rapacity. [26]You blind Pharisee! first cleanse the inside of the cup and of the plate, that the outside also may be clean."

MC, DSM, UR.

Opponents may appear righteous, but harbor faithless rapacity.

Logion 303 (Matthew 23.27-28): "[27]Woe to you, scribes and Pharisees, hypocrites! for you are like whitewashed tombs, which outwardly appear beautiful, but within they are full of dead men's bones and all uncleanness. So you also outwardly appear righteous to men, but within you are full of hypocrisy and iniquity."

MC, DSM, UR.

Yeshua teaches that scribes and Pharisees, apparently honorable, harbor dead faith within. Do not emulate them.

Logion 304 (Matthew 23.29-36): "[29]Woe to you, scribes and Pharisees, hypocrites! for you build the tombs of the prophets and adorn the monuments of the righteous, [30]saying, 'If we had lived in the days of our fathers, we would have not taken part with them in shedding the blood of the prophets.' [31]Thus you witness against yourselves, that you are sons of those who murdered the prophets. [32]Fill up, then, the measure of your fathers. [33]You serpents, you brood of vipers, how are you to escape being sentenced to hell? [34]Therefore, I send you prophets and wise men and scribes, some of whom you will kill and crucify, and some you will scourge in your synagogues and persecute from town to town, [35]that upon you may come all the righteous blood shed on earth, from the blood of the innocent Abel to the blood of Zechariah the son of Barachiah, whom you murdered between the sanctuary and the altar. [36]Truly, I say to you, all this will come upon this generation."

MC, DSM, UR, HH.

LOGION SIEVE KEY: Marcan Consistency (MC), Danielic Son of man (DSM), Hagiographical Hurdle (HH), Urgency of Repentance (UR), Hagiographical Excess (HE), Anachronisms and Post-Yeshuan concerns (APY)

Yeshua disparages the scribes and Pharisees for their ancestor rituals. They deem themselves unlike their fathers, who murdered prophets. This logion suffers some interpolation from the post-Yeshuan period. Yeshua indicates that he personally sent Israel prophets. There is also a crucifixion reference, which is not impossible, but raises doubts about the reliability of the logion. Finally, there is a hagiographical hurdle in the last verse, where Yeshua promises that judgment will fall upon the living generation.

Logion 305 (Matthew 23.37-39): "[37]O Jerusalem, Jerusalem, killing the prophets and stoning those who are sent to you! How often would I have gathered your children together as a hen gathers her brood under her wings, and you would not! [38]Behold, your house is forsaken and desolate. [39]For I tell you, you will not see me again, until you say, 'Blessed is he who comes in the name of the Lord.'"

MC, DSM, UR.

This logion retains the condemnations of earlier "Woe to you" logia. It turns, however, to lamentation. The last two verses may be post-Yeshua importations. The final citation may derive from Psalm 118:26, in which a man laid low is exalted by Yahweh. It may be an explanation of the non-return of Yeshua in judgment following his death. The verses also, however, bear other interpretations, at least some of which Yeshua may have uttered. With reservations, I retain the logion.

Logion 306 (Matthew 24.2): (concerning the Temple buildings) "You see all these, do you not? Truly, I say to you, there will not be left here one stone upon another, that will not be thrown down."

MC, DSM, UR, HH.

Yeshua condemns Temple practice, even the buildings themselves. The logion may present a hagiographical hurdle because, at the time of writing of Matthew (if one accepts its earliest date), the Temple may not have yet been razed by Titus (70 A.D.). If one accepts a later date of construction for Matthew (say, the mid 80s), then one wonders why the writer made so little of this logion, since it might have proved a rhetorical boon. Regardless, in the mouth of Yeshua, this logion promised that Temple worship will cease upon judgment by the Son of man.

LOGION SIEVE KEY: Marcan Consistency (MC), Danielic Son of man (DSM), Hagiographical Hurdle (HH), Urgency of Repentance (UR), Hagiographical Excess (HE), Anachronisms and Post-Yeshuan concerns (APY)

Logion 376 (Luke 7.31-35): "[31]To what then shall I compare the men of this generation, and what are they like? [32]They are like children sitting in the market place and calling to one another, 'We piped to you, and you did not dance; we wailed, and you did not weep.' [33]For John the Baptist has come eating no bread and drinking no wine; and you say, 'He has a demon.' [34]The Son of man has come eating and drinking; and you say, 'Behold, a glutton and a drunkard, a friend of tax collectors and sinners!' [35]Yet wisdom is justified by all her children."

MC, DSM, UR.

Yeshua teaches that his Jewish generation is condemned for its heartless superficiality. His contemporaries criticize John the Baptist's asceticism, and the Son of man's indulgences. They are never satisfied. Compare Matthew 11:19. Luke tries to make sense of this indeterminate final verse.

Logion 407 (Luke 10.13-15): "[13]Woe to you, Chorazin! Woe to you, Bethsaida! For if the mighty works done in you had been done in Tyre and Sidon, they would have repented long ago, sitting in sackcloth and ashes. [14]But it shall be more tolerable in the judgment for Tyre and Sidon than for you. [15]And you, Capernaum, will you be exalted to heaven? You shall be brought down to Hades."

MC, DSM, UR.

Yeshua rebukes his home town and neighboring hamlets sharply.

Logion 417 (Luke 11.17-20): "Every kingdom divided against itself is laid waste, and house falls upon house. [18]And if Satan also is divided against himself, how will his kingdom stand? For you say that I cast out demons by Beelzebul. [19]And if I cast out demons by Beelzebul, by whom do your sons cast them out? Therefore they shall be your judges. [20]But if it is by the finger of God that I cast out demons, then the kingdom of God has come upon you."

MC, DSM, UR.

Yeshua criticizes critics, and summons repentance.

Logion 425 (Luke 11.39-41): "Now you Pharisees cleanse the outside of the cup and of the dish, but inside you are full of extortion and wickedness. [40]You fools! Did not he who made the outside make the inside also? [41]But give for alms those things which are within; and behold, everything is clean for you."

MC, DSM, UR.

Yeshua criticizes the concern for appearances in the religious rites of the Temple, to the neglect of inner pollutions. Luke turns this logion to serve the needs of the post-Yeshua church, in intra-mural debates about compliance with Toranic law for gentile Christians. Invisible repentance suffices. Compare Matthew 23.25-26. With reservations, I retain this logion.

Logion 426 (Luke 11.42): "[42]But woe to you Pharisees! For you tithe mint and rue and every herb, and neglect justice and the love of God; these you ought to have done, without neglecting the others."

MC, DSM, UR.

Yeshua holds the eighth century prophetic magnifying glass up to Pharisaic religiosity. Focus on human relations, not rote compliance.

Logion 427 (Luke 11.43): "[43]Woe to you Pharisees! For you love the best seat in the synagogues and salutations in the market places."

MC, DSM, UR.

Yeshua repeats his litany of derogation for the religion of appearances, not substance.

Logion 428 (Luke 11.44): "[44]Woe to you: for you are like graves which are not seen, and men walk over them without knowing it."

MC, DSM, UR.

Yeshua emphasizes that his opponents mislead their followers, polluting them in the eyes of Yahweh.

Logion 429 (Luke 11.46): "Woe to you lawyers also! For you load men with burdens hard to bear, and you yourselves do not touch the burdens with one of your fingers."

MC, DSM, UR.

Yeshua criticizes the rabbis who build a hedge around Toranic law to "safeguard" commoners, without complying themselves.

LOGION SIEVE KEY: Marcan Consistency (MC), Danielic Son of man (DSM), Hagiographical Hurdle (HH), Urgency of Repentance (UR), Hagiographical Excess (HE), Anachronisms and Post-Yeshuan concerns (APY)

Logion 430 (Luke 11.47-51): "[47]Woe to you! For you build the tombs of the prophets whom your fathers killed. [48]So you are witnesses and consent to the deeds of your fathers; for they killed them, and you build their tombs. [49]Therefore also the Wisdom of God said, 'I will send them prophets and apostles, some of whom they will kill and persecute,' [50]that the blood of all the prophets, shed from the foundation of the world, may be required of this generation, [51]from the blood of Abel to the blood of Zechariah, who perished between the altar and the sanctuary. Yes, I tell you, it shall be required of this generation."

MC, DSM, UR, HH.

Yeshua lumps his opponents with those who executed previous prophets. He promises that guilt for all such deaths will fall of the present generation of sinners. Hence, there exists here a hagiographic hurdle, since Yeshua's anticipated judgment failed to materialize.

Logion 431 (Luke 11.52): "[52]Woe to you lawyers! For you have taken away the key of knowledge; you did not enter yourselves, and you hindered those who were entering."

MC, DSM, UR.

Yeshua heaps scorn on the religious scholars of his day. They know how to enter the kingdom of God, but allow none in.

Logion 432 (Luke 12.1b): "Beware of the leaven of the Pharisees, which is hypocrisy."

MC, DSM, UR.

Yeshua likens the role of hypocrisy in one's inner life to yeast in bread. Hypocrisy comes to dominate all.

Logion 451 (Luke 13.15b-16): (answering criticism of healing on the Sabbath) "You hypocrites! Does not each of you on the Sabbath untie his ox or his ass from the manger, and lead it away to water it? [16]And ought not this woman, a daughter of Abraham whom Satan bound for eighteen years, be loosed from this bond on the Sabbath day?"

MC, DSM, UR.

LOGION SIEVE KEY: Marcan Consistency (MC), Danielic Son of man (DSM), Hagiographical Hurdle (HH), Urgency of Repentance (UR), Hagiographical Excess (HE), Anachronisms and Post-Yeshuan concerns (APY)

Yeshua teaches that time is short, and Toranic law flexes to pressing demands. He also spits at the synagogue ruler's inability to distinguish between watering asses and healing a tormented woman.

Logion 457 (Luke 13.34-35): "[34]O Jerusalem, Jerusalem, killing the prophets and stoning those who are sent to you! How often would I have gathered your children together as a hen gathers her brood under her wings, and you would not! [35]Behold, your house is forsaken. And I tell you, you will not see me until you say, 'Blessed is he who comes in the name of the Lord!'"

MC, DSM, UR.

Yeshua expresses care for his damned generation. He invites them to welcome Yeshua as Son of man. Until they do, no reprieve will issue. This last verse may be rhetoric addressing the post-Yeshua non-parousia.

Logion 474 (Luke 16.15): "You are those who justify yourselves before men, but God knows your hearts; for what is exalted among men is an abomination in the sight of God."

MC, DSM, UR.

Yeshua calls Pharisees to heartfelt repentance. One cannot please men and please Yahweh.

Logion 505 (Luke 19.46): "It is written, 'My house shall be a house of prayer'; but you have made it a den of robbers."

MC, DSM, UR.

Yeshua criticizes Temple practices.

Logion 506 (Luke 20.3-4, 8): "I also will ask you a question; now tell me, [4]Was the baptism of John from heaven or from men? . . . Neither will I tell you by what authority I do these things."

MC, DSM.

Yeshua evades a trap set by critics, turning the tables on them.

Logion 508 (Luke 20.24-25): "[24]Show me a coin. Whose likeness and inscription has it? . . . Then render to Caesar the things that are Caesar's, and to God the things that are God's."

MC, DSM.
Yeshua evades opponent traps.

Logion 511 (Luke 20.46-47): "[46]Beware of the scribes, who like to go about in long robes, and love salutations in the market places and the best seats in the synagogues and the places of honor at feasts, [47]who devour widows' houses and for a pretense make long prayers. They will receive the greater condemnation."

MC, DSM, UR.
Yeshua condemns hypocritical religiosity.

LAW LOGIA

Yeshua's law logia contain a deep correlation to the opponent logia. In Yeshua's view, one rudimentary problem lay in how religious authorities of his day viewed law. The strictures of law demanded obedience. Yeshua's opponents built behavioral moats around the Torah's 613 demands, meant to insure that none even approached disobedience. Yeshua looked for the Torah's fulfillment. He boiled down Toranic fundaments to two precepts. He pierced the Law to find its deep rationale, as had others before him. Yeshua advocated compliance with divine purposes. He castigated shallow rule-following. The Law guided one to deep self-knowledge, where one found humility toward oneself and compassion toward others.

Logion 14 (Mark 2.25-26): (Pharisees criticize disciples for plucking grain on the Sabbath) "Have you never read what David did, when he was in need and was hungry, he and those who were with him: [26]how he entered the house of God, when Abiathar was high priest, and ate the bread of the Presence, which was not lawful for any but the priests to eat, and also gave it to those who were with him?"

MC, DSM.

Yeshua teaches that law flexes to human needs, and compliance does not outweigh necessity. See I Samuel 21.1-6.

Logion 15 (Mark 2.27-28): "The Sabbath was made for man, not man for the Sabbath; so the Son of man is lord even of the Sabbath."

MC, DSM, UR.

Yeshua asserts his authority as Son of man, and contradicts the compliance fixation of the Temple authorities.

LOGION SIEVE KEY: Marcan Consistency (MC), Danielic Son of man (DSM), Hagiographical Hurdle (HH), Urgency of Repentance (UR), Hagiographical Excess (HE), Anachronisms and Post-Yeshuan concerns (APY)

Logion 16 (Mark 3.3-5) (to a man with withered hand) "Come here. . . . Is it lawful on the Sabbath to do good or to do harm, to save life or to kill? . . . Stretch out your hand."

MC, DSM, UR.

Mark sets this story in conflict with Pharisees, who then take counsel with the Herodians to kill Yeshua. Doing well by others is more important than complying with Temple regulations surrounding Sabbath observance. The logion is marred by its showy healing, given before others, which may well be hagiographical excess.

Logion 43 (Mark 7.14-15): "Hear me, all of you, and understand: [15]there is nothing outside a man which by going into him can defile him; but the things which come out of a man are what defile him."

MC, DSM, UR.

Yeshua asserts the principle underlying his view of the sacral. It is human hearts and the actions they inspire that build or erode a man. This is the core message of the eighth century prophets as well, to whom Yeshua shows much deference. He derives his self-concept from those authors (Daniel is an inter-testamental work, possibly from the second century B.C., but that fact would have been unknown to Yeshua.)

Logion 44 (Mark 7.18-19): "Then are you also without understanding? Do you not see that whatever goes into a man from outside cannot defile him, [18]since it enters, not his heart but his stomach, and so passes on?"

MC, DSM, UR.

Yeshua evidences a non-physical understanding of sacral impurity. The disciples, in Mark's telling, fail to understand.

Logion 71 (Mark 10.3, 5-9): "What did Moses command you? . . . For your hardness of heart he wrote you this commandment. [6]But from the beginning of creation, God made them male and female. [7]For this reason a man shall leave his father and mother and be joined to his wife, [8]and the two shall become one. So they are no longer two but one. [9]What therefore God has joined together, let not man put asunder."

MC, DSM, UR.

Yeshua contradicts Temple divorce law, and the Torah. See Deuteronomy 24.1-4.

Logion 72 (Mark 10.11-12): "Whoever divorces his wife and marries another, commits adultery against her; [12]and if she divorces her husband and marries another, she commits adultery."

MC, DSM, UR.

Yeshua establishes a new rule for marriage.

Logion 75 (Mark 10.19, 21): "[19]You know the commandments: 'Do not kill, do not commit adultery, Do not steal, Do not bear false witness, Do not defraud, Honor your father and mother,' . . . You lack one thing; go, sell what you have, and give to the poor, and you will have treasure in heaven; and come, follow me."

MC, DSM, UR.

Yeshua demotes money, reiterates the Decalogue, and calls the rich young man to follow.

Logion 97 (Mark 12.29-31): "The first is, 'Hear, O Israel: The Lord our God, the Lord is one; [30]and you shall love the Lord your God with all your heart, and with all your soul, and with all your mind, and with all your strength.' [31]The second is this, 'You shall love your neighbor as yourself.' There is no other commandment greater than these."

MC, DSM.

Yeshua reaffirms his summary of Toranic law, which conforms to the teaching of other rabbis. See Deuteronomy 6.4 and Leviticus 19.18.

Logion 101 (Mark 12.43-44): (observing a widow's Temple treasury payment) "Truly, I say to you, this poor widow has put in more than all those who are contributing to the treasury. [44]For they all contributed out of their abundance; but she out of her poverty has put in everything she had, her whole living."

MC, DSM.

Yeshua makes of money a matter of the heart, and inverts the priorities of the Jerusalem Temple authorities.

LOGION SIEVE KEY: Marcan Consistency (MC), Danielic Son of man (DSM), Hagiographical Hurdle (HH), Urgency of Repentance (UR), Hagiographical Excess (HE), Anachronisms and Post-Yeshuan concerns (APY)

Logion 140 (Matthew 5.17-19): "[17]Think not that I have come to abolish the law and the prophets; I have come not to abolish them but to fulfill them. [18]For truly, I say to you, till heaven and earth pass away, not an iota, not a dot, will pass from the law until all is accomplished. [19]Whoever then relaxes one of the least of these commandments and teaches men so, shall be called least in the kingdom of heaven; but he who does them and teaches them shall be called great in the kingdom of heaven."

MC, DSM, UR.

Yeshua, with some self-contradiction, urges that the law must be punctiliously observed and fulfilled.

Logion 142 (Matthew 5.21-22): "[21]You have heard that it was said to the men of old,' You shall not kill; and whoever kills shall be liable to judgment.' [22]But I say to you that every one who is angry with his brother shall be liable to judgment; whoever insults his brother shall be liable to the council, and whoever says, 'You fool!' shall be liable to the hell of fire."

MC, DSM, UR.

Yeshua increases the demands of the law, and makes them a matter of the heart.

Logion 143 (Matthew 5.23-24): "[23]So if you are offering your gift at the altar, and there remember that your brother has something against you, [24]leave your gift there before the altar and go; first be reconciled to your brothers, and then come and offer your gift."

MC, DSM, UR.

Yeshua prioritizes human amity over legal compliance, with neglect of neither.

Logion 145 (Matthew 5.27-28): "[27]You have heard that it was said, 'You shall not commit adultery.' [28]But I say to you that every one who looks at a woman lustfully has already committed adultery with her in his heart."

MC, DSM, UR.

Yeshua increases the demands of law, making them a matter of the heart.

LOGION SIEVE KEY: Marcan Consistency (MC), Danielic Son of man (DSM), Hagiographical Hurdle (HH), Urgency of Repentance (UR), Hagiographical Excess (HE), Anachronisms and Post-Yeshuan concerns (APY)

Logion 147 (Matthew 5.31-32): "[31]It is also said, 'Whoever divorces his wife, let him give her a certificate of divorce.' [32]But I say to you that every one who divorces his wife, except on the ground of unchastity, makes her an adulteress; and whoever marries a divorced woman commits adultery."

MC, DSM, UR.

Yeshua's rule for singular marriage exceeds the Toranic rule, which permitted divorce for many reasons.

Logion 148 (Matthew 5.33-37): "[33]Again you have heard that it was said to the men of old, 'You shall not swear falsely, but shall perform to the Lord what you have sworn.' [34]But I say to you, Do not swear at all, either by heaven, for it is the throne of god, [35]or by the earth, for it is his footstool, or by Jerusalem, for it is the city of the great King. [36]And do not swear by your head, for you cannot make one hair white or black. [37]Let what you say be simply 'Yes' or 'No'; anything more than this comes from evil."

MC, DSM, UR.

Yeshua demotes oaths, urging simple language.

Logion 149 (Matthew 5.38-41): "[38]You have heard that it was said, 'An eye for an eye and a tooth for a tooth.' [39]But I say to you, Do not resist one who is evil. But if any one strikes you on the right cheek, turn to him the other also; [40]and if any one would sue you and take your coat, let him have your cloak as well; [41]and if any one forces you to go one mile, go with him two miles."

MC, DSM, UR.

The rules of the kingdom of God are not those of this world. One wins by losing, keeps by giving, and defeats rapacity by generosity.

Logion 152 (Matthew 5.48): "[48]You, therefore, must be perfect, as your heavenly Father is perfect."

MC, DSM, UR.

Yeshua teaches that kingdom conduct must exceed that which has preceded it. The ultimate breaks in upon the penultimate.

Logion 167 (Matthew 7.12): "[12]So whatever you wish that men would do to you, do so to them; for this is the law and the prophets."

MC, DSM, UR.

Yeshua captures the law in a sentence. Note the similarity to Tobit 4.15 (a deutero-canonical work of the second century B.C.): "And what you hate, do not do to any one."

Logion 209 (Matthew 12.3-8): "Have you not read what David did, when he was hungry, and those who were with him: [4]how he entered the house of God and ate the bread of the Presence, which it was not lawful for him to eat nor for those who were with him, but only for the priests? [5]Or have you not read in the law how on the Sabbath the priests in the temple profane the Sabbath, and are guiltless? [6]I tell you, something greater than the temple is here. [7]And if you had known what this means, 'I desire mercy and not sacrifice,' you would not have condemned the guiltless. [8]For the Son of man is lord of the Sabbath."

MC, DSM, UR.

Yeshua asserts the eighth century prophetic perspective on legal compliance, and asserts his personal prerogatives as Son of man.

Logion 210 (Matthew 12.11-13): "What man of you, if he has one sheep and it falls into a pit on the Sabbath, will not lay hold of it and lift it out? [12]Of how much more value is a man than a sheep! So it is lawful to do good on the Sabbath. . . . Stretch out your hand."

MC, DSM, UR.

Matthew adds endangered sheep to the Marcan version (Logion 16: Mark 3.3-5) of his teaching on Sabbath leisure.

Logion 234 (Matthew 15.3-9): "And why do you transgress the commandment of God for the sake of your tradition? [4]For God commanded, 'Honor your father and your mother,' and, 'He who speaks evil of father or mother, let him surely die.' [5]But you say, 'If any one tells his father or his mother, What you would have gained from me is given to God, he need not honor his father.' [6]So for the sake of your tradition, you have made void the word of God. [7]You hypocrites! Well did Isaiah prophesy of you, when he said: [8]'This people honors me with their lips, but their hearts are far from me; [9]in vain do they worship me, teaching as doctrines the precepts of men.'"

MC, DSM, UR.

Yeshua contradicts rabbinical hedges concerning Temple gifts. He recurs to Isaiah and the sentiment of the eighth century prophets generally.

Logion 235 (Matthew 15.10-11): "Hear and understand: [11]not what goes into the mouth defiles a man, but what comes out of the mouth, this defiles a man."

MC, DSM, UR.

Yeshua adjusts Toranic law, emphasizing the inner aspect of ritual purity. This was the great message of the eighth century prophets.

Logion 237 (Matthew 15.15-20): "Are you also still without understanding? [17]Do you not see that whatever goes into the mouth passes into the stomach, and so passes on? [18]But what comes out of the mouth proceeds from the heart, and this defiles a man. [19]For out of the heart come evil thoughts, murder, adultery, fornication, theft, false witness, slander. [20]These are what defile a man; but to eat with unwashed hands does not defile a man."

MC, DSM, UR.

Yeshua explains his emphasis on inner purity.

Logion 264 (Matthew 19.4-6, 9): "Have you not read that he who made them from the beginning made them male and female, [5]and said, 'For this reason a man shall leave his father and mother and be joined to his wife, and the two shall become one'? [6]So they are no longer two but one. What therefore God has joined together, let no man put asunder. . . . For your hardness of heart, Moses allowed you to divorce your wives, but from the beginning it was not so. [9]And I say to you: whoever divorces his wife, except for unchastity, and marries another, commits adultery."

MC, DSM, UR.

Yeshua adjusts Toranic law, parsing Moses' intentions.

Logion 292 (Matthew 22.37-40): "You shall love the Lord your God with all your heart, and with all your soul, and with all your mind. [38]This is the great and first commandment. [39]And a second is like it, You shall love your neighbor as yourself. [40]On these two commandments depend all the law and the prophets."

LOGION SIEVE KEY: Marcan Consistency (MC), Danielic Son of man (DSM), Hagiographical Hurdle (HH), Urgency of Repentance (UR), Hagiographical Excess (HE), Anachronisms and Post-Yeshuan concerns (APY)

MC, DSM, UR.

Yeshua epitomizes the law, in accord with its own provisions.

Logion 348 (Luke 6.3-5): "Have you not read what David did when he was hungry, he and those who were with him: [4]how he entered the house of God, and took and ate the bread of the Presence, which it is not lawful for any but the priests to eat, and also gave it to those with him? . . . The Son of man is lord of the Sabbath."

MC, DSM, UR.

Yeshua asserts his authority over Toranic obedience, and cites an historical precedent for such deviations.

Logion 349 (Luke 6.8-10): (to a man with withered hand) "Come and stand here. . . . I ask you, is it lawful on the Sabbath to do good or to do harm, to save life or to destroy it? . . . Stretch out your hand."

MC, DSM, UR.

Yeshua teaches that one may do well by others, despite Sabbath regulations. This logion suffers its showy healing. The message, however, appears essentially Yeshua's. I retain the logion.

Logion 412 (Luke 10.26-28, 30-37): (to lawyer inquiring after eternal life, the law, and neighbors) "What is written in the law? How do you read? . . . You have answered right; do this, and you will live. . . . A man was going down from Jerusalem to Jericho, and he fell among robbers, who stripped him and beat him, and departed, leaving him half dead. [31]Now by chance a priest was going down that road; and when he saw him he passed by on the other side. [32]So likewise a Levite, when he came to the place and saw him, passed by on the other side. [33]But a Samaritan, as he journeyed, came to where he was; and when he saw him, he had compassion, [34]and went to him and bound up his wounds. Pouring on oil and wine; then he set him on his own beast and brought him to an inn, and took care of him. [35]And the next day he took out two denarii and gave them to the innkeeper, saying, 'Take care of him; and whatever more you spend, I will repay you when I come back.' [36]Which of these three, do you think, proved neighbor to the man who fell among the robbers?' . . . Go and do likewise."

MC, DSM, UR.

Yeshua teaches of compassion, its proper purposes and application. He also disparages the wan piety of opponent priests.

LOGION SIEVE KEY: Marcan Consistency (MC), Danielic Son of man (DSM), Hagiographical Hurdle (HH), Urgency of Repentance (UR), Hagiographical Excess (HE), Anachronisms and Post-Yeshuan concerns (APY)

Logion 421 (Luke 11.28): "Blessed rather are those who hear the word of God and keep it!"

MC, DSM, UR.

This logion suffers for its hagiographical context. The logion proper emphasizes the kingdom and response to it, which are core messages of Yeshua.

Logion 458 (Luke 14.3, 5): "Is it lawful to heal on the Sabbath, or not? . . . Which of you, having an ass or an ox that has fallen into a well, will not immediately pull him out on a Sabbath day?"

MC, DSM.

Yeshua again sets ritual observance in a life context, and offers a counter-example.

Logion 475 (Luke 16.16): "[16]The law and the prophets were until John; since then the good news of the kingdom of God is preached, and every one enters it violently."

MC, DSM, UR, HH.

Yeshua teaches of the imminent kingdom, now preached, and offers violence as the means of entry into that kingdom. Such a saying may have proved a hagiographical hurdle for the early church. Such words may have spurred response from Roman and Temple authorities, whom messianic rebels of the first century plagued.

Logion 476 (Luke 16.17): "[17]But it is easier for heaven and earth to pass away, than for one dot of the law to become void."

MC, DSM.

Yeshua continues to balance on the razor edge of affirming the law and asserting that it is passing away in the kingdom of God.

LOGION SIEVE KEY: Marcan Consistency (MC), Danielic Son of man (DSM), Hagiographical Hurdle (HH), Urgency of Repentance (UR), Hagiographical Excess (HE), Anachronisms and Post-Yeshuan concerns (APY)

Logion 477 (Luke 16.18): "[18]Every one who divorces his wife and marries another commits adultery, and he who marries a woman divorced from her husband commits adultery."

MC, DSM, UR.

Yeshua confutes the Mosaic tradition of divorce, and moves the emphasis to what occurs within a person.

Logion 489 (Luke 18.10-14): "[10]Two men went up into the temple to pray, one a Pharisee and the other a tax collector. [11]The Pharisee stood and prayed thus with himself, 'God, I thank thee that I am not like other men, extortioners, unjust, adulterers, or even like this tax collector. [12]I fast twice a week, I give tithes of all that I get.' [13]But the tax collector, standing far off, would not even lift up his eyes to heaven, but beat his breast, saying, 'God, be merciful to me a sinner!' [14]I tell you, this man went down to his house justified rather than the other; for every one who exalts himself will be humbled, but he who humbles himself will be exalted."

MC, DSM, UR.

Yeshua disparages pride in ritual purity, and emphasizes heartfelt repentance. The kingdom of God inverts Temple priorities.

Logion 512 (Luke 21.3-4): (on a poor woman's small gift) "Truly I tell you, this poor widow has put in more than all of them; [4]for they all contributed out of their abundance, but she out of her poverty put in all the living that she had."

MC, DSM, UR.

Yeshua contextualizes giving. To give much when one has little counts most.

MISSION LOGIA

Logion 2 (Mark 1.17): "Follow me and I will make you become fishers of men."

MC, DSM, UR.

Yeshua issues his most basic invitation.

Logion 4 (Mark 1.38): "Let us go on to the next towns, that I may preach there also; for that is why I came out."

MC, DSM, UR.

Yeshua seeks to tell his story to many.

Logion 9A (Mark 2.14): "Follow me."

MC, DSM, UR.

Again, Yeshua invites.

Logion 18A (Mark 3.33-35): "Who are my mother and my brothers? . . . Here are my mother and my brothers! [35]Whoever does the will of God is my brother, and sister, and mother."

MC, DSM, UR, HH.

Yeshua states one of his more controversial views. He overturns the role of family, redefining who are its members. This view would have offended many in his audience, and may have presented a hagiographic hurdle to the early church.

Logion 19 (Mark 4.3-9): "[3]Listen! A sower went out to sow. [4]And as he sowed, some seed fell along the path, and the birds came and devoured it. [5]Other seed fell on rocky ground, where it had not much soil, and immediately it sprang up, since it had no depth of soil; [6]and when the sun rose it was scorched, and since it had no root it withered away. [7]Other seed fell among thorns and the thorns grew up and choked it, and it yielded no grain. [8]And other seeds fell into good soil and brought forth grain, growing up and increasing and yielding thirtyfold and sixtyfold and a hundredfold. . . . He who has ears to hear, let him hear."

MC, DSM, UR.

Yeshua teaches his mission to a crowd. The message is the mission.

Logion 22 (Mark 4.21-23): "Is a lamp brought in to be put under a bushel, or under a bed, and not on a stand? [22]For there is nothing hid, except to be made manifest; nor is anything secret, except to come to light. [23]If any man has ears to hear, let him hear."

MC, DSM, UR.

Yeshua's message urgently requires hearing and response.

Logion 26 (Mark 4.35): "Let us go across to the other side."

MC.

This logion may be nothing more than a narrative bridge to a logion of patent hagiographical excess. On the other hand, Yeshua was often moving, and was sometimes distressed by crowds of people. He may well have been in the habit of escaping by boat across the Sea of Galilee. I retain the logion, for what it is worth.

Logion 35 (Mark 6.4): "A prophet is not without honor, except in his own country, and among his own kin, and in his own house."

MC, DSM, UR.

Yeshua may have found rejection even in his own region of Galilee and among family.

Logion 36 (Mark 6.10-11): "Where you enter a house, stay there until you leave the place. [11]And if any place will not receive you and they refuse to hear you, when you leave, shake off the dust that is on your feet for a testimony against them."

MC, DSM, UR.

Yeshua delegates his mission to disciples. Since repentance is urgent, one may not dawdle.

LOGION SIEVE KEY: Marcan Consistency (MC), Danielic Son of man (DSM), Hagiographical Hurdle (HH), Urgency of Repentance (UR), Hagiographical Excess (HE), Anachronisms and Post-Yeshuan concerns (APY)

Logion 37 (Mark 6.31): "Come away by yourselves to a lonely place, and rest a while."

MC.

Yeshua teaches tired laborers to seek silence and solitude.

Logion 38 (Mark 6.37): (In feeding the 5,000) "You give them something to eat. . . . How many loaves have you? Go and see."

MC, DSM.

This logion is marred by its showy context, and may be nothing more than invented narrative. Nevertheless, explanations for these events (people sharing their food) other than a miraculous multiplication of fishes and loaves might be accurate. I retain the logion with reticence.

Logion 48 (Mark 8.2-3, 5): (On feeding the four thousand) "[2]I have compassion on the crowd, because they have been with me now three days, and have nothing to eat; [3]and if I send them away hungry to their homes, they will faint on the way; and some of them have come a long way. . . . How many loaves have you?"

MC, DSM.

The logion is a likely dittography of oral tradition. Still, the concern Yeshua shows remains consistent with both his customary compassion for poor people and his confidence as Son of man.

Logion 53 (Mark 8.33): (To Peter when Yeshua spoke of Yeshua's death) "Get behind me, Satan! For you are not on the side of God, but of men."

MC, DSM, UR.

Yeshua chastises Peter for Peter's rejection of Yeshua's revised mission concept.

Logion 62 (Mark 9.33): "What were you discussing on the way?"

MC, DSM, UR.

Yeshua embarrasses his clueless students.

LOGION SIEVE KEY: Marcan Consistency (MC), Danielic Son of man (DSM), Hagiographical Hurdle (HH), Urgency of Repentance (UR), Hagiographical Excess (HE), Anachronisms and Post-Yeshuan concerns (APY)

Logion 63 (Mark 9.35): "If any one would be first, he must be last of all and servant of all."

MC, DSM, UR.

Yeshua asserts inverted values in the kingdom of God.

Logion 64 (Mark 9.37): "[37]Whoever receives one such child in my name receives me; and whoever receives me, receives not me but him who sent me."

MC, DSM, UR.

Yeshua again emphasizes simplicity in repentance, and its social evidences. One receives the kingdom of God by receiving the Son of man by receiving children.

Logion 65 (Mark 9.39-40): (of a non-disciple casting out demons in Yeshua's name) "Do not forbid him; for no one who does a mighty work in my name will be able soon after to speak evil of me. [40]For he that is not against us is for us."

MC, DSM, UR.

Yeshua believes in exorcism of demons, and commends those who undertake exorcism, viewing them as colleagues or unwitting followers.

Logion 73 (Mark 10.14-15): "Let the children come to me, do not hinder them; for to such belongs the kingdom of God. [15]Truly, I say to you, whoever does not receive the kingdom of God like a child shall not enter it."

MC, DSM, UR.

Yeshua teaches simplicity of heart as evident repentance.

Logion 83 (Mark 10.36, 38, 39b, 40): "What do you want me to do for you? . . . You do not know what you are asking. Are you able to drink the cup that I drink, or to be baptized with the baptism with which I am baptized? . . . The cup that I drink you will drink; and with the baptism with which I am baptized you will be baptized; [40]but to sit at my right hand or at my left is not mine to grant, but it is for those for whom it has been prepared."

MC, DSM, UR.

LOGION SIEVE KEY: Marcan Consistency (MC), Danielic Son of man (DSM), Hagiographical Hurdle (HH), Urgency of Repentance (UR), Hagiographical Excess (HE), Anachronisms and Post-Yeshuan concerns (APY)

Yeshua continues teaching disciples his revised mission, which ends in Yeshua's death. The disciples continue missing Yeshua's point.

Logion 84 (Mark 10.42-45a): "You know that those who are supposed to rule over the Gentiles lord it over them, and their great men exercise authority over them. [43]But it shall not be so among you; but whoever would be great among you must be your servant, [44]and whoever would be first among you must be slave of all. [45]For the Son of man also came not to be served but to serve."

MC, DSM, UR.

Yeshua teaches servant leadership and his role as Son of man.

Logion 107 (Mark 14.13-15): "Go into the city, and a man carrying a jar of water will meet you; follow him, [14]and wherever he enters, say to the householder, 'The Teacher says, Where is my guest room, where I am to eat the passover with my disciples? [15]And he will show you a large upper room furnished and ready; there prepare for us."

MC.

Yeshua makes ready the last supper. The logion may attribute to Yeshua super-human powers of foreknowledge, and hence be hagiographical excess. But Yeshua's knowledge in this regard might have come naturally.

Logion 108 (Mark 14.18, 20-21): "Truly, I say to you, one of you will betray me, one who is eating with me. . . . It is one of the twelve, one who is dipping bread in the same dish with me. [21]For the Son of man goes as it is written of him, but woe to that man by whom the Son of man is betrayed! It would have been better for that man if he had not been born."

MC, DSM, UR.

Yeshua acknowledges that a disciple will betray him. There is no indication how Yeshua knew such. So this logion might be an attempt at hagiographical excess, by attributing foreknowledge of future events. Other possibilities exist, and so, I retain the logion.

Logion 109 (Mark 14.22, 24-25): "Take; this is my body. . . . This is my blood of the covenant, which is poured out for many. [25]Truly, I say to you, I shall not drink again of the fruit of the vine until that day when I drink it new in the kingdom of God."

MC, DSM, UR, HH.

Yeshua teaches of his imminent death, and promises prompt resurrection.

Logion 110 (Mark 14.27): "You will all fall away; for it is written, 'I will strike the shepherd, and the sheep will be scattered.'"

MC, DSM.

Yeshua cites Zechariah 13.7, and pessimizes about his disciples' perseverance in adversity.

Logion 113 (Mark 14.32): "Sit here, while I pray."

MC.

Yeshua asks the disciples to sit with him while he prays.

Logion 114 (Mark 14.34): (Speaking to Peter, James, and John) "My soul is very sorrowful, even to death; remain here, and watch."

MC, DSM, UR.

Yeshua asks core disciples to watch with him. He confides his trepidation at the prospect of imminent death.

Logion 115 (Mark 14.36): "Abba, Father, all things are possible to thee; remove this cup from me; yet not what I will, but what thou wilt."

MC, DSM, UR.

Yeshua prays to live, submissively.

Logion 116 (Mark 14.37): "Simon, are you asleep? Could you not watch one hour? [38]Watch and pray that you may not enter into temptation; the spirit indeed is willing, but the flesh is weak."

MC, DSM, UR.

Yeshua upbraids Peter for napping.

Logion 117 (Mark 14.41-42): "Are you still sleeping and taking your rest? It is enough; the hour has come; the Son of man is betrayed into the hands of sinners. [42]Rise, let us be going; see, my betrayer is at hand."

MC, DSM, UR.

Yeshua expresses disappointment in disciple napping. All must wake to oncoming betrayal.

Logion 118 (Mark 14.48-49): "Have you come out as against a robber, with swords and clubs to capture me? [19]Day after day I was with you in the temple teaching, and you did not seize me. But let the scriptures be fulfilled."

MC, DSM, UR.

Yeshua criticizes his surreptitious arrest. Yet, the matter fulfills his revised Son of man mission.

Logion 126 (Matthew 4.19): "Follow me, and I will make you fishers of men."

MC, DSM, UR.

Yeshua calls his commoner disciples.

Logion 134 (Matthew 5.10): "[10]Blessed are those who are persecuted for righteousness' sake, for theirs is the kingdom of heaven."

MC, DSM, UR.

This logion certainly reflects later church concerns about persecution, and so may be suspect. But the logion might derive from Yeshua, who was frequently concerned about the persecution of John the Baptist and the eighth century prophets. He held both dear. The logion's proximity to Matthew 5.11-12, which I take to be a late interpolation to the beatitudes, may weigh against this logion. On the other hand, this logion may have inspired the suspect subsequent logion. I retain this logion.

Logion 136 (Matthew 5.13): "[13]You are the salt of the earth; but if salt has lost its taste, how shall its saltness be restored? It is no longer good for anything except to be thrown out and trodden under foot by men."

MC, DSM, UR.

Yeshua teaches that his students must be distinguishable from others, and useful to them.

Logion 137 (Matthew 5.14a): "[14]You are the light of the world. A city set on a hill cannot be hid."

LOGION SIEVE KEY: Marcan Consistency (MC), Danielic Son of man (DSM), Hagiographical Hurdle (HH), Urgency of Repentance (UR), Hagiographical Excess (HE), Anachronisms and Post-Yeshuan concerns (APY)

MC, DSM, UR.

Yeshua teaches the legibility of his students, and their import.

Logion 138 (Matthew 5.15): "[15]Nor do men light a lamp and put it under a bushel, but on a stand, and it gives light to all in the house."

MC, DSM, UR.

Yeshua teaches his students' visibility and their role.

Logion 139 (Matthew 5.15): "[16]Let your light so shine before men, that they may see your good works and give glory to your Father who is in heaven."

MC, DSM, UR.

Yeshua teaches that his students' good acts bring repentance to others.

Logion 150 (Matthew 5.42): "[42]Give to him who begs from you, and do not refuse him who would borrow from you."

MC, DSM, UR.

Yeshua calls his students to give freely.

Logion 151 (Matthew 5.43-47): "[43]You have heard that it was said, 'You shall love your neighbor and hate your enemy.' [44]But I say to you, Love your enemies and pray for those who persecute you, [45]so that you may be sons of your Father who is in heaven; for he makes his sun rise on the evil and on the good, and sends rain on the just and on the unjust. [46]For if you love those who love you, what reward have you? Do not even the tax collectors do the same? [47]And if you salute only your brethren, what more are you doing than others?"

MC, DSM, UR.

Yeshua teaches love of enemies. None knows Yahweh's judgment. This logion is troubled by inclusion of the persecution reference, which is likely a later church interpolation. Yeshua's students must surpass the love shown by others to their friends and acquaintances.

Logion 173 (Matthew 8.11-12): "[11]I tell you, many will come from east and west and sit at table with Abraham, Isaac, and Jacob in the kingdom of heaven, [12]while the sons of the kingdom will be thrown into the outer darkness; there men will weep and gnash their teeth."

LOGION SIEVE KEY: Marcan Consistency (MC), Danielic Son of man (DSM), Hagiographical Hurdle (HH), Urgency of Repentance (UR), Hagiographical Excess (HE), Anachronisms and Post-Yeshuan concerns (APY)

MC, DSM, UR.

Yeshua opens Yahweh's table to gentiles, and warns unrepentant Jews.

Logion 174 (Matthew 8.20): "Foxes have holes, and birds of the air have nests; but the Son of man has nowhere to lay his head."

MC, DSM, UR.

Yeshua teaches that repentance is so urgent that one grows homeless.

Logion 175 (Matthew 8.22): "Follow me, and leave the dead to bury their own dead."

MC, DSM, UR.

There is no time. Usual practices notwithstanding, allegiance to the kingdom of God predominates all.

Logion 178A (Matthew 9.9): (to Matthew) "Follow me."

MC, DSM, UR.

Yeshua makes his most fundamental command, to join in announcing the irruptive kingdom of God.

Logion 186 (Matthew 9.37-38): "The harvest is plentiful, but the laborers are few; [38]pray therefore the Lord of the harvest to send out laborers into his harvest."

MC, DSM, UR.

Yeshua prepares his students to undertake independent excursions.

Logion 188 (Matthew 10.7-15): "[7]And preach as you go, saying, 'The kingdom of heaven is at hand.' [8]Heal the sick, raise the dead, cleanse lepers, cast out demons. You received without pay, give without pay. [9]Take no gold, nor silver, nor copper in your belts, [10]no bag for your journey, nor two tunics, nor sandals, nor a staff; for the laborer deserves his food. [11]And whatever town or village you enter, find out who is worthy in it, and stay with him until you depart. [12]As you enter the house, salute it. [13]And if the house is worthy, let your peace come upon it; but if it is not worthy, let your peace return to you. [14]And if any one will not receive you or listen to your words, shake off the dust from your feet as you leave that house or town. [15]Truly, I say to you, it shall be more tolerable on the day of judgment of the land of Sodom and Gomorrah than for that town."

MC, DSM, UR.

Yeshua charges his students in their independent foray into the countryside.

Logion 191 (Matthew 10.24-26a): "[24]A disciple is not above his teacher, nor a servant above his master; [25]it is enough for the disciple to be like his teacher, and the servant like his master. If they have called the master of the house Beelzebul, how much more will they malign those of his household. [26]So have no fear of them."

MC, DSM, UR.

Yeshua warns of harsh treatment awaiting his students.

Logion 192 (Matthew 10.26b-27) "For nothing is covered that will not be revealed, or hidden that will not be known. [27]What I tell you in the dark, utter in the light; and what you hear whispered, proclaim upon the housetops."

MC, DSM, UR.

The irruptive kingdom of God exposes secrets and illuminates mysteries. The kingdom of God is to be proclaimed.

Logion 193 (Matthew 10.28): "[28]And do not fear those who kill the body but cannot kill the soul; rather fear him who can destroy both soul and body in hell."

MC, DSM, UR.

Yeshua teaches avoidance of divine judgment.

Logion 194 (Matthew 10.29-31): "[29]Are not two sparrows sold for a penny? And not one of them will fall to the ground without your Father's will. [30]But even the hairs of your head are all numbered. [31]Fear not, therefore; you are of more value than many sparrows."

MC, DSM, UR.

Yeshua teaches Yahweh's universal control and knowledge.

Logion 196 (Matthew 10.34-37): "[34]Do not think that I have come to bring peace on earth; I have not come to bring peace, but a sword. [35]For I have come to set a man against his father, and a daughter against her mother, and a daughter-in-

LOGION SIEVE KEY: Marcan Consistency (MC), Danielic Son of man (DSM), Hagiographical Hurdle (HH), Urgency of Repentance (UR), Hagiographical Excess (HE), Anachronisms and Post-Yeshuan concerns (APY)

law against her mother-in-law; 36and a man's foes will be those of his own household. 37He who loves father or mother more than me is not worthy of me; and he who loves son or daughter more than me is not worthy of me."

MC, DSM, UR, HH.

Yeshua teaches the conflict his mission entails. Allegiance will disrupt families. This logion may have proved a hagiographical hurdle in the early church. But it is clear that Yeshua's sense of urgency would have necessitated such views.

Logion 198 (Matthew 10.39): "39He who finds his life will lose it, and he who loses his life for my sake will find it."

MC, DSM, UR.

Yeshua teaches the expense of being a student of the kingdom of God.

Logion 201 (Matthew 11.4-6): "Go and tell John [the Baptist] what you hear and see: 5the blind receive their sight and the lame walk, lepers are cleansed and the deaf hear, and the dead are raised up, and the poor have good news preached to them. 6And blessed is he who takes no offense at me."

MC, DSM, UR.

Note Yeshua's affinity for John the Baptist. The logion is possibly a reference to Isaiah 61.1-2, corresponding (lightly) to Luke 4.18-19. The logion refers to Yeshua's belief in astounding interventions in his role as Son of man. He reports to John to confirm to that free spirit that the kingdom is poised to irrupt.

Logion 203 (Matthew 11.12): "12From the days of John the Baptist until now the kingdom of heaven has suffered violence, and men of violence take it by force."

MC, DSM, UR, HH.

Yeshua teaches that entering the kingdom requires exigent response. The days before the kingdom of God irrupts are days of violence. It seems likely that this logion proved a hurdle to the early church, given the church's emphasis on Yeshua's compassion. This logion may also have contributed to Peter's and Judas's conclusion that Yeshua was a messiah, destined to throw off the Roman yoke and restore Israel to self-governance.

Logion 212 (Matthew 12.30): "30He who is not with me is against me, and he who does not gather with me scatters."

MC, DSM, UR.

Yeshua teaches his students to close ranks and recognize opponents. Yeshua also expressed the opposite view, teaching his disciples to open ranks and welcome people of similar, but not identical, sentiment. See Mark 9.39-40 and Luke 9.50 for this polar teaching.

Logion 220 (Matthew 12.48-50): "[48]Who is my mother, and who are my brothers? . . . Here are my mother and my brothers! [50]For whoever does the will of my Father in heaven is my brother, and sister, and mother."

MC, DSM, UR.

Yeshua teaches that kingdom loyalty supersedes all other loyalties, including those of familial obligation.

Logion 221 (Matthew 13.3-9): "A sower went out to sow. [4]And as he sowed, some seeds fell along the path, and the birds came and devoured them. [5]Other seeds fell on rocky ground, where they had not much soil, and immediately they sprang up, since they had no depth of soil, [6]but when the sun rose they were scorched; and since they had no root they withered away. [7]Other seeds fell upon thorns, and the thorns grew up and choked them. [8]Other seeds fell on good soil and brought forth grain, some a hundredfold, some sixty, some thirty. [9]He who has ears, let him hear."

MC, DSM, UR.

Yeshua teaches dangers that prevent recognizing the kingdom of God.

Logion 231 (Matthew 13.57): "A prophet is not without honor except in his own country and in his own house."

MC, DSM, UR.

Yeshua notes that his home precincts are unreceptive to his message. It has ever been so with Israeli prophets.

Logion 232 (Matthew 14.16, 18): "They need not go away; you give them something to eat. . . . Bring them [loaves and fish] here to me."

MC, DSM, UR.

This episode of feeding the five thousand is the quintessential miracle story, and hence suffers from hagiographical excess. However, the logion itself might have been spoken by Yeshua, and the event might have occurred without miraculous excursions by sharing among the people. I retain the logion with reluctance.

Logion 239 (Matthew 15.32): "I have compassion on the crowd, because they have been with me now three days, and have nothing to eat; and I am unwilling to send them away hungry, lest they faint on the way. . . . How many loaves have you?"

MC, DSM, UR.

This logion suffers as does its predecessor from hagiographical excess. Further, the two episodes, feeding five thousand and feeding four thousand, may be oral transmission errors in which each logion took on a life of its own. I retain the logion as I did Logion 232, with substantial reluctance.

Logion 244 (Matthew 16.23): (to Peter, upon Yeshua's change in mission concept) "Get behind me, Satan! You are a hindrance to me; for you are not on the side of God, but of men."

MC, DSM, UR.

Yeshua rebukes Peter for insisting on a messianic model for Yeshua's role.

Logion 249 (Matthew 17.9): "Tell no one the vision, until the Son of man is raised from the dead."

MC, DSM.

This logion suffers by its conflation with the transfiguration hagiograph, but the Son of man attribution renders it sufficiently reliable. Yeshua, once his view of his mission came to include fatal conflict with authorities in Jerusalem, would have anticipated resurrection into power as the only course open for the Son of man in his cosmic role.

Logion 250 (Matthew 17.11-12): "Elijah does come, and he is to restore all things; [12]but I tell you that Elijah has already come, and they did not know him, but did to him whatever they pleased. So also the Son of man will suffer at their hands."

MC, DSM, UR.

Yeshua teaches of John the Baptist's ministry, and Yeshua's coming death.

LOGION SIEVE KEY: Marcan Consistency (MC), Danielic Son of man (DSM), Hagiographical Hurdle (HH), Urgency of Repentance (UR), Hagiographical Excess (HE), Anachronisms and Post-Yeshuan concerns (APY)

Logion 253 (Matthew 17.22-23): "The Son of man is to be delivered into the hands of men, [23]and they will kill him, and he will be raised on the third day."

MC, DSM.

Though this logion attributes impossible foreknowledge to Yeshua concerning the timing of resurrection, the remainder of the logion was accessible to him. Yeshua probably surmised that going to Jerusalem would entail his arrest and execution, which would have necessitated his resurrection in order to fulfill his role as Son of man.

Logion 260 (Matthew 18.19): "[19]Again I say to you, if two of you agree on earth about anything they ask, it will be done for them by my Father in heaven."

MC, DSM.

Yeshua teaches his students of their collective power in the kingdom of God. Though the early church bootstrapped this saying into a defense of church authority, it seems likely that Yeshua entertained such convictions, just as he sent out the students to heal in independent sojourns. Standing well in the kingdom of God grants power.

Logion 262 (Matthew 18.22): (to Peter's inquiry about forgiveness) "I do not say to you seven times, but seventy times seven."

MC, DSM, UR.

Yeshua teaches limitless forgiveness.

Logion 265 (Matthew 19.11-12): (concerning never marrying) "Not all men can receive this precept, but only those to whom it is given. [12]For there are eunuchs who have been so from birth, and there are eunuchs who have been made eunuchs by men, and there are eunuchs who have made themselves eunuchs for the sake of the kingdom of heaven. He who is able to receive this, let him receive it."

MC, DSM, UR.

Yeshua teaches celibacy for those who can manage it. The kingdom takes priority.

LOGION SIEVE KEY: Marcan Consistency (MC), Danielic Son of man (DSM), Hagiographical Hurdle (HH), Urgency of Repentance (UR), Hagiographical Excess (HE), Anachronisms and Post-Yeshuan concerns (APY)

Logion 266 (Matthew 19.14): "Let the children come to me, and do not hinder them; for to such belongs the kingdom of heaven."

MC, DSM, UR.

Yeshua teaches the sort of person who enters the kingdom of God.

Logion 276 (Matthew 20.21, 22-23): "What do you want? . . . You do not know what you are asking. Are you able to drink the cup that I am to drink? . . . You will drink my cup, but to sit at my right hand and at my left is not mine to grant, but it is for those for whom it has been prepared by my Father."

MC, DSM, UR.

Yeshua entertains the request of the mother of the sons of Zebedee that her boys should sit at Yeshua's right and left in the kingdom. Yeshua expresses doubt about their ability to persevere. He refers them to Yahweh.

Logion 277 (Matthew 20.25-28a): "You know that the rulers of the Gentiles lord it over them, and their great men exercise authority over them. [26]It shall not be so among you; but whoever would be great among you must be your servant, [27]and whoever would be first among you must be your slave; [28]even as the Son of man came not to be served but to serve."

MC, DSM, UR.

Yeshua teaches servant leadership, the essence of kingdom rule.

Logion 296 (Matthew 23.11): "[11]He who is greatest among you shall be your servant."

MC, DSM, UR.

Yeshua reiterates his social ranking criterion.

Logion 297 (Matthew 23.12): "[12]Whoever exalts himself will be humbled, and whoever humbles himself will be exalted."

MC, DSM, UR.

Yeshua teaches Yahweh's sentiment concerning promotion. The humble heart rules.

Logion 315 (Matthew 26.18): "Go into the city to such a one, and say to him, 'The Teacher says, My time is at hand; I will keep the passover at your house with my disciples.'"

MC, DSM, UR.

Yeshua prepares a place for the final meal. The logion suffers the implication that Yeshua had foreknowledge of unknowable events. Since the passage bears other interpretations, the implication is not fatal for the logion.

Logion 316 (Matthew 26.21, 23-24): "Truly, I say to you, one of you will betray me. . . . He who has dipped his hand in the dish with me, will betray me. [24]The Son of man goes as it is written of him, but woe to that man by whom the Son of man is betrayed! It would have been better for that man if he had not been born."

MC, DSM, UR.

Yeshua predicts a betrayer among his disciples. This deeply flawed logion may be spurious, the later church spitting upon Judas. Yet, Yeshua might well have detected disaffection among disciples, and suspected betrayal. I retain the logion with reluctance.

Logion 318 (Matthew 26.26-27, 29): "Take, eat; this is my body. . . .Drink of it, all of you. . . . [29]I tell you I shall not drink again of this fruit of the vine until that day when I drink it new with you in my Father's kingdom."

MC, DSM, UR, HH.

Yeshua makes a ritual of his anticipated death and resurrection. The logion would have proved a hurdle to the early church, as the days of Yeshua's non-return wore into years.

Logion 320 (Matthew 26.31, 34): "You will all fall away because of me this night; for it is written, 'I will strike the shepherd, and the sheep of the flock will be scattered.'"

MC, DSM, UR.

Yeshua recurs to his beloved eighth century prophets for interpretation. It is possible that this logion speaks the church's after-the-fact proof-texting about events of Yeshua's life. Still, Yeshua was deeply critical of his disciples, and may well have found them generally wanting.

LOGION SIEVE KEY: Marcan Consistency (MC), Danielic Son of man (DSM), Hagiographical Hurdle (HH), Urgency of Repentance (UR), Hagiographical Excess (HE), Anachronisms and Post-Yeshuan concerns (APY)

Logion 323 (Matthew 26.36, 38-42, 44-46): "Sit here, while I go yonder and pray. . . . My soul is very sorrowful, even to death; remain here, and watch with me. . . . My Father, if it be possible, let this cup pass from me; nevertheless, not as I will, but as thou wilt. . . . So, could you not watch with me one hour? [41]Watch and pray that you may not enter into temptation; the spirit indeed is willing, but the flesh is weak. . . . My Father, if this cannot pass unless I drink it, thy will be done. . . . Are you still sleeping and taking your rest? Behold the hour is at hand and the Son of man is betrayed into the hands of sinners. [46]Rise, let us be going; see, my betrayer is at hand."

MC, DSM, UR.

Yeshua asks Yahweh for his life, criticizes his students, and acknowledges betrayal.

Logion 324 (Matthew 26.50): (to Judas) "Friend, why are you here?"

MC.

Yeshua greets Judas mid-betrayal.

Logion 325 (Matthew 26.52-53, 55): "Put your sword back into its place; for all who take the sword will perish by the sword. [53]Do you think that I cannot appeal to my Father, and he will at once send me more than twelve legions of angels? . . . Have you come out as against a robber, with swords and clubs to capture me? Day after day I sat in the temple teaching, and you did not seize me."

MC, DSM, UR.

Yeshua teaches non-violence. He reminds his students that he can marshal divine resources.

Logion 328 (Matthew 27.11b): (to governor asking whether Yeshua is king of the Jews) "You have said so."

MC, DSM.

Yeshua declines to defend himself or claim a political role.

Logion 329 (Matthew 27.46b): "Eli, Eli, lama sabachthani?"

MC, DSM.

Yeshua cites Psalm 22:1, "My God, my God, why hast thou forsaken me?" Such a citation calls into question the reliability of this logion. Still, Yeshua would have been familiar with the psalm, and might have cited it. That Yeshua would have been experiencing sore distress is consistent with his circumstance. That he would have been trying to point out that his circumstances mirror those described in a particular psalm is not consistent with his circumstance. I retain the logion with reservations.

Logion 337 (Luke 4.23-27): "Doubtless you will quote to me this proverb, 'Physician, heal yourself; what we have heard you did at Capernaum, do here also in your own country.' . . . Truly, I say to you, no prophet is acceptable in his own country. [25]But in truth, I tell you, there were many widows in Israel in the days of Elijah when the heaven was shut up three years and six months, when there came a great famine over all the land; [26]and Elijah was sent to none of them but only to Zarephath, in the land of Sidon, to a woman who was a widow. [27]And there were many lepers in Israel in the time of the prophet Elisha; and none of them was cleansed, but only Naaman the Syrian.'"

MC, DSM, UR.

Yeshua teaches Yahweh's choices. None knows divine intentions. Perhaps those who question Yeshua have had their ears shut.

Logion 339 (Luke 4.43): "I must preach the good news of the kingdom of God to the other cities also; for I was sent for this purpose."

MC, DSM, UR.

Yeshua leaves some for others. He has a mission.

Logion 343 (Luke 5.27): (to a tax collector) "Follow me."

MC, DSM, UR.

Yeshua issues his core request.

Logion 344 (Luke 5.31-32): "Those who are well have no need of a physician, but those who are sick; [32]I have not come to call the righteous, but sinners to repentance."

MC, DSM, UR.

Yeshua seeks people with a particular sort of attitude, one that turns from past error in a heartfelt manner, preferring divine forgiveness.

Logion 358 (Luke 6.27-28): "[27]But I say to you that hear, Love your enemies, do good to those who hate you, [28]bless those who curse you, pray for those who abuse you."

MC, DSM, UR.

Yeshua teaches that the kingdom of God inverts retributive impulses.

Logion 359 (Luke 6.29a): "[29]To him who strikes you on the cheek, offer the other also."

MC, DSM, UR.

Yeshua's students do not defend themselves, but rather agree to abuse. Thus, this is another inversion in the kingdom of God.

Logion 360 (Luke 6.29b): "And from him who takes away your cloak do not withhold your coat as well."

MC, DSM, UR.

Yeshua's ethical inversion extends to property as well as person.

Logion 361 (Luke 6.30): "[30]Give to every one who begs from you; and of him who takes away your goods do not ask them again."

MC, DSM, UR.

People of the kingdom of God give without assessment of return, and do not cling to their goods, even in the face of pilfering.

Logion 362 (Luke 6.31): "[31]And as you wish that men would do to you, do so to them."

MC, DSM.

Yeshua repeats the universal rule of anticipatory reciprocity.

Logion 363 (Luke 6.32-35): "[32]If you love those who love you, what credit is that to you? For even sinners love those who love them. [33]And if you do good to those who do good to you, what credit is that to you? For even sinners do the same. [34]And if you lend to those from whom you hope to receive, what credit is that to you? Even sinners lend to sinners, to receive as much again. [35]But love

> **LOGION SIEVE KEY:** Marcan Consistency (MC), Danielic Son of man (DSM), Hagiographical Hurdle (HH), Urgency of Repentance (UR), Hagiographical Excess (HE), Anachronisms and Post-Yeshuan concerns (APY)

your enemies, and do good, and lend, expecting nothing in return; and your reward will be great, and you will be sons of the Most High; for he is kind to the ungrateful and the selfish."

MC, DSM, UR.

Yeshua emphasizes the differences between the priorities of the unrepentant and those of the sons of Yahweh.

Logion 364 (Luke 6.36): "[36]Be merciful, even as your Father is merciful."

MC, DSM, UR.

Yeshua teaches the most basic moral lesson: treat others with the mercy Yahweh shows you.

Logion 374 (Luke 7.22-23): (to John the Baptist's envoys) "Go and tell John what you have seen and heard: The blind receive their sight, the lame walk, lepers are cleansed, and the deaf hear, the dead are raised up, the poor have good news preached to them. [23]And blessed is he who takes no offense at me."

MC, DSM, UR.

Yeshua reassures John the Baptist that Yeshua's work evidences the irruptive kingdom.

Logion 378 (Luke 8.5-8): "[5]A sower went out to sow his seed; and as he sowed, some fell along the path, and was trodden under foot, and the birds of the air devoured it. [6]And some fell on the rock; and as it grew up, it withered away, because it had no moisture. [7]And some fell among thorns; and the thorns grew with it and choked it. [8]And some fell into good soil and grew, and yielded a hundredfold. . . . He who has ears to hear, let him hear."

MC, DSM, UR.

Yeshua teaches of his good news about the kingdom of God, and coming judgment. Many will hear; few will profit.

Logion 381 (Luke 8.16): "[16]No one after lighting a lamp covers it with a vessel, or puts it under a bed, but puts it on a stand, that those who enter may see the light."

MC, DSM, UR.

Those who bring Yeshua's good news must do so publicly.

LOGION SIEVE KEY: Marcan Consistency (MC), Danielic Son of man (DSM), Hagiographical Hurdle (HH), Urgency of Repentance (UR), Hagiographical Excess (HE), Anachronisms and Post-Yeshuan concerns (APY)

Logion 382 (Luke 8.17): "[17]For nothing is hid that shall not be made manifest, nor anything secret that shall not be known and come to light."

MC, DSM, UR.

The irruptive kingdom exposes what has been hitherto hidden.

Logion 383 (Luke 8.18): "[18]Take heed then how you hear; for to him who has will more be given, and from him who has not, even what he thinks that he has will be taken away."

MC, DSM, UR.

Yeshua continues his concern with listening, and relates it to ultimate judgment.

Logion 384 (Luke 8.21): "My mother and my brothers are those who hear the word of God and do it."

MC, DSM, UR.

Yeshua teaches the primacy among human values of Yahweh's kingdom.

Logion 385 (Luke 8.22): "Let us go across to the other side of the lake."

MC.

Yeshua makes a suggestion for itinerary. This logion suffers as a potential narrative bridge to the hagiographical storm calming story, and so may be nothing more than a component of that excess. Yet, Yeshua must certainly have said such things in the course of living near the Sea of Galilee with fishermen.

Logion 391 (Luke 9.3-5): "Take nothing for your journey, no staff, nor bag, nor bread, nor money; and do not have two tunics. [4]And whatever house you enter, stay there, and from there depart. [5]And wherever they do not receive you, when you leave that town shake off the dust from your feet as a testimony against them."

MC, DSM, UR.

Yeshua sends his students on their critical, kingdom-inviting mission. Response to the student's message, was, for the early Yeshua, the defining moment of the divine judgment to come. Once announced, Yahweh would act, so Yeshua thought.

LOGION SIEVE KEY: Marcan Consistency (MC), Danielic Son of man (DSM), Hagiographical Hurdle (HH), Urgency of Repentance (UR), Hagiographical Excess (HE), Anachronisms and Post-Yeshuan concerns (APY)

Logion 392 (Luke 9.13, 14): "You give them something to eat. . . . Make them sit down in companies, about fifty each."

MC, DSM.

Yeshua feeds five thousand with a pittance of food. Note that Luke's and Mark's narrative contain the detail concerning sitting in groups, while Matthew's story lacks it. Compare Matthew 14.19 and Mark 6.40. This logion suffers from the hagiographical excess of its miraculous setting.

Logion 393 (Luke 9.22): "The Son of man must suffer many things, and be rejected by the elders and chief priests and scribes, and be killed, and on the third day be raised."

MC, DSM, UR.

This logion reflects the content of Yeshua's fundamental change mid-ministry in his conception of the path of the Son of man. The logion suffers from the church's importation of later knowledge of the time lapse to claims of resurrection.

Logion 398 (Luke 9.44): "[44]Let these words sink into your ears; for the Son of man is to be delivered into the hands of men."

MC, DSM, UR.

Yeshua reiterates his understanding of what lies ahead for him.

Logion 399 (Luke 9.48a): "Whoever receives this child in my name receives me, and whoever receives me receives him who sent me."

MC, DSM, UR.

Yeshua corrects his students. How they treat others determines rank in the kingdom of God.

Logion 400 (Luke 9.48b): "For he who is least among you all is the one who is great."

MC, DSM, UR.

Yeshua links ranking in the kingdom of God to a direct inversion of worldly prestige.

LOGION SIEVE KEY: Marcan Consistency (MC), Danielic Son of man (DSM), Hagiographical Hurdle (HH), Urgency of Repentance (UR), Hagiographical Excess (HE), Anachronisms and Post-Yeshuan concerns (APY)

Logion 401 (Luke 9.50): (on forbidding others to use Yeshua's name) "Do not forbid him; for he that is not against you is for you."

MC, DSM, UR.

Yeshua welcomes assistance from strangers.

Logion 402 (Luke 9.58): "Foxes have holes, and birds of the air have nests; but the Son of man has nowhere to lay his head."

MC, DSM, UR.

Yeshua notes that those who recognize the urgency of repentance he teaches grow homeless.

Logion 403 (Luke 9.59a, 60): (to a person who wished to bury his father before following Yeshua) "Follow me. . . . Leave the dead to bury their own dead; but as for you, go and proclaim the kingdom of God."

MC, DSM, UR.

Yeshua teaches that no normal obligations bind as the irruptive kingdom trembles at the verge of consuming all.

Logion 404 (Luke 9.62): (to a person who wished to say farewell to family before following) "No one who puts his hand to the plow and looks back is fit for the kingdom of God."

MC, DSM, UR.

Yeshua teaches that none who have regrets about following will be admitted to the kingdom of God.

Logion 405 (Luke 10.2): "The harvest is plentiful, but the laborers are few; pray therefore the Lord of the harvest to send out laborers into his harvest."

MC, DSM, UR.

Yeshua complains that his followers are too few in number to accomplish what he anticipates.

LOGION SIEVE KEY: Marcan Consistency (MC), Danielic Son of man (DSM), Hagiographical Hurdle (HH), Urgency of Repentance (UR), Hagiographical Excess (HE), Anachronisms and Post-Yeshuan concerns (APY)

Logion 406 (Luke 10.3-12): "[3]Go your way; behold, I send you out as lambs in the midst of wolves. [4]Carry no purse, no bag, no sandals; and salute no one on the road. [5]Whatever house you enter, first say, 'Peace be to this house!' [6]And if a son of peace is there, your peace shall rest upon him; but if not, it shall return to you. [7]And remain in the same house, eating and drinking what they provide, for the laborer deserves his wages; do not go from house to house. [8]Whenever you enter a town and they receive you, eat what is set before you; heal the sick in it and say to them, 'The kingdom of God has come near to you.' [10]But whenever you enter a town and they do not receive you, go into its streets and say, [11]'Even the dust of your town that clings to our feet, we wipe off against you; nevertheless know this, that the kingdom of God has come near.' [12]I tell you, that it shall be more tolerable on that day for Sodom than for that town."

MC, DSM, UR.

Yeshua instructs his students in their independent work. Their ministries are the kingdom of God approaching the towns they visit.

Logion 413 (Luke 10.41-42): "Martha, Martha, you are anxious and troubled about many things: [42]one thing is needful. Mary has chosen the good portion, which shall not be taken away from her."

MC, DSM, UR.

Yeshua commends a focused student, and gently corrects the serving, but anxiety-ridden, Martha.

Logion 414A (Luke 11.5-8): "Which of you who has a friend will go to him at midnight and say to him, 'Friend, lend me three loaves; [6]for a friend of mine has arrived on a journey, and I have nothing to set before him;' [7]and he will answer from within, 'Do not bother me; the door is now shut, and my children are with me in bed; I cannot get up and give you anything'? [8]I tell you, though he will not get up and give him anything because he is his friend, yet because of his importunity he will rise and give him whatever he needs."

MC, DSM, UR.

Yeshua teaches persistence, and perhaps a pinch of resolute rudeness.

Logion 419 (Luke 11.23): "[23]He who is not with me is against me, and he who does not gather with me scatters."

MC, DSM, UR.

Yeshua teaches the opposite of his inclusive saying. See Logion 401 (Luke 9.50).

Logion 423 (Luke 11.33): "[33]No one after lighting a lamp puts it in a cellar or under a bushel, but on a stand, that those who enter may see the light."

MC, DSM, UR.

Yeshua teaches that his students must make themselves socially visible.

Logion 424 (Luke 11.34-36): "[34]Your eye is the lamp of your body; when your eye is sound, your whole body is full of light; but when it is not sound, your body is full of darkness. [35]Therefore be careful lest the light in you be darkness. [36]If then your whole body is full of light, having no part in dark, it will be wholly bright, as when a lamp with its rays gives you light."

MC, DSM, UR.

This logion suffers because its focus recalls Gnostic or Manichean concern for light and darkness. Yet, the motif is a commonplace. Yeshua might have said something like this. So, too, might the later church in elaborating Yeshua's "light" logion. With reservations, I retain the logion.

Logion 434 (Luke 12.6-7): "[6]Are not five sparrows sold for two pennies? And not one of them is forgotten before God. [7]Why, even the hairs of your head are all numbered. Fear not; you are of more value than many sparrows."

MC, DSM, UR.

Yeshua teaches of Yahweh's affectionate attention to detail.

Logion 437 (Luke 12.14): (to a brother seeking his inheritance) "Man, who made me a judge or divider over you?"

MC, DSM, UR, HH.

Yeshua grows peevish with a misdirected inquirer. His short dismissal may have proved an embarrassment to the early church.

Logion 445 (Luke 12.51-53): "[51]Do you think that I have come to give peace on earth? No, I tell you, but rather division; [52]for henceforth in one house there will be five divided, three against two and two against three; [53]they will be divided father against son and son against father, mother against daughter and daughter against her mother, mother-in-law against her daughter-in-law and daughter-in-law against her mother-in-law."

MC, DSM, UR.

Yeshua teaches that the onrushing kingdom of God will create divisions within families.

Logion 459 (Luke 14.8-10): "[8]When you are invited by any one to a marriage feast, do not sit down in a place of honor, lest a more eminent man than you be invited by him; [9]and he who invited you both will come and say to you, 'Give place to this man,' and then you will begin with shame to take the lowest place. [10]But when you are invited, go and sit in the lowest place, so that when your host comes he may say to you, 'Friend, go up higher'; then you will be honored in the presence of all who sit at table with you."

MC, DSM, UR.

Yeshua teaches humility and a danger of presumption.

Logion 460 (Luke 14.11): "For every one who exalts himself will be humbled, and he who humbles himself will be exalted."

MC, DSM, UR.

Yeshua teaches the inverted social ranking of the kingdom of God.

Logion 463 (Luke 14.26): "[26]If any one comes to me and does not hate his own father and mother and wife and children and brothers and sisters, yes, and even his own life, he cannot be my disciple."

MC, DSM, UR, HH.

Yeshua requires absolute loyalty. This logion would have, by Luke's time, embarrassed the early church. The logion marks Yeshua as a fanatical eschatologist.

Logion 465 (Luke 14.28-32): "[28]For which of you, desiring to build a tower, does not first sit down and count the cost, whether he has enough to complete it? [29]Otherwise, when he has laid a foundation, and is not able to finish, all who see it begin to mock him, [30]saying, 'This man began to build, and was not able to finish.' [31]Or what king, going to encounter another king in war, will not sit down first and take counsel whether he is able with ten thousand to meet him who comes against him with twenty thousand? [32]And if not, while the other is yet a great way off, he sends an embassy and asks terms of peace."

MC, DSM, UR.

Yeshua asks students to count the cost, and not begin if they cannot finish their tenure with Yeshua.

Logion 466 (Luke 14.33): "So therefore, whoever of you does not renounce all that he has cannot be my disciple."

MC, DSM, UR.

Yeshua asks that his students forsake distractions.

Logion 480 (Luke 17.3-4): "[3]Take heed to yourselves; if your brother sins, rebuke him, and if he repents, forgive him; [4]and if he sins against you seven times in the day, and turns to you seven times, and says, 'I repent,' you must forgive him."

MC, DSM, UR.

Yeshua teaches the expansive parameters of interpersonal forgiveness.

Logion 481 (Luke 17.6): "If you had faith as a grain of mustard seed, you could say to this sycamine tree, 'Be rooted up, and be planted in the sea,' and it would obey you."

MC, DSM, UR.

Although Matthew17.20 uses this logion in the context of a healing, Luke employs it in response to the disciples' request for an increase of their faith. The logion may be a mash-up of Yeshua's teaching on mustard seed and the kingdom of God (Logion 25: Mark 4.30-32) and his teaching on the powers of prayer (Logion 90: Mark 11.23). Oral transmission would facilitate such confusions. Still, Yeshua might have said such a thing, and the sentiment expressed is not inconsistent with his other sayings. I retain this logion, with reservations.

Logion 482 (Luke 17.7-10): "[7]Will any one of you, who has a servant plowing or keeping sheep, say to him when he has come in from the field, 'Come at once and sit down at table'? [8]Will he not rather say to him, 'Prepare supper for me, and gird yourself and serve me, till I eat and drink; and afterward you shall eat and drink'? [9]Does he thank the servant because he did what was commanded?

[10]So you also, when you have done all that is commanded you, say, 'We are unworthy servants; we have only done what was our duty.'"

MC, DSM, UR.

Yeshua teaches humility and obedience to the kingdom of God. This logion might also be interpreted as a saying invented to address laxity among early church members and their criticisms of the relative leisure leaders enjoyed. I retain the logion with reservations.

Logion 518 (Luke 22.8, 10-12): "Go and prepare the passover for us, that we may eat it. . . . Behold, when you have entered the city, a man carrying a jar of water will meet you; follow him into the house which he enters, [11]and tell the householder, 'The Teacher says to you, Where is the guest room, where I am to eat the Passover with my disciples?' [12]And he will show you a large upper room furnished; there make ready."

MC, DSM, UR, HE.

Yeshua sends students to prepare the Passover meal. The logion contains elements trending toward foreknowledge unavailable to humans, and so hagiographical excess. Yet it bears other, less fantastic, interpretations. With reservations, I retain the logion.

Logion 519 (Luke 22.15-22): "I have earnestly desired to eat this Passover with you before I suffer; [16]for I tell you I shall not eat it until it is fulfilled in the kingdom of God. . . . Take this, and divide it among yourselves; for I tell you that from now on I shall not drink of the fruit of the vine until the kingdom of God comes. . . . This is my body. [21]But behold the hand of him who betrays me is with me on the table. [22]For the Son of man goes as it has been determined; but woe to that man by whom he is betrayed!"

MC, DSM, UR, HH.

Yeshua teaches of his death by a last meal, and chastises his betrayer. Yeshua's non-return would have been a source of embarrassment to the early church.

Logion 520 (Luke 22.25-27): "The kings of the Gentiles exercise lordship over them; and those in authority over them are called benefactors. [26]But not so with you; rather let the greatest among you become as the youngest, and the leader as one who serves. [27]For which is the greater, one who sits at table, or one who

LOGION SIEVE KEY: Marcan Consistency (MC), Danielic Son of man (DSM), Hagiographical Hurdle (HH), Urgency of Repentance (UR), Hagiographical Excess (HE), Anachronisms and Post-Yeshuan concerns (APY)

serves? Is it not the one who sits at table? But I am among you as one who serves."

MC, DSM, UR.

Yeshua teaches service and ranking in the kingdom of God.

Logion 524 (Luke 22.40): "Pray that you may not enter into temptation."

MC, DSM, UR.

Yeshua teaches prayer.

Logion 525 (Luke 22.42): "[42]Father, if thou art willing, remove this cup from me; nevertheless, not my will, but thine, be done."

MC, DSM, UR, HH.

Yeshua prays for delivery from his fate. The prayer shows Yeshua's fear, wishing for different outcomes, and so may have proved a hagiographical hurdle for an early church seeking a resolute deity. The logion suffers from its improbability, given that in the context Luke gives the logion, none could have heard this prayer of Yeshua. He had moved away from the group, who were, nevertheless, sleeping. This concern is counterbalanced by the hagiographical hurdle presented. I retain the logion.

Logion 526 (Luke 22.46): "Why do you sleep? Rise and pray that you may not enter into temptation."

MC, DSM, UR.

Yeshua expresses frustration with the underwhelming fortitude of his students.

Logion 527 (Luke 22.48): "Judas, would you betray the Son of man with a kiss?"

MC, DSM, UR.

Yeshua rebukes Judas's duplicity.

Logion 528 (Luke 22.51): (to a disciple who cut off a slave's ear) "No more of this!"

MC, DSM, UR.

Yeshua demands no violence in his arrest. The hagiographical excess of Luke's setting can be ignored.

Logion 529 (Luke 22.52b-53): "Have you come out as against a robber, with swords and clubs? [53]When I was with you day after day in the temple, you did not lay hands on me. But this is your hour, and the power of darkness."

MC, DSM, UR.

Yeshua confronts his captors about their skulking arrest.

Logion 530 (Luke 22.67b-70): (to inquiry whether Yeshua is the *christos*) "If I tell you, you will not believe; [68]and if I ask you, you will not answer. [69]But from now on the Son of man shall be seated at the right hand of the power of God." . . . You say that I am."

MC, DSM, UR.

Yeshua declines to confess he is the Christ. He warns of his role as Son of man.

Logion 531 (Luke 23.3): (to Pilate's inquiry whether Yeshua is king of the Jews) "You have said so."

MC, DSM, UR.

Yeshua declines to say that he is king of the Jews.

Logion 532 (Luke 23.28-31): "Daughters of Jerusalem, do not weep for me, but weep for yourselves and for your children. [29]For behold, the days are coming when they will say, 'Blessed are the barren, and the wombs that never bore, and the breasts that never gave suck!' [30]Then they will begin to say to the mountains, 'Fall on us'; and to the hills, 'Cover us.' [31]For if they do this when the wood is green, what will happen when it is dry?"

MC, DSM, UR.

This logion may reflect the later church's persecution concerns and its angst at the non-return of Yeshua. But the logion is not inconsistent with a Yeshua under duress who believes that he will, by submitting to the depredations of his enemies, be rapidly vindicated by Yahweh in demonstrated power. This logion's reliability is a close call. I retain it.

LOGION SIEVE KEY: Marcan Consistency (MC), Danielic Son of man (DSM), Hagiographical Hurdle (HH), Urgency of Repentance (UR), Hagiographical Excess (HE), Anachronisms and Post-Yeshuan concerns (APY)

Logion 533 (Luke 23.34): "Father, forgive them; for they know not what they do."

MC, DSM, UR.

Yeshua seeks forgiveness for his tormentors.

CHAPTER 10
SUSPECT LOGIA ATTRIBUTED TO YESHUA

All of these suspect logia exhibit inconsistency with the Marcan Yeshua.[96] *Each also exhibits a tendency either to idealize Yeshua or inject post-Yeshuan concerns into his sayings. Many of these logia exhibit all three problems.*

LOGIA MORE HE THAN APY

⊘

Logion 3 (Mark 1.25): "Be silent, and come out of him!"

HE.

Messianic secret sayings serve to explain why those who heard Yeshua failed to understand that he was the Messiah. Christian messianism is a mostly post-Yeshua phenomenon, that mashes together Son of Man apocalypticism with Jewish nationalist aspiration and Hellenistic and Mithraic son of god expectations. Some among Yeshua's followers (Judas and Peter, for example) believed Yeshua to be a Messiah, bringing earthly power and dominion, not divine rule. These persons pressed Yeshua's ministry in that deeply political direction.

---

[96] Jan Oppermann asks whether consistency is all that important in seminal thinkers. Perhaps Yeshua proceeded intuitionally, at least some of the time, and so, tolerated some *non sequiturs*. Private correspondence with the author, spring 2017. In my view, one encounters difficulty sorting white zebras with black stripes from black zebras with white stripes. My sort of the Yeshuan logia may be terribly unreliable. Or, perhaps, all black-striped zebras serve an identifiable ecclesiastical predilection. The reader will have to make a judgment in this regard.

Logion Sieve Key: Marcan Consistency (MC), Danielic Son of man (DSM), Hagiographical Hurdle (HH), Urgency of Repentance (UR), Hagiographical Excess (HE), Anachronisms and Post-Yeshuan concerns (APY)

⃠

Logion 20 (Mark 4.11-12): "To you has been given the secret of the kingdom of God, but for those outside everything is in parables; [12]so that they may indeed see but not perceive, and may indeed hear but not understand; lest they should turn again, and be forgiven."

HE.

This logion is suspect for its messianic secret overtones which serve to explain why eyewitnesses could not confirm that these are, in fact, Yeshua's teachings. This logion accompanies Yeshua calming a storm, which humans lack the ability to do.

⃠

Logion 27 (Mark 4.39, 40): (to a storm on the Sea of Galilee, and then to his students) "Peace! Be still! . . . Why are you afraid? Have you no faith?"

HE.

Yeshua calms a storm, which lies beyond human capacity.

⃠

Logion 31 (Mark 5.30): (in response to a woman touching Yeshua's garment and feeling "power" go forth from him) "Who touched my garments?"

HE.

Humans lack the capacity to transfer power by contact with their clothing or to detect power leaving them upon another's contact with clothing.

⃠

Logion 39 (Mark 6.50): (while walking on water) "Take heart, it is I; have no fear."

HE.

This logion is suspect for its association with the hagiographic walking-on-water story.

⃠

Logion 54 (Mark 8.34-37): "If any man would come after me, let him deny himself and take up his cross and follow me. [35]For whoever would save his life will lose it; and whoever loses his life for my sake and the gospel's will save it. For what does it profit a man, to gain the whole world and forfeit his life? For what can man give in return for his life?"

HE, APY.

This logion has been altered by the church's addition of the cross detail and the loyalty to gospel detail. It addresses the difficulty of the early church in retaining the loyalty of members under the pressure of sporadic Jewish and Roman persecutions.

LOGION SIEVE KEY: Marcan Consistency (MC), Danielic Son of man (DSM), Hagiographical Hurdle (HH), Urgency of Repentance (UR), Hagiographical Excess (HE), Anachronisms and Post-Yeshuan concerns (APY)

⊘

Logion 61 (Mark 9.31): "The Son of man will be delivered into the hands of men, and they will kill him; and when he is killed, after three days he will rise."

HE.

Yeshua could not have had this sort of detailed foreknowledge, though the narrative train seems to require that Yeshua recognized things would not go well for him in Jerusalem. Luke excises from the Marcan logion Yeshua's foreknowledge of death and resurrection (see Luke 9.44). I reject this logion with reservations.

⊘

Logion 175A (Matthew 8.25): "Why are you afraid, O men of little faith?"

HE.

This logion suffers by its association with this hagiographical narrative. Humans cannot control storms.

⊘

Logion 206 (Matthew 11.25-26): "I thank thee, Father, Lord of heaven and earth, that thou hast hidden these things from the wise and understanding and revealed them to babes; [26]yea, Father, for such was thy gracious will."

HE, APY

This logion evidences ostentation uncharacteristic of Yeshua. The logion's conjunction with Matthew 11.27 also reduces its reliability.

⊘

Logion 207 (Matthew 11.27): "[27]All things have been delivered to me by my Father; and no one knows the Son except the Father, and no one knows the Father except the Son and any one to whom the Son chooses to reveal him."

HE, APY.

This logion reflects a much later Christology, and evidences the later Matthean shift from the kingdom to Yeshua himself.

⊘

Logion 218 (Matthew 12.40): "[40]For as Jonah was three days and three nights in the belly of the whale, so will the Son of man be three days and three nights in the heart of the earth."

HE, APY.

This logion puts foreknowledge of the details of Yeshua's death and missing body in his mouth, and makes reference to the Writings, as was Matthew's penchant. Note also that this logion is missing from Luke's rendition at Luke 11:29-32.

LOGION SIEVE KEY: Marcan Consistency (MC), Danielic Son of man (DSM), Hagiographical Hurdle (HH), Urgency of Repentance (UR), Hagiographical Excess (HE), Anachronisms and Post-Yeshuan concerns (APY)

⦸

Logion 233 (Matthew 14.27, 29, 31): "Take heart, it is I; have no fear. . . . Come. . . . O man of little faith, why did you doubt?"

HE.

This logion places Yeshua walking on water, which humans cannot do, and assisting Peter to do the same.

⦸

Logion 242 (Matthew 16.13, 15, 17): "Who do men say that the Son of man is? . . . But who do you say that I am? . . . Blessed are you, Simon Bar-Jona! For flesh and blood has not revealed this to you, but my father who is in heaven."

HE, APY.

This logion places later church views about Yeshua in the mouth of Yeshua. Its close conjunction with the Petros church logion (Matthew 15.18-20) and an attenuated version of the Marcan messianic secret concept (Matthew 16.20) further weakens it.

⦸

Logion 248 (Matthew 17.7): "Rise, and have no fear."

HE.

This logion, mired in the transfiguration, is suspect for its hagiographical impetus.

⦸

Logion 254 (Matthew 17.24-27): "What do you think, Simon? From whom do kings of the earth take toll or tribute? From their sons or from others? . . .Then the sons are free. [27]However, not to give offense to them, go to the sea and cast a hook, and when you open its mouth you will find a shekel; take that and give it to them for me and for yourself."

HE.

This logion invokes a pointless miracle.

⦸

Logion 284 (Matthew 21.21b): "You will not only do what has been done to the fig tree . . ."

HE.

Matthew has hyperbolized the mysterious fig tree curse to cause immediate death of the tree, and attached this exhortation to magical powers.

⦸

Logion 312 (Matthew 26.2): "You know that after two days the Passover is coming, and the Son of man will be delivered up to be crucified."

HE.

Yeshua could not have known the time of arrest or manner of punishment.

⊘

Logion 317 (Matthew 26.25): (to Judas asking if Yeshua knew it was he who betrayed him) "You have said so."

HE.

Yeshua could not have known that Judas had betrayed him (nor would Judas have asked).

⊘

Logion 330 (Matthew 28.9, 10): "Hail! . . . Do not be afraid; go and tell my brethren to go to Galilee, and there they will see me."

HE, APY.

Yeshua speaks to women post-resurrection, which is beyond human capacity.

⊘

Logion 331 (Matthew 28.18-20): "All authority in heaven and on earth has been given to me. [19]Go therefore and make disciples of all nations, baptizing them in the name of the Father and of the Son and of the Holy Spirit, [20]teaching them to observe all that I have commanded you; and lo, I am with you always, to the close of the age."

HE, APY.

Yeshua speaks post-resurrection to the assembled surviving disciples. The theology represented here is very late, with a fully developed Trinitarian formulation, and full resolution of the non-return-despite-promise-to-return issue.

⊘

Logion 332 (Luke 2.49): "How is it that you sought me? Did you not know that I must be in my Father's house?"

HE.

Yeshua teaches at the Jerusalem temple, though too immature to have done so.

⊘

Logion 333 (Luke 4.4): "It is written, 'Man shall not live by bread alone.'"

HE.

Humans do not directly confront or speak with hypostatized ideas like the "devil."

⊘

Logion 334 (Luke 4.8): "It is written, 'You shall worship the Lord your God, and him only shall you serve.'"

HE.

Humans do not directly confront or speak with the devil, nor does the devil levitate humans.

⦸

Logion 335 (Luke 4.12): "It is said, 'You shall not tempt the Lord your God.'"

HE.

Humans do not directly confront or speak with the devil, nor does the devil place humans on building pinnacles.

⦸

Logion 336 (Luke 4.18-19, 21): "[18]The Spirit of the Lord is upon me, because he has anointed me to preach good news to the poor. He has sent me to proclaim release to the captives and recovering of sight to the blind, to set at liberty those who are oppressed, [19]to proclaim the acceptable year of the Lord. . . . Today this scripture has been fulfilled in your hearing."

HE, APY.

This logion conflates Isaiah 61.1-2 with other thoughts, and is clearly out of character for the Marcan Yeshua, who worked more and provided less riveting explanations of himself. The story provides context for Yeshua's compelling speaking skills, and though the Marcan Yeshua was captivated by the Son of man eschatology, he eventually linked that complex of ideas to deutero-Isaiah's suffering servant passages. This passage tends to import Yeshua's conclusions into the commencement of his ministry, glossing over the painful moment of realization when Yeshua grasped that he would not be Yahweh's strong arm, but rather his broken reed, barring a resurrection. This logion loses the reference to John the Baptist, present in Matthew 11:5, and so appears more suspect in Luke's synagogue context. Though I reject this logion, I nevertheless accept that Yeshua linked his ministry to Isaiah 61. In rejecting this logion, I have reservations.

⦸

Logion 340 (Luke 5.4, 10): "Put out in to the deep and let down your nets for a catch. . . . Do not be afraid; henceforth you will be catching men."

HE.

This logion expands Yeshua's call of Galilean fishermen into a gaudy miracle. It is wholly inconsistent with the Marcan Yeshua.

⦸

Logion 373 (Luke 7.13, 14): "Do not weep. . . . Young man, I say to you, arise."

HE.

Humans cannot cause the dead to live again. Yeshua's compassion and comfort are typical of the Marcan character. Ostentation in this healing renders it suspect.

Logion 386 (Luke 8.25): (to cowed disciples in a storm) "Where is your faith?"

HE.

Humans, whether faithful or unfaithful, cannot control storms.

Logion 388 (Luke 8.45, 46): "Who was it that touched me? . . . Some one touched me; for I perceive that power has gone forth from me."

HE.

Humans cannot sense power drain from clothing, nor can bleeding be stemmed by touching fringes.

Logion 410 (Luke 10.21-22): "I thank thee, Father, Lord of heaven and earth, that thou hast hidden these things from the wise and understanding and revealed them to babes; yea, Father, for such was thy gracious will. [22]All things have been delivered to me by my Father; and no one knows who the Son is except the Father, or who the Father is except the Son and any one to whom the Son chooses to reveal him."

HE, APY.

This logion is suspect for rampant hagiography and late Christology. It also contains hints of secret knowledge concepts typical of Gnostic theologies.

Logion 411 (Luke 10.23-24): "Blessed are the eyes which see what you see! [24]For I tell you that many prophets and kings desired to see what you see, and did not see it, and to hear what you hear, and did not hear it."

HE, APY.

This logion looks back from the perspective of the later church, and has a triumphalist tone inconsistent with the Marcan Yeshua.

Logion 496 (Luke 18.31-33): "Behold, we are going up to Jerusalem, and everything that is written of the Son of man by the prophets will be accomplished. [32]For he will be delivered to the Gentiles, and will be mocked and shamefully treated and spit upon, [33]they will scourge him and kill him, and on the third day he will rise."

HE, APY.

LOGION SIEVE KEY: Marcan Consistency (MC), Danielic Son of man (DSM), Hagiographical Hurdle (HH), Urgency of Repentance (UR), Hagiographical Excess (HE), Anachronisms and Post-Yeshuan concerns (APY)

This logion attributes foreknowledge to Yeshua of a sort unavailable to humans. It also oddly describes Yeshua's course in third person, as might a member of the early church.

⃠

Logion 516 (Luke 21.33): "[33]Heaven and earth will pass away, but my words will not pass away."

HE.

This logion makes of Yeshua a cosmic speaker beyond time, which is not possible for humans.

⃠

Logion 521 (Luke 22.28-30): "[28]You are those who have continued with me in my trials; [29]as my Father appointed a kingdom for me, so do I appoint for you [30]that you may eat and drink at my table in my kingdom, and sit on thrones judging the twelve tribes of Israel."

HE, APY.

This logion reassures the early church, shaken by Yeshua's non-return, of their place in the divine scheme of the irruptive kingdom. When Yeshua's students sought such an appointment from Yeshua, he often declined, urging them to serve others.

⃠

Logion 534 (Luke 23.43): (to criminal crucified next to Yeshua) "Truly, I say to you, today you will be with me in Paradise."

HE, APY.

This logion is inconsistent with Yeshua's circumstance. It further reflects a salvation theory distinct from Yeshua's. Yeshua believed himself about to be vindicated, via his voluntary suffering, by Yahweh. He was not going to Paradise, but to resurrection and to reign upon the earth as Yahweh's divine proxy.

⃠

Logion 535 (Luke 23.46): "Father into thy hands I commit my spirit!"

HE, APY.

Yeshua cites Psalm 31.5. Scriptural citations under such stressful circumstances render this logion suspect. The gospel writer may be supplying language he deems appropriate. The sentiment expressed by Psalm 31 may have characterized what Yeshua was feeling: confidence in Yahweh, his redeeming rock and impregnable fortress. Yeshua had been having less confident feelings as recently as Gethsemane. Note the reversed direction of divine action. The Marcan Yeshua is sent by Yahweh. Now, the tortured Christ returns to paradise.

LOGION SIEVE KEY: Marcan Consistency (MC), Danielic Son of man (DSM), Hagiographical Hurdle (HH), Urgency of Repentance (UR), Hagiographical Excess (HE), Anachronisms and Post-Yeshuan concerns (APY)

⊘

Logion 536 (Luke 24.17, 19a, 25-26): "What is this conversation which you are holding with each other as you walk? . . . What things? . . . O foolish men, and slow of heart to believe all that the prophets have spoken! [26]Was it not necessary that the Christ should suffer these things and enter into his glory?"

HE, APY.

This logion claims that the resurrected Yeshua spoke to women who failed to recognize him. Dead people cannot speak. The christos *emphasis places this logion in the post-Yeshua period, as does its fully developed theological interpretation of Yeshua's death.*

⊘

Logion 537 (Luke 24.38-41): "Why are you troubled, and why do questionings arise in your hearts? [39]See my hands and my feet, that it is I myself; handle me, and see; for a spirit has not flesh and bones as you see that I have. . . . Have you anything here to eat?"

HE, APY.

This logion attempts to give substance to eyewitness accounts of post-death Yeshua. It fails to persuade.

⊘

Logion 538 (Luke 24.44, 46-49): "These are my words which I spoke to you, while I was still with you, that everything written about me in the law of Moses and the prophets and the psalms must be fulfilled. . . . Thus it is written, that the Christ should suffer and on the third day rise from the dead, [47]and that repentance and forgiveness of sins should be preached in his name to all nations, beginning from Jerusalem. [48]You are witnesses of these things. [49]And behold, I send the promise of my Father upon you; but stay in the city, until you are clothed with power from on high."

HE, APY.

This logion sets the stage for the resurrected Yeshua stories of Acts, which narrative is the companion volume to the gospel of Luke. Dead men do not speak.

LOGIA MORE APY THAN HE

⊘

Logion 21 (Mark 4.13-20): "Do you not understand this parable? How then will you understand all the parables? [14]The sower sows the word. [15]And these are the ones along the path, where the word is sown; when they hear, Satan immediately comes and takes away the word which is sown in them. [16]And these in like manner are the ones sown upon rocky ground, who, when they hear the word, immediately receive it with joy; [17]and they have no root in themselves, but endure for a while; then, when tribulation or persecution arises on account of the word, immediately they fall away. [18]And others are the ones sown among thorns; they are those who hear the word, [19]but the cares of the world, and the delight in riches, and the desire for other things, enter in and choke the word, and it proves unfruitful. [20]But those that were sown upon the good soil are the ones who hear the word and accept it and bear fruit, thirtyfold and sixtyfold and a hundredfold."

APY.

Emphasis on "the word" would appear to be a post-Yeshua homiletic concern, as well as concern to educate the disciples in the secret meaning of Yeshua's parables, thereby keeping the messianic secret. The logion also includes concerns about persecution, which concerns did not arise until late in Yeshua's ministry, but were prominent in the early church's experience.

Logion 52 (Mark 8.27b, 29): (Of Peter's confession that Jesus is the Christ) "Who do men say that I am? . . . But who do you say that I am?"

HE, APY.

This passage is suspect for its messianic secret emphasis and its interest in the christos *theory.*

Logion 55 (Mark 8.35b): "And the gospel's."

APY.

This passage reflects homiletic concerns of the post-Yeshua church.

Logion 66 (Mark 9.41): "[41]For truly I say to you, whoever gives you a cup of water to drink because you bear the name of Christ, will by no means lose his reward."

APY.

This formulation post-dates Yeshua, and reflects the early church's christos *theology.*

Logion 80 (Mark 10.29-30): "Truly, I say to you, there is no one who has left house or brother or sisters or mother or father or children or lands, for my sake and for the gospel, [30]who will not receive a hundredfold now in this time, houses and brothers and sisters and mothers and children and lands, with persecutions, and in the age to come eternal life."

LOGION SIEVE KEY: Marcan Consistency (MC), Danielic Son of man (DSM), Hagiographical Hurdle (HH), Urgency of Repentance (UR), Hagiographical Excess (HE), Anachronisms and Post-Yeshuan concerns (APY)

APY.

This well-loved logion about reward for suffering evidences concerns of the early persecuted church, not those of Yeshua mid-ministry. The age is "to come," rather than presently breaking in, as Yeshua believed. One suffers for the sake of Yeshua, not the kingdom, which is a theological move the later church made. This logion is not characteristic of the teaching emphases of the Marcan Yeshua.

Logion 82 (Mark 10.33-34): Behold, we are going up to Jerusalem; and the Son of man will be delivered to the chief priests and the scribes, and they will condemn him to death, and deliver him to the Gentiles; [34]and they will mock him and spit upon him, and scourge him, and kill him, and after three days he will arise."

HE, APY.

This logion attributes to Yeshua a specificity of knowledge unavailable to humans.

Logion 85 (Mark 10.45b): ". . .and to give his life as a ransom for many."

HE, APY.

This dangling clause imports a post-Yeshua theological view of Yeshua's death.

Logion 94 (Mark 12.1-11): "A man planted a vineyard, and set a hedge around it, and dug a pit for the wine press, and built a tower, and let it out to tenants, and went into another country. [2]When the time came, he sent a servant to the tenants, to get from them some of the fruit of the vineyard. [3]And they took him and beat him, and sent him away empty-handed. [4]Again he sent to them another servant, and they wounded him in the head, and treated him shamefully. [5]And he sent another, and him they killed; and so with many others, some they beat and some they killed. [6]He had still one other, a beloved son; finally he sent him to them, saying, 'They will respect my son.' [7]But those tenants said to one another, "This is the heir, let us kill him, and the inheritance will be ours.' [8]And they took him and killed him, and cast him out of the vineyard. [9]What will the owner of the vineyard do? He will come and destroy the tenants, and give the vineyard to others. [10]Have you not read this scripture: 'The very stone which the builders rejected has become the head of the corner; [12]this was the Lord's doing and it is marvelous in our eyes'?"

HE, APY.

LOGION SIEVE KEY: Marcan Consistency (MC), Danielic Son of man (DSM), Hagiographical Hurdle (HH), Urgency of Repentance (UR), Hagiographical Excess (HE), Anachronisms and Post-Yeshuan concerns (APY)

This logion contains a post-Yeshuan view of the role of Yeshua as son of God, rather than Son of man. It also emphasizes that the Jews have generally rejected Yeshua, which sentiment occurred long after Yeshua's death.

Logion 99 (Mark 12.35-37): "How can the scribes say that the Christ is the son of David? [36]David himself, inspired by the Holy Spirit, declared, 'The Lord said to my Lord, Sit at my right hand, till I put thy enemies under thy feet.' [37]David himself calls him Lord; so how is he his son?"

HE, APY.

This logion reflects the early church's ongoing rhetoric favoring a christos *theology. Yeshua was concerned to be known as the Danielic Son of man.*

Logion 103 (Mark 13.5-37): "Take heed that no one leads you astray. [6]Many will come in my name, saying, 'I am he!' and they will lead many astray. [7]And when you hear of wars and rumors of wars, do not be alarmed; this must take place, but the end is not yet. [8]For nation will rise against nation, and kingdom against kingdom; there will be earthquakes in various places, there will be famines; this is but the beginning of the sufferings. [9]But take heed to yourselves; for they will deliver you up to councils; and you will be beaten in synagogues; and you will stand before governors and kings for my sake, to bear testimony before them. [10]And the gospel must first be preached to all nations. [11]And when they bring you to trial and deliver you up, do not be anxious beforehand what you are to say; but say whatever is given you in that hour, for it is not you who speak, but the Holy Spirit. [12]And brother will deliver up brother to death, and the father his child, and the children will rise against parents and have them put to death; [13]and you will be hated by all for my name's sake. But he who endures to the end will be saved. [14]But when you see the desolating sacrilege set up where it ought not to be (let the reader understand), then let those who are in Judea flee to the mountains; [15]let him who is on the housetop not go down, nor enter his house, to take anything away; [16]and let him who is in the field not turn back to take his mantle. [17]And alas for those who are with child and for those who give suck in those days! [18]Pray that it may not happen in winter. [19]For in those days there will be such tribulation as has not been from the beginning of the creation which God created until now, and never will be. [20]And if the Lord had not shortened the days, no human being would be saved; but for the sake of the elect, whom he chose, he shortened the days. [21]And then if any one says to you, 'Look, here is the Christ!' or 'Look, there he is!' do not believe it. [22]False Christs and false prophets will arise and show signs and wonders, to lead astray, if possible, the elect. [23]But take heed; I have told you all things beforehand. 24But in those days, after that tribulation, the sun will be darkened, and the moon will not give its light, 25and the stars will be falling from heaven, and the powers in the heavens will be shaken. 26And then they will see the Son of man coming in clouds with great power and glory. 27And then he will send out the angels, and gather his elect from the four winds, from the ends of the earth to the ends of heaven. 28From the fig tree learn its lesson: as soon as its branch becomes tender and puts forth its leaves, you know that summer is near. 29So also, when you see these things taking place, you know that he is near, at the very gates. 30Truly, I say to you, this generation will not pass away before all these things take place. 31Heaven and earth will pass away, but my words will not pass away. 32But of that day or that hour no one knows, not even the angels in heaven, not the Son, but only the Father. 33Take heed, watch; for you do not know when the time will come. 34It is like a man going on a journey, when he leaves home and puts his servants in charge, each with his work and commands the doorkeeper to be on the watch. 35Watch therefore—for you do not know when the master of the house will come, in the evening, or at midnight, or at cockcrow, or in the morning—36lest he come suddenly and find you asleep. 37And what I say to you I say to all: Watch."

HE, APY.

This entire apocalyptic vision reflects the post-Yeshuan church's internal struggle with the failure of Yeshua to prevail in his role as Son of man. Two portions of this reflect Yeshua's other teaching: the section on the Son of man in the clouds (Mark 13.26), and the section on the end time arriving during the lifetime of the hearers (Mark 13.30). The logion addresses the reader as a reader, and so loses track of its own pretense as a saying of Yeshua.

Logion 106 (Mark 14.9): "9And truly I say to you, wherever the gospel is preached in the whole world, what she has done will be told in memory of her."

HE, APY.

This logion expresses the concern of the church for its legacy and evangelism.

Logion 111 (Mark 14.28): "28But after I am raised up, I will go before you to Galilee."

HE, APY.

Yeshua could not possess this sort of specific knowledge. Yeshua expected to be resurrected to power as the Son of man, not to comfort his stricken students.

Logion 112 (Mark 14.30): "Truly, I say to you, this very night, before the cock crows twice, you will deny me three times."

HE.

Yeshua could not know what would happen specifically with respect to Peter's cowardice.

Logion 119 (Mark 14.62a): (to an inquiry whether Yeshua is the *christos*) "I am."

HE, APY.

The christos *designation and Son of Yahweh designations reflect post-Yeshuan developments in the church's thinking about Yeshua.*

Logion 123 (Matthew 3.15): "Let it be so now; for thus it is fitting for us to fulfil all righteousness."

HE, APY.

The late first century church found itself asserting Yeshua's sinlessness, and was embarrassed by the fact he sought John's baptism for the forgiveness of sins.

Logion 124 (Matthew 4.4, 7, 10): "It is written, 'Man shall not live by bread alone, but by every word that proceeds from the mouth of God.' . . . Again it is written, 'You shall not tempt the Lord your God.' . . . Begone, Satan! For it is written, 'You shall worship the Lord your God and him only shall you serve.'"

HE, APY.

The story indicates Yeshua was alone. Yeshua's answers are all references from Deuteronomy: 8.3, 6.16, and 6.13 (this latter, vaguely). Humans cannot speak with Satan.

Logion 135 (Matthew 5.11-12): "[11]Blessed are you when men revile you and persecute you and utter all kinds of evil against you falsely on my account. [12]Rejoice and be glad, for your reward is great in heaven, for so men persecuted the prophets who were before you."

APY.

This logion reflects later church struggles with sporadic persecution.

Logion 169 (Matthew 7.21-23): "[21]Not every one who says to me, 'Lord, Lord,' shall enter the kingdom of heaven, but he who does the will of my Father who is in heaven. [22]On that day many will say to me, 'Lord, Lord, did we not prophesy in your name, and cast out demons in your name, and do many mighty works in your name?' [23]And then will I declare to them, 'I never knew you; depart from me, you evildoers.'"

HE, APY.

This logion reflects later church concerns about imposters and claimants to authority in the flailing early church.

⊘

Logion 187 (Matthew 10.5-6): "Go nowhere among the Gentiles, and enter no town of the Samaritans, [6]but go rather to the lost sheep of the house of Israel."

APY.

This logion reflects disputes in the early church about the role of Jew and Gentile in the church, not a problem Yeshua was having in his Galilean ministry. Yeshua contemplated non-Jews in the kingdom of God. Heartfelt repentance, not ethnic origin, offered admission, in Yeshua's view.

⊘

Logion 189 (Matthew 10.16-23a): "[16]Behold, I send you out as sheep in the midst of wolves; so be wise as serpents and innocent as doves. [17]Beware of men; for they will deliver you up to councils, and flog you in their synagogues, [18]and you will be dragged before governors and kings for my sake, to bear testimony before them and the Gentiles. [19]When they deliver you up, do not be anxious how you are to speak or what you are to say; for what you are to say will be given to you in that hour; [20]for it is not you who speak, but the spirit of your Father speaking through you. [21]Brother will deliver up brother to death, and the father his child, and children will rise against parents and have them put to death; [22]and you will be hated by all for my name's sake. But he who endures to the end will be saved. [23]When they persecute you in one town, flee to the next."

APY.

This logion reflects concerns of the early church in preaching the gospel, not problems of the disciples when Yeshua sent them to the Galilean villages. It contains resonances of Yeshua (family member conflict, going from village to village), but reflects mostly concerns of the post-Yeshuan church.

⊘

Logion 195 (Matthew 10.32-33): "[32]So every one who acknowledges me before men, I also will acknowledge before my Father who is in heaven; [33]but whoever denies me before men, I also will deny before my Father who is in heaven."

HE, APY.

This logion reflects persecution and perseverance concerns of the early church.

⊘

Logion 197 (Matthew 10.38): "[38]And he who does not take his cross and follow me is not worthy of me."

LOGION SIEVE KEY: Marcan Consistency (MC), Danielic Son of man (DSM), Hagiographical Hurdle (HH), Urgency of Repentance (UR), Hagiographical Excess (HE), Anachronisms and Post-Yeshuan concerns (APY)

APY.

This beloved logion reflects knowledge of the outcome in Jerusalem, and therefore cannot come from Yeshua.

⦸

Logion 199 (Matthew 10.40-41): "[40]He who receives you receives me, and he who receives me receives him who sent me. [41]He who receives a prophet because he is a prophet shall receive a prophet's reward, and he who receives a righteous man because he is a righteous man shall receive a righteous man's reward."

HE, APY.

This logion reflects the concerns of the proselytizing early church.

⦸

Logion 208 (Matthew 11.28-30): "[28]Come to me, all who labor and are heavy laden, and I will give you rest. [29]Take my yoke upon you, and learn from me; for I am gentle and lowly in heart, and you will find rest for your souls. [30]For my yoke is easy, and my burden light."

HE, APY.

Yet another beloved logion shifts emphasis from the kingdom to Yeshua personally, which change of focus is characteristic of post-Yeshuan theological developments. It also seems to reflect concerns that occupied the later church: the heavy burdens of Jewish dietary and circumcision compliance. The section, of which this logion is one component (Matthew 11.25-30), may be a much later interpolation into the Matthean narrative.

⦸

Logion 218A (Matthew 13.13-17): "[13]This is why I speak to them in parables, because seeing they do not see, and hearing they do not hear, nor do they understand. [14]With them indeed is fulfilled the prophecy of Isaiah which says: 'You shall indeed hear but never understand, and you shall indeed see but never perceive, [15]For this people's heart has grown dull, and their ears are heavy of hearing, and their eyes they have closed, lest they should perceive with their eyes and hear with their ears, and understand with their heart, and turn for me to heal them.' [16]But blessed are your eyes, for they see, and your ears, for they hear. [17]Truly, I say to you, many prophets and righteous men longed to see what you see, and did not see it, and to hear what you hear, and did not hear it."

HE, APY.

This explanation expresses Matthew's interest in prophetic proof texting. This passage also evidences hagiographical excess and a Messianic secret leaning.

LOGION SIEVE KEY: Marcan Consistency (MC), Danielic Son of man (DSM), Hagiographical Hurdle (HH), Urgency of Repentance (UR), Hagiographical Excess (HE), Anachronisms and Post-Yeshuan concerns (APY)

⊘

Logion 219A (Matthew 13.18-23): "[18]Hear then the parable of the sower. [19]When any one hears the word of the kingdom and does not understand it, the evil one comes and snatches away what is sown in his heart; this is what was sown along the path. [20]As for what was sown on rocky ground, this is he who hears the word and immediately receives it with joy; [21]yet he has no root in himself, but endures for a while, and when tribulation or persecution arises on account of the word, immediately he falls away. [22]As for what was sown among thorns, this is he who hears the word, but the cares of the world and the delight in riches choke the word, and it proves unfruitful. [23]As for what was sown on good soil, this is he who hears the word and understands it; he indeed bears fruit, and yields, in one case a hundredfold, in another sixty, in another thirty."

APY.

This explanation, as in Mark, demonstrates post-Yeshuan homiletic concerns about the "word."

⊘

Logion 243 (Matthew 16.18-20): "[18]And I tell you, you are Peter, and on this rock I will build my church, and the powers of death shall not prevail against it. [19]I will give you the keys of the kingdom of heaven, and whatever you bind on earth shall be bound in heaven, and whatever you loose on earth shall be loosed in heaven."

HE, APY.

This logion reflects post-Yeshuan church concern for the primacy of the Jewish church and Petrine authority over that church, as the church faced an increasingly gentile constituency, as well as the later interest in christos *designations (at Matthew 16.16).*

⊘

Logion 245 (Matthew 16.24-26): "If any man would come after me, let him deny himself and take up his cross and follow me. [25]For whoever would save his life will lose it, and whoever loses his life for my sake will find it. [26]For what will it profit a man, if he gains the whole world and forfeits his life? Or what shall a man give in return for his life?"

HE, APY.

This logion reflects the church's later concern about recantation in the face of Roman persecution, and attributes to Yeshua foreknowledge of the means of his demise.

⊘

Logion 259 (Matthew 18.15-18): "[15]If your brother sins against you, go and tell him his fault, between you and him alone. If he listens to you, you have gained your brother. [16]But if he does not listen, take one or two others along with you, that every word may be confirmed by the evidence of two or three witnesses. [17]If he refuses to listen to them, tell it to the church; and if he refuses to listen even to the church, let him be to you as a Gentile and a tax collector. [18]Truly, I say to you, whatever you bind on earth shall be bound in heaven, and whatever you loose on earth shall be loosed in heaven."

HE, APY.

This logion reflects post-Yeshuan concerns of the early church about its congregational discipline, not Yeshua's concerns mid-ministry. Yeshua did not contemplate a church forming after his non-return.

⦸

Logion 261 (Matthew 18.20): "[20]For where two or three are gathered in my name, there am I in the midst of them."

HE, APY.

This logion reflects the early church's conviction that Yeshua, though he had failed to return as promised, remained in their midst. Yeshua, contrary to the post-Yeshuan church, anticipated resurrection, as a vindication of his suffering and ministry, followed by rule of the kingdom of God by Yahweh through his designee, the Son of man.

⦸

Logion 272 (Matthew 19.28-29): "Truly, I say to you, in the new world, when the Son of man shall sit on his glorious throne, you who have followed me will also sit on twelve thrones, judging the twelve tribes of Israel. [29]And every one who has left houses or brothers or sisters or father or mother or children or lands, for my name's sake, will receive a hundredfold, and inherit eternal life."

HE, APY.

This logion answers post-Yeshuan church's dissenters who alleged that since Yeshua had failed to return, they had been duped. It also seeks to augment apostolic authority in the face of challenge. Gone is Yeshua's emphasis, when considering questions of rank, on servitude.

⦸

Logion 275 (Matthew 20.18-19): "[18]Behold, we are going up to Jerusalem; and the Son of man will be delivered to the chief priests and scribes, and they will condemn him to death, [19]and deliver him to the Gentiles to be mocked and scourged and crucified, and he will be raised on the third day."

HE, APY.

This logion asserts Yeshua had foreknowledge of specific future events, which knowledge is unavailable to humans.

LOGION SIEVE KEY: Marcan Consistency (MC), Danielic Son of man (DSM), Hagiographical Hurdle (HH), Urgency of Repentance (UR), Hagiographical Excess (HE), Anachronisms and Post-Yeshuan concerns (APY)

⃠

Logion 278 (Matthew 20.28b): "And to give his life as a ransom for many."

HE, APY.

The appended language imports a post-Yeshuan theological interpretation of Yeshua's death.

⃠

Logion 288 (Matthew 21.33-40, 42-44): "[33]Hear another parable. There was a householder who planted a vineyard, and set a hedge around it and dug a wine press in it, and built a tower, and let it out to tenants, and went into another country. [34]When the season of fruit drew near, he sent his servants to the tenants, to get his fruit; [35]and the tenants took his servants and beat one, killed another, and stoned another. [36]Again he sent other servants, more than the first, and they did the same to them. [37]Afterward he sent his son to them, saying, 'They will respect my son.' [38]But when the tenants saw the son, they said to themselves,' This is the heir; come, let us kill him and have his inheritance.' [39]And they took him and cast him out of the vineyard, and killed him. [40]When therefore the owner of the vineyard comes, what will he do to those tenants? . . . Have you never read in the scriptures: 'The very stone which the builders rejected has become the head of the corner; this was the Lord's doing, and it is marvelous in our eyes'? [43]Therefore I tell you, the kingdom of God will be taken away from you and given to a nation producing the fruits of it."

HE, APY.

This logion contains a late view of the role of Yeshua as son of God, rather than Son of man. It also emphasizes that the Jews have rejected Yeshua as a whole, which did not occur in Yeshua's days.

⃠

Logion 293 (Matthew 22.42a, 43-45): (Yeshua questions Pharisees) "What do you think of the Christ? Whose son is he? . . . How is it then that David, inspired by the Spirit, calls him Lord, saying, [44]'The Lord said to my Lord, Sit at my right hand, till I put thy enemies under thy feet'? If David thus calls him Lord, how is he his son?"

HE, APY.

This logion reflects the early church's later interests in portraying Yeshua as messiah.

⃠

Logion 295 (Matthew 23.8-10): "[8]But you are not to be called rabbi, for you have one teacher, and you are all brethren. [9]And call no man your father on earth, for you have one Father, who is in heaven. [10]Neither be called masters, for you have one master, the Christ."

LOGION SIEVE KEY: Marcan Consistency (MC), Danielic Son of man (DSM), Hagiographical Hurdle (HH), Urgency of Repentance (UR), Hagiographical Excess (HE), Anachronisms and Post-Yeshuan concerns (APY)

HE, APY.

This logion addresses concerns in the early church about status and authority, even calling Yeshua by the term christos, *utilized as a proper name, not a title.*

Logion 307 (Matthew 24.4-33, 35-51): "Take heed that no one leads you astray. 5For many will come in my name, saying, 'I am the Christ,' and they will lead many astray. 6And you will hear of wars and rumors of wars; see that you are not alarmed; for this must take place, but the end is not yet. 7For nation will rise against nation, and kingdom against kingdom, and there will be famines and earthquakes in various places: 8all this is but the beginning of the sufferings. 9Then they will deliver you up to tribulation, and put you to death; and you will be hated by all nations for my name's sake. 10And then many will fall away, and betray one another, and hate one another. 11And many false prophets will arise and lead many astray. 12And because wickedness is multiplied, most men's love will grow cold. 13But he who endures to the end will be saved. 14And this gospel of the kingdom will be preached throughout the whole world, as a testimony to all nations; and then the end will come. 15So when you see the desolating sacrilege spoken of by the prophet Daniel, standing in the holy place (let the reader understand), 16then let those who are in Judea flee to the mountains; 17let him who is on the housetop not go down to take what is in his house; 18and let him who is in the field not turn back to take his mantle. 19And alas for those who are with child and for those who give suck in those days! 20Pray that your flight may not be in winter or on a Sabbath. 21For then there will be great tribulation, such as has not been from the beginning of the world until now, no, and never will be. 22And if those days had not been shortened, no human being would be saved; but for the sake of the elect those days will be shortened. 23Then if any one says to you, 'Lo, here is the Christ!' or 'There he is!' do not believe it. 24For false Christs and false prophets will arise and show great signs and wonders, so as to lead astray, if possible, even the elect. 25Lo, I have told you beforehand. 26So, if they say to you, 'Lo, he is in the wilderness,' do not go out; if they say, 'Lo, he is in the inner rooms,' do not believe it. 27For as lightning comes from the east and shines as far as the west, so will be the coming of the Son of man. 28Wherever the body is, there the eagles will be gathered together. 29Immediately after the tribulation of those days the sun will be darkened, and the moon will not give its light, and the stars will fall from heaven, and the powers of the heavens will be shaken; 30then will appear the sign of the Son of man in heaven, and then all the tribes of the earth will mourn, and they will see the Son of man coming on the clouds of heaven with power and great glory; 31and he will send out his angels with a loud trumpet call, and they will gather his elect from the four winds, from one end of heaven to the other. 32From the fig tree learn its lessons: as soon as its branch becomes tender and puts forth its leaves, you know that summer is near. [33]So also, when you see all these things, you know that he is near, at the very gates. . . . [35]Heaven and earth will pass away, but my words will not pass away. [36]But of that day and hour no one knows, not even the angels of heaven, not the Son, but the Father only. [37]As were the days of Noah, so will be the coming of the Son of man. [38]For as in those days before the flood they were eating and drinking, marrying and giving in marriage, until the day when Noah entered the ark, [39]and they did not know until the flood came and swept them all away, so will be the coming of the Son of man. [40]Then two men will be in the field; one is taken and one is left. [41]Two women will be grinding at the mill; one is taken and one is left. [42]Watch therefore, for you do not know on what day your Lord is coming. [43]But know this, that if the householder had known in what part of the night the thief was coming, he would have watched and would not have let his house be broken into. [44]Therefore you also must be ready; for the Son of man is coming at an hour you do not expect. [45]Who then is the faithful and wise servant, whom his master has set over his household, to give them their food at the proper time? [46]Blessed is that servant whom his master when he comes will find so doing. [47]Truly, I say to you, he will set him over all his possessions. [48]But if that wicked servant says to himself, 'My master is delayed,' [49]and begins to beat his fellow servants, and eats and drinks with the drunken, [50]the master of that servant will come on a day when he does not expect him and at an hour he does not know, [51]and will punish him and put him with the hypocrites; there men will weep and gnash their teeth."

HE, APY.

This long apocalypse addresses the church's dilemma with the never-forthcoming parousia of vindicated Yeshua.

⃠

Logion 309 (Matthew 25.1-13): "Then the kingdom of heaven shall be compared to ten maidens who took their lamps and went to meet the bridegroom. [2]Five of them were foolish, and five were wise. [3]For when the foolish took their lamps, they took no oil with them; [4]but the wise took flasks of oil with their lamps. [5]As the bridegroom was delayed, they all slumbered and slept. [6]But at midnight there was a cry, 'Behold, the bridegroom! Come out to meet him.' [7]Then all those maidens rose and trimmed their lamps. [8]And the foolish said to the wise, 'Give us some of your oil, for our lamps are going out.' [9]But the wise replied, 'Perhaps there will not be enough for us and for you; go rather to the dealers and buy for yourselves.' [10]And while they went to buy, the bridegroom came, and those who were ready went in with him to the marriage feast; and the door was shut. [11]Afterwards the other maidens came also, saying, 'Lord, lord, open to us.' [12]But he replied, 'Truly, I say to you, I do not know you.' [13]Watch therefore for you know neither the day nor the hour."

HE, APY.

This logion reflects the struggles of the early church with the delayed parousia of Yeshua, and the crisis created by the ineluctable passing of the eyewitness generation.

⦸

Logion 310 (Matthew 25.14-28,30): "[14]For it will be as when a man going on a journey called his servants and entrusted to them his property; [15]to one he gave five talents, to another two, to another one, to each according to his ability. Then he went away. [16]He who had received five talents went at once and traded with them; and he made five talents more. [17]So also, he who had two talents made two talents more. [18]But he who had received the one talent went and dug in the ground and hid his master's money. [19]Now after a long time the master of those servants came and settled accounts with them. [20]And he who had received the five talents came forward, bringing five talents more, saying, 'Master, you delivered to me five talents; here I have made five talents more.' [21]His master said to him, 'Well done, good and faithful servant; for you have been faithful over a little, I will set you over much; enter into the joy of your master.' [22]And he also who had the two talents came forward, saying, 'Master, you delivered to me two talents; here I have made two talents more.' [23]His master said to him, 'Well done, good and faithful servant; you have been faithful over a little, I will set you over much; enter into the joy of your master.' [24]He also who had received the one talent came forward, saying, 'Master, I knew you to be a hard man, reaping where you did not sow, and gathering where you did not winnow; [25]so I was afraid, and I went and hid your talent in the ground. Here you have what is yours.' [26]But his master answered him, 'You wicked and slothful servant! You knew that I reap where I have not sowed, and gather where I have not winnowed? [27]Then you ought to have invested my money with the bankers, and at my coming I should have received what was my own with interest. [28]So take the talent from him, and give it to him who has the ten talents. . . . [30]And cast the worthless servant into the outer darkness; there men will weep and gnash their teeth.'"

HE, APY.

This logion reflects the struggles of the early church with the non-parousia of Yeshua, and the crisis created by the passing of the eyewitness generation.

⦸

Logion 311 (Matthew 25.31-46): "[31]When the Son of man comes in his glory, and all the angels with him, then he will sit on his glorious throne. [32]Before him will be gathered all the nations, [33]and he will separate one from another as shepherd separates the sheep from the goats, and he will place the sheep at his right hand, but the goats at the left. [34]Then the King will say to those at his right hand,

'Come, O blessed of my Father, inherit the kingdom prepared for you from the foundation of the world; [35]for I was hungry and you gave me food, I was thirsty and you gave me drink, I was a stranger and you welcomed me. [36]I was naked and you clothed me, I was sick and you visited me, I was in prison and you came to me.' [37]Then the righteous will answer him, 'Lord, when did we see thee hungry and feed thee, or thirsty and give thee drink? [38]When did we see thee a stranger and welcome thee, or naked and clothe thee? [39]And when did we see thee sick or in prison and visit thee?' [40]And the King will answer, 'Truly, I say to you, as you did it to the least of these my brethren, you did it to me.' [41]Then he will say to those at his left hand, 'Depart from me, you cursed, into the eternal fire prepared for the devil and his angels; [42]for I was hungry and you gave me no food, I was thirsty and you gave me no drink, [43]I was a stranger and you did not welcome me, naked and you did not clothe me, sick and in prison and did not visit me.' [44]Then they also will answer, 'Lord, when did we see thee hungry or thirsty or a stranger or naked or sick or in prison, and did not minister to three? [45]Then he will answer them, 'Truly, I say to you, as you did it not to one of the least of these, you did it not to me.' [46]And they will go away into eternal punishment, but the righteous into eternal life."

HE, APY.

This luminous logion reflects the church's struggle with the delayed parousia, and suggests a way forward in understanding fealty to Yeshua in social justice and service. It does not, however, derive from Yeshua, though its sentiment is deeply consistent with that of Yeshua and the eighth-century prophets.

Logion 314 (Matthew 26.13): "[13]Truly, I say to you, wherever this gospel is preached in the whole world, what she has done will be told in memory of her."

APY.

This logion reflects the later concern of the church about extending the gospel into the Roman world.

Logion 319 (Matthew 26.28): ". . . [28]for this is my blood of the covenant, which is poured out for many for the forgiveness of sins."

This logion reflects later theological developments in the church, not Yeshua's interpretation of these events.

Logion 321 (Matthew 26.31-32): "You will all fall away because of me this night; for it is written, 'I will strike the shepherd, and the sheep of the flock will be scattered.' [32]But after I am raised up, I will go before you to Galilee.'"

HE, APY.

Yeshua could not possess such specific foreknowledge.

⃠

Logion 322 (Matthew 26.34): "Truly, I say to you, this very night, before the cock crows, you will deny me three times."

HE, APY.

Yeshua could not foreknow such an event.

⃠

Logion 326 (Matthew 26.54, 56a): "[54]But how then should the scriptures be fulfilled, that it must be so? . . . [56]But all this has taken place, that the scriptures of the prophets might be fulfilled."

HE, APY.

This logion represents the rhetorical purpose of the author of Matthew in portraying Yeshua's ministry as fulfillment of Jewish prophecies.

⃠

Logion 379 (Luke 8.10): "To you it has been given to know the secrets of the kingdom of God; but for others they are in parables, so that seeing they may not see, and hearing they may not understand."

HE, APY.

This is a continuation of the Marcan messianic secret tradition, which served to explain why so few recognized Yeshua as the christos *during his ministry. Messianic secret passages are suspect as rhetorical devices.*

⃠

Logion 380 (Luke 8.11-15): "[11]Now the parable is this: The seed is the word of God. [12]The ones along the path are those who have heard; then the devil comes and takes away the word from their hearts, that they may not believe and be saved. [13]And the ones on the rock are those who, when they hear the word, receive it with joy; but these have no root, they believe for a while and in time of temptation fall away. [14]And as for what fell among the thorns, they are those who hear, but as they go on their way they are choked by the cares and riches and pleasures of life, and their fruit does not mature. [15]And as for that in the good soil, they are those who, hearing the word, hold it fast in an honest and good heart, and bring forth fruit with patience."

HE, APY.

Emphasis on "the word" would appear to be a post-Yeshua homiletic concern, as well as concern to educate the disciples in the secret meaning of Yeshua's parables, thereby preserving the messianic secret.

⊘

Logion 394 (Luke 9.23-24): "If any man would come after me, let him deny himself and take up his cross daily and follow me. [24]For whoever would save his life will lose it; and whoever loses his life for my sake, he will save it."

HE, APY.

This logion reflects the post-Yeshuan church's concerns about congregant recantation in the face of sporadic persecution. Its express reference to the cross rules out its origin in Yeshua.

⊘

Logion 396 (Luke 9.26): "[26]For whoever is ashamed of me and of my words, of him will the Son of man be ashamed when he comes in his glory and the glory of the Father and of the holy angels."

HE, APY.

This logion reflects a later church concern about recantation under persecution.

⊘

Logion 408 (Luke 10.16): "[16]He who hears you hears me, and he who rejects you rejects me, and he who rejects me rejects him who sent me."

APY.

This logion expresses the concerns of the early church in its authority struggles and proselytizing. Its sentiment reflects Yeshua's at the time he sent out students to short independent ministries. I reject the logion for its forceful assertion, which I take to reflect a later time during which the early church struggled with congregational compliance. I reject this logion with reservations.

⊘

Logion 409 (Luke 10.18-20): "I saw Satan fall like lightning from heaven. [19]Behold, I have given you authority to tread upon serpents and scorpions, and over all the powers of the enemy; and nothing shall hurt you. [20]Nevertheless do not rejoice in this, that the spirits are subject to you; but rejoice that your names are written in heaven."

HE, APY.

This logion reflects post-Yeshuan church concerns about dangers of and authority for proselytizing, and a fascination with odd religious phenomena.

⊘

Logion 436 (Luke 12.11-12): "[11]And when they bring you before the synagogues and the rulers and the authorities, do not be anxious how or what you are

LOGION SIEVE KEY: Marcan Consistency (MC), Danielic Son of man (DSM), Hagiographical Hurdle (HH), Urgency of Repentance (UR), Hagiographical Excess (HE), Anachronisms and Post-Yeshuan concerns (APY)

to answer or what you are to say; [12]for the Holy Spirit will teach you in that very hour what you ought to say."

APY.

This logion evidences the later church's concerns under persecution.

⊘

Logion 442 (Luke 12.35-40): "[35]Let your loins be girded and your lamps burning, [36]and be like men who are waiting for their master to come home from the marriage feast, so that they may open to him at once when he comes and knocks. [37]Blessed are those servants whom the master finds awake when he comes; truly, I say to you, he will gird himself and have them sit at table, and he will come and serve them. [38]If he comes in the second watch, or in the third, and finds them so, blessed are those servants! [39]But know this, that if the householder had known at what hour the thief was coming, he would have been awake and would not have left his house to be broken into. [40]You also must be ready; for the Son of man is coming at an hour you do not expect."

HE, APY.

This logion heartens church members discouraged by the non-return of Yeshua, contrary to Yeshua's oft-repeated promise of imminent return in power. This was a significant problem for the post-Yeshuan church.

⊘

Logion 443 (Luke 12.42-48): "Who then is the faithful and wise steward, whom his master will set over his household, to give them their portion of food at the proper time? [43]Blessed is that servant whom his master when he comes will find so doing. [44]Truly I tell you, he will set him over all his possessions. [45]But if that servant says to himself, 'My master is delayed in coming,' and begins to beat the menservants and the maidservants, and to eat and drink and get drunk, [46]the master of that servant will come on a day when he does not expect him and at an hour he does not know, and will punish him, and put him with the unfaithful. [47]And that servant who knew his master's will, but did not make ready or act according to his will, shall receive a severe beating. [48]But he who did not know, and did what deserved a beating, shall receive a light beating. Every one to whom much is given, of him will much be required; and of him to whom men commit much they will demand the more."

HE, APY.

This logion reflects later concerns of the early church, as discouragement attending the delayed parousia led to backsliding in behavior and attitude.

LOGION SIEVE KEY: Marcan Consistency (MC), Danielic Son of man (DSM), Hagiographical Hurdle (HH), Urgency of Repentance (UR), Hagiographical Excess (HE), Anachronisms and Post-Yeshuan concerns (APY)

Logion 456 (Luke 13.32-33): (to Pharisees warning of Herod's plots) "Go and tell that fox, 'Behold, I cast out demons and perform cures today and tomorrow, and the third day I finish my course. [33]Nevertheless I must go on my way today and tomorrow and the day following; for it cannot be that a prophet should perish away from Jerusalem."

HE.

Yeshua's precise foreknowledge of events is hagiographical excess. Humans cannot predict such matters.

Logion 464 (Luke 14.27): "[27]Whoever does not bear his own cross and come after me, cannot be my disciple."

HE, APY.

This logion expresses foreknowledge of the manner of Yeshua's death and addresses concerns of the post-Yeshuan first-century church.

Logion 472 (Luke 16.1-12): "There was a rich man who had a steward, and charges were brought to him that this man was wasting his goods. [2]And he called him and said to him, 'What is this that I hear about you? Turn in the account of your stewardship, for you can no longer be steward.' [3]And the steward said to himself, 'What shall I do, since my master is taking the stewardship away from me? I am not strong enough to dig, and I am ashamed to beg. [4]I have decided what to do, so that people may receive me into their houses when I am put out of the stewardship.' [5]So, summoning his master's debtors one by one, he said to the first, 'How much do you owe my master?' [6]He said, 'A hundred measures of oil.' And he said to him, 'Take your bill, and sit down quickly and write fifty.' [7]Then he said to another, 'And how much do you owe?' He said, "A hundred measures of wheat.' He said to him, 'Take your bill, and write eighty.' [8]The master commended the dishonest steward for his prudence; for the sons of this world are wiser in their own generation than the sons of light. [9]And I tell you, make friends for yourselves by means of unrighteous mammon, so that when it fails they may receive you into the eternal habitations. [10]He who is faithful in a very little is faithful also in much; and he who is dishonest in a very little is dishonest also in much. [11]If then you have not been faithful in the unrighteous mammon, who will entrust to you the true riches? [12]And if you have not been faithful in that which is another's who will give you that which is your own?"

APY.

This odd logion contains the locutions "sons of light" and "eternal habitations," both of which emerge from the later church's (possibly Gnostic) influences and modes of expression. The primary concern of the parable is the steward's prudence in bad circumstances, which reflects the later church's plight. In favor of this logion stands its embarrassment quotient, but that embarrassment relates not to the church's disappointment in Yeshua, but to its own ineptitude.

⦸

Logion 478 (Luke 16.19-31): "[19]There was a rich man, who was clothed in purple and fine linen and who feasted sumptuously every day. [20]And at his gate lay a poor man named Lazarus, full of sores, [21]who desired to be fed with what fell from the rich man's table; moreover the dogs came and licked his sores. [22]The poor man died and was carried by the angels to Abraham's bosom. The rich man also died and was buried; [23]and in Hades, being in torment, he lifted up his eyes, and saw Abraham far off and Lazarus in his bosom. [24]And he called out, 'Father Abraham, have mercy upon me, and send Lazarus to dip the end of his finger in water and cool my tongue; for I am in anguish in this flame.' [25]But Abraham said, 'Son, remember that you in your lifetime received your good things, and Lazarus in like manner evil things; but now he is comforted here, and you are in anguish. [26]And besides all this, between us and you a great chasm has been fixed, in order that those who would pass from here to you may not be able, and none may cross from there to us.' [27]And he said, 'Then I beg you, father, to send him to my father's house, [28]for I have five brothers, so that he may warn them, lest they also come into this place of torment.' [29]But Abraham said, 'They have Moses and the prophets; let them hear them.' [30]And he said, 'No, father Abraham; but if some one goes to them from the dead, they will repent.' [31]He said to him, 'If they do not hear Moses and the prophets, neither will they be convinced if some one should rise from the dead."

HE, APY.

This logion reflects foreknowledge of what the church later came to believe, that Yeshua was resurrected. It also reflects an intermediary theory that developed later in church history. The thrust of the logion reflects the later church's concerns with proselytizing Jews.

⦸

Logion 484 (Luke 17.17-18): "Were not ten cleansed? Where are the nine? [18]Was no one found to return and give praise to God except this foreigner?"

HE, APY.

This logion evidences hagiography of Yeshua, intimating that praising him is to praise God, which is a much later development in the history of the church, and the later church's struggles with the role of foreigners in its midst.

LOGION SIEVE KEY: Marcan Consistency (MC), Danielic Son of man (DSM), Hagiographical Hurdle (HH), Urgency of Repentance (UR), Hagiographical Excess (HE), Anachronisms and Post-Yeshuan concerns (APY)

Logion 485 (Luke 17.20-21): "The kingdom of God is not coming with signs to be observed; [21]nor will they say, 'Lo, here it is!' or 'There! for behold, the kingdom of God is in the midst of you."

APY.

This logion addresses the later church's concern about the non-return of the resurrected Yeshua as the eyewitness generation passed. It seeks to revise the kingdom of God as Yeshua proclaimed it, making of the kingdom a psychological state.

Logion 486 (Luke 17.22-32, 34-37): "The days are coming when you will desire to see one of the days of the Son of man, and you will not see it. [23]And they will say to you, 'Lo, there!' or 'Lo, here!' Do not go, do not follow them. [24]For as the lightning flashes and lights up the sky from one side to the other, so will the Son of man be in his day. [25]But first he must suffer many things and be rejected by this generation. [26]As it was in the days of Noah, so will it be in the days of the Son of man. [27]They ate, they drank, they married, they were given in marriage, until the day when Noah entered the ark, and the flood came and destroyed them all. [28]Likewise as it was in the days of Lot—they ate, they drank, they bought, they sold, they planted, they built, [29]but on the day when Lot went out from Sodom fire and brimstone rained from heaven and destroyed them all—[30]so will it be on the day when the Son of man is revealed. [31]On that day, let him who is on the housetop, with his goods in the house, not come down to take them away; and likewise let him who is in the field not turn back. [32]Remember Lot's wife. . . . [34]I tell you, in that night there will be two men in one bed; one will be taken and the other left. [35]There will be two women grinding together; one will be taken and the other left. . . . [37]Where the body is, there the eagles will be gathered together."

HE, APY.

This logion reflects the church's dilemma confronting the non-return of Yeshua. The author seeks a non-falsifiable basis for Yeshua's inbreaking Son of man powers post-resurrection.

Logion 488 (Luke 18.2-8): "In a certain city there was a judge who neither feared God nor regarded man; [3]and there was a widow in that city who kept coming to him and saying, 'Vindicate me against my adversary.' [4]For a while he refused; but afterward he said to himself, 'Though I neither fear God nor regard man, [5]yet because this widow bothers me, I will vindicate her, or she will wear me out by her continual coming.' . . . Hear what the unrighteous judge says. [7]And will not God vindicate his elect, who cry to him day and night? Will he delay long over them? [8]I tell you, he will vindicate them speedily. Nevertheless, when the Son of man comes, will he find faith on earth?"

HE, APY.

This logion addresses the non-return of Yeshua in power, which failure casts doubt for the early community upon the claims of Yeshua.

⃠

Logion 495 (Luke 18.29-30): "Truly, I say to you, there is no man who has left house or wife or brothers or parents or children, for the sake of the kingdom of God, [30]who will not receive manifold more in this time, and in the age to come eternal life."

HE, APY.

This logion reflects attempts to address the dysphoria in the early church over the non-return of Yeshua, despite his promises to do so. Challenges in awaiting Yeshua turn out harder than some were prepared to endure.

⃠

Logion 500 (Luke 19.12-27): "A nobleman went into a far country to receive kingly power and then return. [13]Calling ten of his servants, he gave them ten pounds, and said to them, 'Trade with these till I come.' [14]But his citizens hated him and sent an embassy after him saying, 'We do not want this man to reign over us.' [15]When he returned, having received the kingly power, he commanded these servants to whom he had given the money, to be called to him, that he might know what they had gained by trading. [16]The first came before him, saying, 'Lord, your pound has made ten pounds more.' [17]And he said to him, 'Well done, good servant! Because you have been faithful in very little, you shall have authority over ten cities.' [18]And the second came, saying, 'Lord, your pound has made five pounds.' [19]And he said to him, 'And you are to be over five cities.' [20]Then another came, saying, 'Lord, here is your pound, which I kept laid away in a napkin; [21]for I was afraid of you, because you are a severe man; you take up what you did not lay down, and reap what you did not sow.' [22]He said to him, 'I will condemn you out of your own mouth, you wicked servant! You knew that I was a severe man, taking what I did not lay down and reaping what I did not sow? [23]Why then did you not put my money into the bank, and at my coming I should have collected it with interest?' [24]And he said to those who stood by, 'Take the pound from him and give it to him who has the ten pounds.' [25](And they said to him, 'Lord, he has ten pounds!') [26]I tell you, that to every one who has will more be given; but from him who has not, even what he has will be taken away. [27]But as for these enemies of mine, who did not want me to reign over them, bring them here and slay them before me."

APY.

This logion addresses the later church's internal concerns about the non-return of Yeshua, and seeks to hold the faithful in line despite their doubts.

Logion 504 (Luke 19.42-44): "Would that even today you knew the things that make for peace! But now they are hid from your eyes. [43]For the days shall come upon you, when your enemies will cast up a bank about you and surround you, and hem you in on every side, [44]and dash you to the ground, you and your children within you, and they will not leave one stone upon another in you; because you did not know the time of your visitation."

APY.

This logion places in Yeshua's mouth foreknowledge of the Roman destruction of the Temple and subjugation of Jewish rebels in 70 A.D. by Titus Flavius.

Logion 507 (Luke 20.9-18): "A man planted a vineyard, and let it out to tenants, and went into another country for a long while. [10]When the time came, he sent a servant to the tenants, that they should give him some of the fruit of the vineyard; but the tenants beat him, and sent him away empty-handed. [11]And he sent another servant; him also they beat and treated shamefully, and sent him away empty-handed. And he sent yet a third; this one they wounded and cast out. [13]Then the owner of the vineyard said, 'What shall I do? I will send my beloved son; it may be they will respect him." [14]But when the tenants saw him, they said to themselves, 'This is the heir; let us kill him, that the inheritance may be ours.' [15]And they cast him out of the vineyard and killed him. What then will the owner of the vineyard do to them? [16]He will come and destroy those tenants, and give the vineyard to others.' When they heard this, they said, 'God forbid!' [17]But he looked at them and said, 'What then is this that is written: 'The very stone which the builders rejected has become the head of the corner'? [18]Every one who falls on that stone will be broken to pieces; but when it falls on any one it will crush him."

HE, APY.

This logion contains a late view of the role of Yeshua as son of God, rather than Son of man. It also emphasizes that the Jews have generally rejected Yeshua.

Logion 510 (Luke 20.41-44): "How can they say that the Christ is David's son? [42]For David himself says in the Book of Psalms, 'The Lord said to my Lord, Sit at my right hand, [43]till I make thy enemies a stool for thy feet.' [44]David thus calls him Lord; so how is he his son?"

HE, APY.

LOGION SIEVE KEY: Marcan Consistency (MC), Danielic Son of man (DSM), Hagiographical Hurdle (HH), Urgency of Repentance (UR), Hagiographical Excess (HE), Anachronisms and Post-Yeshuan concerns (APY)

This logion reflects the post-Yeshuan church's interest in proving Yeshua to be the christos. *Yeshua rejected this designation, in favor of the Son of man title. The disciples were more interested in Yeshua's possibilities as an earthly ruler and king.*

Logion 513 (Luke 21.6, 8-31): "[6]As for these things which you see, the days will come when there shall not be left here one stone upon another that will not be thrown down. . . . Take heed that you are not led astray; for many will come in my name, saying, 'I am he!' and, 'The time is at hand!' Do not go after them. [9]And when you hear of wars and tumults, do not be terrified; for this must first take place, but the end will not be at once. . . . Nation will rise against nation, and kingdom against kingdom; [11]there will be great earthquakes, and in various places famines and pestilences; and there will be terrors and great signs from heaven. [12]But before all this they will lay their hands on you and persecute you, delivering you up to the synagogues and prisons, and you will be brought before kings and governors for my name's sake. [13]This will be a time for you to bear testimony. [14]Settle it therefore in your minds, not to meditate beforehand how to answer; [15]for I will give you a mouth and wisdom, which none of your adversaries will be able to withstand or contradict. [16]You will be delivered up even by parents and brothers and kinsmen and friends, and some of you they will put to death; [17]for you will be hated by all for my name's sake. [18]But not a hair of your head will perish. [19]By your endurance you will gain your lives. [20]But when you see Jerusalem surrounded by armies, then know that its desolation has come near. [21]Then let those who are in Judea flee to the mountains, and let those who are inside the city depart, and let not those who are out in the country enter it; [22]for these are days of vengeance, to fulfil all that is written. [23]Alas for those who are with child and for those who give suck in those days! For great distress shall be upon the earth and wrath upon this people; [24]they will fall by the edge of the sword, and be led captive among all nations; and Jerusalem will be trodden down by the Gentiles, until the times of the Gentiles are fulfilled. [25]And there will be signs in sun and moon and stars, and upon the earth distress of nations in perplexity at the roaring of the sea and the waves, [26]men fainting with fear and with foreboding of what is coming on the world; for the powers of the heavens will be shaken. [27]And then they will see the Son of man coming in a cloud with power and great glory. [28]Now when these things begin to take place, look up and raise your heads, because your redemption is drawing near."

HE, APY.

The logion reflects the early church's distress at the non-return of Yeshua, contrary to his promise of return in power, and the passing of the eyewitness gen-

eration before that return in power. This logion attributes foreknowledge of Titus's sack of Jerusalem and the destruction of the Second Temple (70 A.D.) to Yeshua. None foresees the future. This logion is valuable, though suspect as a saying of Yeshua, because Luke 21.27 expressly confirms the church's grasp of Yeshua's Son of man designation (see Daniel 7).

⃠

Logion 514 (Luke 21.29-31): "Look at the fig tree, and all the trees; [30]as soon as they come out in leaf, you see for yourselves and know that the summer is already near. [31]So also, when you see these things taking place, you know that the kingdom of God is near."

HE, APY.

This logion addresses the early church's concern about the non-return of Yeshua, and seeks to address the anxiety and discouragement of the community at this fact.

⃠

Logion 517 (Luke 21.34-36): "[34]But take heed to yourselves lest your hearts be weighed down with dissipation and drunkenness and cares of this life, and that day come upon you suddenly like a snare; [35]for it will come upon all who dwell upon the face of the whole earth. [36]But watch at all times, praying that you may have strength to escape all these things that will take place, and to stand before the Son of man."

HE, APY.

This logion addresses the impatience and lack of resilience among some congregants at their disappointment in Yeshua's non-return.

⃠

Logion 522 (Luke 22.31-32, 34): "[31]Simon, Simon, behold, Satan demanded to have you, that he might sift you like wheat, [32]but I have prayed for you that your faith may not fail; and when you have turned again, strengthen your brethren. . . . I tell you, Peter, the cock will not crow this day, until you three times deny that you know me."

HE, APY.

This logion bolsters Petrine authority, which became a concern of the church much later than Yeshua's time, and places in the mouth of Yeshua the sort of foreknowledge humans cannot possess.

⃠

Logion 523 (Luke 22.35-37, 38b): (the last phrase responds to disciples noting the presence of two swords) "When I sent you out with no purse or bag or sandals, did you lack anything? . . . But now, let him who has a purse take it, and likewise a bag. And let him who has no sword sell his mantle and buy one. [37]For

LOGION SIEVE KEY: Marcan Consistency (MC), Danielic Son of man (DSM), Hagiographical Hurdle (HH), Urgency of Repentance (UR), Hagiographical Excess (HE), Anachronisms and Post-Yeshuan concerns (APY)

I tell you that this scripture must be fulfilled in me, 'And he was reckoned with transgressors'; for what is written about me has its fulfillment. . . . It is enough."

HE, APY.

This logion addresses concerns of the later church at its persecutions. In a sentiment uncharacteristic of the Marcan or Quelle Yeshua, it advises general preparation and the possibility of defensive violence.

TRANSLATIONS FOR GENTILES

Logion 34B (Mark 5.41b): "Little girl, I say to you, arise."

TG.

The author of Mark translates the purported Aramaic saying of Yeshua to the sleeping or dead young daughter of Jairus, "Talitha cumi." Yeshua spoke no Greek of which we know.

Logion 42 (Mark 7.11): "that is, given to God."

TG.

The translation of the word "corban" would not be words of Yeshua speaking to his Aramaic-speaking listeners.

Logion 47A (Mark 7.34c): (Upon restoring sight and speech to the Decapoline deaf and dumb man) "Be opened."

TG.

Mark translates the Aramaic word "ephphatha."

CHAPTER 11
TAILORED YESHUAS

Many shorn Yeshuas have preceded the Yeshua of this *Gethsemane Soliloquy*. Yeshua has been styled a man-god, a wan German civil religionist, a psychobabble namby-pamby, an apocalyptic madman, a best friend, a New Age co-religionist, and a loving advocate in the sky. Other characterizations are legion. Yeshua seems pliant. The Galilean dons the costume and habits his interpreters prefer.

Some modern interpreters, who have been very active in recent years (consider The Jesus Seminar[97] or Rex Weyler[98]), have excised the core apocalyptic message of Yeshua, since they find it inconsistent with the message a modern wisdom-seeker might prefer that Yeshua had preached. Clearly, Yeshua was wrong about the irruptive kingdom and his role in it. That embarrasses those of us who hold Yeshua dear. Apocalyptists are perennial, and often more than a bit

---

[97] "The Jesus Seminar became convinced that Jesus was not an apocalyptic prophet like John, because many of his parables and many of his aphorisms do not portray him as anticipating imminent divine judgment." Robert W. Funk and the Jesus Seminar. *The Gospel of Jesus, According to the Jesus Seminar*. Santa Rosa, California: Polebridge Press, 1999, at page 92.

[98] "Nowhere does Jesus talk about a future apocalyptic kingdom." Rex Weyler. *The Jesus Sayings: The Quest for His Authentic Message*. Toronto: House of Anansi Press Inc., 2008, at page 113.

unhinged. Yeshua's apocalypticism demotes his message.[99] Nevertheless, redacting Yeshua's apocalypticism does violence to his message and person. Yeshua was an errant apocalyptist. His interpreters should bite that bullet, regardless the esteem in which they hold Yeshua. Yeshua's ministry began in John's camp; John was a fiery hermit of unabashed apocalyptic bent (Matthew 3). Yeshua's self-designation was "Son of man," which terminology derives from an intertestamental apocalypse (Daniel 7). Yeshua's sense of urgency, apparent throughout his ministry, underscores the onrushing kingdom he believed to be emergent. Yeshua's change of concept concerning his ministry preserved his faith in the irruptive kingdom when Yahweh failed to act mid-ministry, as had been Yeshua's expectation. Yeshua concluded there was yet one miserable duty to perform in Jerusalem before the kingdom arrived. Yeshua's repudiation of messiah-sayers evidences his conviction of an event exceeding mere earthly rule. Yeshua hoped that, even if killed, resurrection and elevation to divine power would follow close on death's heels. Apocalypticism permeates Yeshua's sayings.[100] In redacting Yeshua's onrushing kingdom, one banishes much of Yeshua. Yeshua was wrong—about the kingdom, about himself. His error demonstrates humanity. Are we not all, to some extent, awry about what might come to pass and who we are? Yeshua remains, apocalypticism intact, a fascinating, compelling, influential thinker, comfortably-situated among the most potent thinkers of humankind's literary heritage.

One may fairly ask why one should prefer the *Gethsemane Soliloquy* Yeshua to others. My answer is this: Do not prefer this Yeshua. I have honestly brokered each logion to the best of my ability and knowledge.[101] The abilities and

---

[99] Albert Schweitzer emphasizes Yeshua's apocalyptic message, making of the Galilean an unabashed John the Baptist redux. Schweitzer says, "We must continually make a fresh effort to realize that Jesus and his immediate followers were at that time in an enthusiastic state of intense eschatological expectation." Schweitzer, *Quest for the Historical Jesus*, 345. In my view, Yeshua's understanding of his message mutated, coming to include, alongside his Son of man irruptive kingdom teaching, the suffering of the servant of deutero-Isaiah (see, for example, Isaiah 52-53).

[100] The early church suffered terribly when Yeshua, contrary to his promises, failed to return in power (the parousia). Yeshua's non-return drove formation of the early church. Yeshua created no congregation of normal people, living out their lifetimes, for Yeshua anticipated imminent resurrection to power as God's scion. Nascent Christianity adapted. Critically, it blended some unblendable ideas. The "Son of man" is a Danielic heavenly wielder of judgment upon mankind. A "messiah" is an earthly warrior who defeats the opponents of Israel (hence, Cyrus of Persia is a "messiah." See Isaiah 44:28-45:1). A "Son of god" is a Hellenic or Mythraic or Zoroastrian metaphysical being, whose filial origin is divine, who may appear human, but is, in fact, a person more deeply divine than might any mere human pretend. The early church, in its illiteracy and post-Yeshuan confusions, conflated these three concepts. See the usage in Acts7:56, 9:20, and 9:22. The church's theological mash-up persists to the present, obscuring the historical Yeshua. Yeshua himself contradicted the mash-up (Matthew 26:62-64).

[101] And, yet, Schweitzer argues that in resolving many largely-unresolvable issues in interpreting Jesus, that "[e]ach view equally involves a violent treatment of the text." Schweitzer, *Quest for the Historical Jesus*, 9.

knowledge of others exceed mine. Yeshua has mattered to me for many decades. No other deceased person has more deeply influenced my decision-making. I have, by this analysis and restatement of Yeshua's message, set to rest certain matters that trouble me. I have made my analysis available for those who share my concerns, especially those who decry the church's monopolization of Yeshua and wince at her hagiographical mania. Though this sketch of Yeshua's teaching remains penultimate and equivocal, no more satisfying result may be possible. For me, it is enough.[102]

For others, my effort will prove underwhelming. Such persons may savor extended debate and speculations of broader scope, poring over Greek *koine* and textual variants. The Synoptic texts bear and require withering scrutiny. The churches' views remain equivocal. So, lavish attention, if you are so inclined. The Synoptics welcome your poking.

So too, if I am right, would Yeshua himself.

[102] Friends, James Max Gossett and Jan Oppermann, have asked for a more personal response to the teaching of Yeshua. Private correspondence with the author, spring 2017. I respond that I am already much too personally present in this analysis. My droning obstructs the purpose of this essay. I wish my reader to be able to hear Yeshua on his mount (or plain).

TABLE OF LOGIA

Reliable logia are in bold italic Times New Roman.
Suspect logia are in Times New Roman without emphasis.

LOGION-CITATION **PAGE**

MENTIONED TEXTS

Aristotle, *Nichomachean Ethics*. Translated by Roger Crisp. Cambridge, United Kingdom: Cambridge University Press, 2000.

Berger, Peter. *The Sacred Canopy: Elements of a Sociological Theory of Religion.* Garden City, New York: Doubleday & Co, Inc., 1967.

Brunner, Emil. *Dogmatics.* (Three volumes.) Eugene, Oregon: Wipf and Stock Publishers, 1950.

Buber, Martin. *I and Thou*. Translated by Walter Kaufmann. New York: Charles Scribner's Sons, 1970.

Cicero. *On Friendship (De Amicitia)*. Translated by William Armistead Falconer. Cambridge, Massachusetts: Harvard University Press, 2001.

Funk, Robert W., Roy W. Hoover, and The Jesus Seminar. *The Five Gospels: What Did Jesus Really Say?* New York: HarperCollins Publishers, 1993.

Jefferson, Thomas. *The Jefferson Bible: The Life and Morals of Jesus of Nazareth Extracted Textually from the Gospels in Greek, Latin, French & English.* Washington, D. C.: Smithsonian Books, 2011.

Kant, Immanuel. *Critique of Pure Reason*. Translated by Allen W. Wood. In *Basic Writings of Kant*. New York: The Modern Library, 2001.

Lancaster, Brad. *Cull: Choosing Well*. Shoreline, Washington: St. George's Hill Press, 2017.

Lancaster, Brad. *Cull: Epitomes*. Shoreline, Washington: St. George's Hill Press, 2017.

Levinas, Emmanuel. *Otherwise Than Being*. Translated by Alphonso Lingis. Pittsburgh, Pennsylvania: Duquesne University Press, 2002.

Schweitzer, Albert. *The Quest of the Historical Jesus.* Translated by W. Montgomery, J. R. Coates, Susan Cupitt, and John Bowden. Minneapolis, Minnesota: Fortress Press, 2001.

Weyler, Rex. *The Jesus Sayings: The Quest for His Authentic Message*. Toronto, Ontario: Anasi Press Inc., 2008.

Wittgenstein, Ludwig. *Philosophical Investigations*. Translated by G. E. M. Anscombe. Malden, Massachusetts: Blackwell Publishing, 2001.

Wittgenstein, Ludwig. *Tractatus Logico-Philosophicus.* Translated by C. K. Ogden. Mineola, New York: Dover Publications, Inc., 1999.

APPRECIATIONS

Many influenced my attachment to Yeshua. The pastor of my home Presbyterian church, an affable old man who treated my father well, taught of Jesus in confirmation classes. There, I learned to appreciate both Yeshua and young women in short skirts. Adolescence flooded mind and bloodstream, mine and theirs. One of those mini-skirted wonders became my dear friend and first love. She is now deceased. Her Yeshuan enthusiasm infected me. I pored over my New Testament. I fell into service of youths. After a time, seminary intruded. In Pasadena, many kind men, and a few cold ones, taught me Greek, Hebrew, and biblical literatures. Most, however, squirmed at my questions. Those (mostly) men were hogtied by an ecclesiastical view of Yeshua. Few could entertain heretical questions concerning the Galilean. Fewer still whispered of church fossilization. Those who dared to converse kept their heads down. Jobs were at stake. They ran risks, that handful who uttered forbidden thoughts with a seditious seminarian.

Dead people live. To the extent we can learn of them, they affect the living as though alive. We drink dead people from books and tales, just as we sip those who, though alive, we shall never meet. Yeshua is one such. I thank him for teaching, for my long, often distressed, gulps from his cup. Yeshua no longer hears. Yet, I feel obliged to thank him.

Like all my teachers, Yeshua mixed a batter of aspiration and confusion. He dosed his concoction with insight and experience. Yeshua baked a cake of reality, one styled to his taste. Some forkfuls of Yeshua's confection taste bitter, even putrid. One would, had we such power, scribble upon Yeshua's recipe a bit.

I aspire to consume Yeshua's cake as he served it. Yet, I am certain I fail. Yeshua suffered ambiguity. He changed his own mind, re-orienting critical features of his own mission. History warps events. Any interpretation of Yeshua remains equivocal. His teaching offers much that beckons. Yeshua refocuses humans who heed him from parochial preoccupations to transcendent concerns, from self to others, from isolation to community. He urges that, as seen by Yahweh, we are what hides deep within, that elusive grub that matures, for good or ill, into social wonders or horrors.

I question Yeshua's teachings. Some I discard. Yet, I cling to Yeshua. I hear him call.

Heartstruck, I limp after the Galilean.

SAINT GEORGE'S HILL PRESS

On St. George's Hill (southwest of London), in 1648, poor people, under the influence of Gerrard Winstanley, tilled and built shacks on public land to feed themselves, when food prices soared during the English Civil War. They called themselves True Levellers, and sought reduction of the financial chasm between the poor and the wealthy. The king sent a representative, who found the group doing no appreciable harm. A local lord felt otherwise, and commissioned thugs to assault the True Levellers. Some were beaten. Their common meal house was burned. Leaders were tried; the judge refused to let them speak in their defense. The True Levellers, dubbed Diggers by opponents, abandoned their plots for less hostile locations. In the twenty-first century, St. George's Hill is home to an exclusive gated and closely-guarded community, consisting in 450 mansions with tennis club and golf course amenities. St. George's Hill claims to be the premier private residential estate in Europe, close to London and Britain's most desirable private preparatory schools. The median price of a residence on St. George's Hill exceeds £3,000,000. St. George's Hill, then, is the dirt upon which clash desperate diggers and entrenched elites, a metaphor barely metaphorical.

www.ingramcontent.com/pod-product-compliance
Lightning Source LLC
LaVergne TN
LVHW051504080426
835509LV00017B/1915
9780998643526